WOMEN AND WILDERNESS

WOMEN
AND
WILDERNESS

Anne LaBastille

SIERRA CLUB BOOKS • San Francisco

The Sierra Club, founded in 1892 by John Muir, has devoted itself to the study and protection of the earth's scenic and ecological resources—mountains, wetlands, woodlands, wild shores and rivers, deserts and plains. The publishing program of the Sierra Club offers books to the public as a nonprofit educational service in the hope that they may enlarge the public's understanding of the Club's basic concerns. The point of view expressed in each book, however, does not necessarily represent that of the Club. The Sierra Club has some fifty chapters coast to coast, in Canada, Hawaii, and Alaska. For information about how you may participate in its programs to preserve wilderness and the quality of life, please address inquiries to Sierra Club, 530 Bush Street, San Francisco, CA 94108.

Library of Congress Cataloging in Publication Data
Main entry entry under title:
Women and Wilderness.

    Bibliography: p.
    Includes index.
    1.   Women naturalists—United States—Biography.
2.   Women naturalists—United States—History.
3.   Outdoor recreation for women—United States—
History.   I.   LaBastille, Anne.   II.   Sierra Club.
QH26.W65   333.78'2'0922   [B]   80-14369
ISBN 0-87156-234-0

Grateful acknowledgment is made to the following for permission to reprint copyrighted material:

Alaska Northwest Publishing Company: Selections from *Two in the Far North,* by Margaret Murie, copyright © 1966 by Margaret E. Murie.

Farrar, Straus & Giroux, Inc: "Women," from *The Blue Estuaries* by Louise Bogan.

Alfred A. Knopf, Inc.: Selections from *Wapiti Wilderness,* by Margaret and Olaus Murie, copyright © 1966 by Margaret E. Murie.

Natural History: Selections from "The Cave of the Guacharos," by Jeanne Gurnee, copyright © 1956 by the American Museum of Natural History.

Jacket design by Drake Jordan
Book design by Wendy Cunkle Calmenson

Printed in the United States of America
10 9 8 7 6 5 4 3 2

To Mac

Contents

Acknowledgments   ix

Introduction   1

PART ONE: FINDING THE WAY

Chapter 1   The Background   11

Chapter 2   Frontier Women—Case Studies   22

Chapter 3   Frontier Women in Fiction   54

Chapter 4   Changing Times   65

Chapter 5   The Making of Professionals   79

PART TWO: THE WILDERNESS WOMEN

Chapter 6   Elaine Rhode   91
               Freelancer in the Aleutians

Chapter 7   Jeanne Gurnee   106
               Explorer Underground

Chapter 8   Krissa Johnson   120
               Architect with a Chainsaw

Chapter 9   Margaret Owings   131
               An Artist in Activism

Chapter 10   Diana Cohen   146
               A School without Walls

Chapter 11   Eugenie Clark   159
               Scientist in a Wetsuit

Chapter 12   Peggy Eckel Duke   173
               Monitoring the Olympics

Chapter 13   Sheila Link   184
               A Modern Diana

Chapter 14   Carol Ruckdeschel   195
               Island Naturalist

Chapter 15   Margaret Stewart   210
               The Frog Professor

Chapter 16   Rebecca Lawton   224
               Crusader for Whitewater

Chapter 17   Margaret Murie   237
               A Long Life in the Wilderness

Chapter 18   Maggie Nichols   254
               Outdoor Journalism in the Urban Jungle

Chapter 19   Nicole Duplaix   263
               The Peripatetic Zoologist

Chapter 20   Joan Daniels   274
               Homesteading on the Alaskan Frontier

Chapter 21   Women and Wilderness   287

Appendix A   Women and Wilderness Questionnaire   296
Appendix B   Wilderness Schools and Courses   298

Bibliography   301
Index   307

Acknowledgments

To all the gallant women who are profiled in this book, and to all those who preceded them in the wilderness, I want to express my heartfelt admiration and friendship.

My deepest appreciation to Dr. Dan Odell, professor of literature at the State University of New York, Albany, for his readiness to discuss my text and his patient help throughout its preparation.

My thanks to the good staff at Crandall Library in Glens Falls, New York, and to the Society of Woman Geographers, who helped enormously with research materials.

And a fond remembrance to the island in beautiful Lake George where I sunned on a sand beach and began this book.

Anne LaBastille

WOMEN

Women have no wilderness in them,
They are provident instead,
Content in the tight hot cell of their hearts
To eat dusty bread.

They do not see cattle cropping red winter grass,
They do not hear
Snow water going down culverts
Shallow and clear.

They wait, when they should turn to journeys,
They stiffen, when they should bend.
They use against themselves that benevolence
To which no man is friend.

They cannot think of so many crops to a field,
Or of clean wood cleft by an ax.
Their love is an eager meaninglessness,
Too tense, too lax.

They hear in every whisper that speaks to them
A shout and a cry.
As like as not, when they take life over their door-sills
They should let it go by.

Louise Bogan
from *Collected Poems 1923–1953*

Introduction

That "women have no wilderness in them" may have seemed true when Louise Bogan penned her poem, and indeed ever since European women first came to North America. But it would be difficult to make such a statement now. In the last fifteen to twenty years a social phenomenon has taken place—women are living, working, and playing, by their own free choice, and in increasing numbers, in the wilderness.

Across our continent women are entering the traditionally male bastions of wilderness work and life. They are out-of-doors as forest technicians, park rangers, marine and wildlife biologists, speleologists, ethologists, herpetologists, conservation officers, professional environmentalists, wilderness guides, survival and firearms experts, hunters, fisherwomen, sportswomen, and just plain backwoods women. Sometimes alone, sometimes with families, they are proving beyond doubt that women *do* have wilderness in them.

One purpose of this book is to examine the historical roles of women in wilderness living and activity. In Chapter One, I explore reasons women traditionally have *not* been ready or willing to confront the wilderness on their own and why they were often hesitant or downright terrified to live there. Then I give a few examples of women who did live in wild places before this century, using original source material to describe their varied reactions to and ways of coping with their circumstances. Chapters 4 and 5 examine some of the factors which have led to the recent and ongoing "revolution" of women entering the wilderness as a working or a living environment.

In Part Two I present profiles of fifteen contemporary wilderness women, and in a final chapter I attempt to draw some general conclusions about them—in what ways they are like or different from other women and from men in comparable positions; how they view the wilderness and their relationship to it; why they feel that this relationship has benefited them.

To write about "women" and "wilderness" is to bring together two subjects that are each large enough to have generated a whole literature, so obviously it's necessary to outline the scope of this book and define my terms.

First of all, the contemporary women discussed at the end of Part One and those profiled in Part Two are all North Americans (though many have mixed heritages or cosmopolitan upbringings). All come from essentially middle-class backgrounds, and all are white. The last two characteristics were not criteria for inclusion, but they almost inevitably follow from my major criterion—that is, women who live full-time or work professionally in the outdoors or have wilderness-oriented careers. In our society at the present time, this translates overwhelmingly as women from the white, well-educated middle class. Seeking exceptions to this rule would be a fascinating and valuable effort, but is not vital to my primary purpose here.*

Secondly, I have chosen to make the distinction—arbitrary but not accidental—between women who are in the wilderness professionally and the much larger group of women who use the wilderness for recreation—backpackers, climbers, cross-country skiers, amateur naturalists, and so on. While the two groups share many characteristics and attitudes, and indeed frequently overlap (a casual interest in this area often leads to a professional career or life change), I have kept my focus narrow for several reasons. An obvious one is manageability; it would require a much larger book to deal adequately with the full range of women's wilderness rec-

---

*My questionnaire and search for subjects drew well over three hundred responses, none of which came from nonwhite women.

reational activities without sacrificing the desired depth of coverage on the professional side. But more important was the question of commitment: I wanted to look at women whose lives or work (and in this field they are often interchangeable and inseparable) center on their interaction with the outdoors. I wanted to learn what this deep involvement means in relation to other aspects of an individual woman's life—family, friends, relationships with men, outside interests—and in comparison to other kinds of careers and lifestyles. I also wanted to form an impression of how their involvement differs from that of men in similar fields. This isn't to say that the subject of women enjoying recreation in the wilderness is not deserving of equally close consideration, but I leave this to others, except where it bears on the lives of the women we meet here.

The historical women whose experiences are discussed in Chapter 2 might in many cases have been the great-great-grandmothers of the subjects of my profiles. These female pioneers came from a somewhat wider social spectrum and variety of backgrounds— East Coast cities, small farms, European ghettoes—but those who left records of their lives on the frontier were again primarily of European extraction and well educated by the standards of their day. In addition to the few available firsthand accounts by such women, I have used as examples fictional portraits of frontier women from the literature of the period. And I could not neglect the opportunity to look briefly at American Indian women. Their adaptation to wilderness surroundings was largely inbred and unself-conscious, and thus it provides a dramatic contrast to the experience of the white women settlers, who nevertheless adopted many skills from them.

The term *wilderness* is used in this book in several ways. Besides being an ecological entity, wilderness is essentially a state of mind, a concept whose meaning has evolved and changed along with the changing relationship of men and women to the natural world. Today it often has a specific meaning to preservationists, public officials, and other people who are concerned with maintaining our natural heritage. I use the word more broadly here. The contemporary women profiled in Part Two themselves define wilderness in various ways, ranging from pockets of open space in

largely settled areas to some of the world's most remote and least-
known places. Some are concerned with specific components, for
example, wildlife or natural features such as caves or coastlines.
The question of what wilderness means to these and other women
is discussed in detail in the last chapter.

In the introductory chapters that deal with the history of
women's interaction with wilderness, my use of the term is at once
very general and quite specific. The historical discussion begins
in the eighteenth century, and to the men and women of that era
our modern concepts have little meaning. Wilderness was not conceived of as something to be cherished; rather, it was a vast and
hostile region to be crossed, acquired, or conquered. In this sense,
its meaning is very broad.

In order to limit my scope, I have taken the North American
continent during the eighteenth- and nineteenth-century period
of exploration and settlement as representative of "wilderness" to
people of that day. This choice of place and time was logical, almost
inescapable, as it was the main arena in our history and culture
where people from developed societies came to grips with nature
in the raw, struggled with it, tried to change it, and were changed
by it. It is also the period for which the most sources exist. Moreover, the frontier experience, which is even now being repeated
in other parts of the world in different cultural and geographical
settings, seems to possess some recurring characteristics and to
evoke similar exploitive human responses wherever and whenever
it occurs.

There are few records of women's presence from the very early
period of European exploration and settlement of the continent.
The earliest explorers seldom if ever had white women accompanying them on their travels through what is now the United States,
Mexico, and Canada. De Soto is reputed to have allowed one woman to travel with him and his 1,500 soldiers. Cortes and his army
of conquistadores had only four Spanish women in their company.
The English sea captains, pirates, and sailors, such as Drake, never
carried their women aboard. And even many of the first colonists
to North America arrived without female companions.

During the seventeenth, eighteenth, and early nineteenth centuries, men and a few women immigrants began venturing away from the Eastern Seaboard colonies, towns, and plantations, which were basically still satellites of Europe in culture and thought, and heading for western New York State, the Midwest, and Ontario. This first wave of wilderness travelers and settlers did not penetrate far. As late as 1836 not a single white woman had ever lived in the wilderness between the Mississippi River and the Rockies, nor crossed this mountain range westward.*

Even after this date, and during the great gold rushes of 1849 and subsequent years, very few women entered the wilderness and set up housekeeping in wild places through *personal* choice or desire. While it was true that tens of thousands of women went West**—with pioneer families emigrating to new lands; as the wives or laundresses of Army men in isolated posts; as wives or prostitutes during the gold rushes; as "companions" to mountain men, *voyageurs*, fur trappers, and traders; more rarely as single school teachers, missionaries, or housekeepers; or as just plain adventurers—they did so through biological and social necessity. They went along as the wives, mothers, concubines, mistresses, or children of wilderness-bound men. They became wilderness women in order to *survive*.

In those days women seldom had any part in the decision to move west, and seldom felt any affinity for their wild surroundings or any desire to test themselves in this challenging arena as men apparently did. Time after time we read of the reluctance and heartbreak of women forced to leave their homes, family, and friends to head west with their menfolk. Their fears and imaginings of wild animals, blood-thirsty Indians, illness and accidents, childbirth at some crude campsite, were all too often realized. Nevertheless, these women went; and although their heroic lives were almost totally unknown, unpraised, and unsung, their presence was critically important in the winning of the new continent.

*Walter O'Meara, *Daughters of the Country. The Women of the Fur Traders and Mountain Men*.

**From 1841 to 1867 nearly 350,000 Americans emigrated to the Pacific coast along the Overland Trail (J. Faragher and C. Stansell, "Women and Their Families").

Of course, a handful of women did love the wilderness for its beauty and the freedom it offered and were not intimidated by its hardships. And an even smaller handful, usually the daughters or widows of wilderness men, did manage alone on the frontier. They had either been brought up to, or had become used to, this way of life, and they handled themselves admirably—riding horseback astride; handling teams; running farms, ranches, Indian schools, and missionary posts; managing hostelries, liveries, inns, and so on. But it is most unusual to find accounts of this type of woman.

Even the most wilderness-oriented of all women, the North American Indians, are practically nonexistent in the annals of frontier life. One hears only of Sacajawea, Malinché (Doña Marina), Pocahontas, a few early medicine women, and a couple of squaws who killed and scalped victims along with the braves. Other than these, Indian women are almost totally neglected as important figures in wilderness history of the United States, Canada, and Mexico. In fact, according to Walter O'Meara, Indian historian, in almost all the early literature of the tribes no Indian woman has spoken for her sisters or for herself.

The material for *Women and Wilderness* was not easy to come by. For records of historical wilderness women I carried out lengthy library research, reading about seventy books and several papers to gain an overview on the subject and to find case histories of outstanding females who survived—or even enjoyed—life in wild places. For the convenience of readers who may wish to pursue certain sources, the Bibliography is presented by chapters. Because this is not a scholarly work, few footnotes are used in the text, but major sources are referred to in context and all are listed in the Bibliography.

To find living subjects for the profiles, I wrote to such organizations as American Women in Science, Society of Woman Geographers, Outdoor Writers of America, National Organization for Women, The Wildlife Society, the U.S. Fish and Wildlife Service, Women in the Wilderness, and several state conservation departments, requesting names of professional women working outdoors. Next I canvassed all my female friends and colleagues in the natural sciences, plus a few male professionals. Finally, I put an ad in *Backpacker* magazine. The responses—some short postcards, others long letters with attached curricula vitae—yielded about 325 names. From these I culled the most interesting sounding down to about fifty individuals. Each of the fifty was sent a questionnaire (see Appendix A) and requested to return it with her resumé and any pertinent publications. On the basis of the responses I subjectively winnowed out thirty-seven exceptional people; then my editor and I chose twenty women whose occupations, locations, ages, marital status, and wilderness philosophies offered the broadest scope for this book.

Personal interviews with these women took me from the Adirondack Mountains of New York State to the Georgia sea islands, across to the mountains of California and the wilds of Alaska, and into the heart of New York City and Washington, D.C. Each woman was so fascinating that by the time I had written fifteen profiles there were enough pages to fill a book. So I stopped there. In addition to what appears in the profiles, each woman provided more information—her definition of wilderness, her personal experiences outdoors, and other observations about women in wilderness-type work and lifestyles. Much of this information has been incorporated into Chapter 5.

My own professions are wildlife ecology and natural history writing and photography; I am not a historian, a social scientist, or a feminist scholar. Therefore, I consider my treatment of the historical, social, psychological, and political material in the first part of this book as a survey of these important areas for study. Others have explored and will explore them in greater depth. But my sketch supplies the necessary background to an understanding of the abilities and attitudes that women today bring to their wilderness lives and careers. In considering the experience of historical women along with that of their contemporary sisters, I hope to show how the wilderness outside has changed women and how the wilderness inside them has emerged.

Part 1

FINDING
THE WAY

Chapter 1

The Background

In this chapter I shall describe in a general way the women who participated in the opening of the American wilderness—who they were, where they came from, why and how they went to the frontier, and what happened to them there. I will concentrate particularly on their responses to this experience and, helped by the work of others who have studied this historical phenomenon, try to reach an understanding of why they reacted as they did.

As I indicated in the Introduction, these historical women fall into several categories, and their background and particular situation had much to do with how they dealt with their experience. In Chapter 2 we will look at these different kinds of women more closely and meet many of them as individuals through their own words. But their experiences also have a great deal in common. Here I shall consider them together and make some observations that seem to apply to them all.

Almost without exception, the women who found themselves moving westward in the late eighteenth and nineteenth centuries had previously led lives that bore no resemblance to what awaited them. Virtually all had spent their lives up to that point in civilized, or at least settled, places. Some came from cities, either in the Atlantic Coast states or in various European countries; others from rural towns or farms, both large and small—again on the eastern seaboard or in Europe. They belonged to a fairly wide range of social classes, and some distinctions can be made here. We can assume, for instance, that women of poor families newly arrived from non-English-speaking countries would have experienced the sharpest culture shock and perhaps the greatest hardships (due to lack of funds to equip themselves comfortably for the trail); or that things might have been somewhat easier for a woman raised on a farm close to the frontier, who would already have learned some skills that would serve her in good stead in her new life. But these differences are relative. The vast majority of the women who went west performed the same role in their adult lives: to make a comfortable home and to rear families—the things that had represented stability and civilized life through the ages.

For these women, then, the move to the wilderness was a series of shocks almost guaranteed to strip away what was most important to them: the secure, carefully constructed environment that defined their sphere of power and their self-worth. And the first of these shocks came with the choice to pick up and go—a decision rarely, if ever, made by the women themselves.

This lack of any voice in the decision to move into wilderness conditions, and the fact that, once under way, they could not stop or change their menfolks' minds must have caused great frustration and concern. Such a feeling is well portrayed in *The Way West*, A. B. Guthrie's powerful novel of pioneer people. In it Rebecca's husband comes home one evening after being with his male buddies and announces that the family is going to move from Missouri to Oregon. The next day his friends ask him if he had checked with his wife about making the trip. The husband replies, "Wouldn't do it. . . . God knows women have aplenty to say, but no say-so." Time after time, women like Rebecca simply had to pull up stakes and follow their men, regardless of their feelings and ties. At that time few had either the financial means or the marketable skills to support themselves independently of their husbands or fathers. This lack of self-sufficiency, combined with the social and psychological difficulties that mature, single, or divorced women had to face, made it virtually impossible to consider staying behind on their own. In Guthrie's book Rebecca enviously wished she would be excited like the men and "not feel such a sadness as a woman did saying goodbye to home."

Not only was the leaving difficult, but once committed to move, these uprooted women were often subjected to abysmal travel conditions, childbirth in remote places, the terror of seeing their children or husbands ill without medical help, starvation and thirst, attack by Indians, the fear of wild animals, social deprivation, homesickness, primitive living conditions, and the possibility of widowhood in an environment where few women could cope alone. Normally only a one-day stopover was allowed for a woman to give birth. Diseases such as malaria, dysentery, pneumonia, and cholera were encountered often and were largely untreatable. Usually the wagons would creep along at twenty miles per day for at.least six months until they reached their destination two thousand miles or more from where they started. Thus it is not surprising that many women entered the wilderness with far more trepidation than we can possibly imagine today.

Take, for example, one Ohio-born woman who spent six months living in a covered wagon on the way to her new home in Wyoming. Throughout this time she never saw another white woman. Or a young wife from Missouri who went into labor during a blizzard out on the open prairie. She had only her husband to help and a tent for shelter. Her newly delivered twins were washed with melted sleet in an iron skillet. The family survived only by huddling under heaps of blankets in their wagon until the storm played itself out.

Whatever the reason and method by which women encountered frontier life for the first time, a great many of them were appalled, frightened, or depressed by what they found, both on the journey and at their destination. Nothing in their upbringing, nor in the American colonies' close dependence on European and British culture, had prepared women for roughing it. In an era when the broadaxe was the most essential tool and an appropriate symbol of America, especially west of the eastern seaboard, and when nature was usually seen as an adversary, it is not surprising that most women looked upon their new environment as a "howling wilderness." They were often visually horrified by the American landscape. Many emigrants were accustomed to the gentle pastoral lands of England, Germany, and Scandinavia, and our own eastern coastal plain. The dense woods, mountains, and wild prairie country from the Appalachians west through the Rockies and to the

Pacific Coast were just not appealing or comforting to the eigh-
teenth- or nineteenth-century eye.

Many diaries, letters, and memoirs clearly illustrate that women
reacted to the wilderness much more critically than men did. Annette Kolodny, a Guggenheim Fellow and author of articles in
feminist criticism, has researched many sources from this period
which reveal womens' varied feelings about wilderness landscapes.*
They expressed frustration at being trapped in new kinds of countryside and settings upon which they could make no significant
imprint—other than small garden plots of their own cultivation.

One such lady was Elizabeth House Trist, who traveled from
Philadelphia to Louisiana in 1783–84 to meet her husband. Though
she often commented on "the delightful prospects" of mountain
passes and historical sites, Elizabeth clearly preferred to see farms
and settlements. She wrote, "I felt oppress'd with so much wood
towering above me in every direction and such a continuance of
it." Of the Mississippi River she commented, "Its appearance is
awful and Melancholy and sometimes terrific." The environment
left her bewildered and depressed, and a short while later she
wrote, "My spirits were condanc'd to nothing; my head began to
ache and I returned to town quite sick." All through her journey
she recorded "violent headaches" and complained, "I can hardly
keep myself alive." For Elizabeth, the wilderness became a place
of almost claustrophobic oppression.

The experience of wilderness as a confining rather than a liberating environment seems to have been common among women,
in sharp contrast to the freedom men found in it. Another woman,
Eliza Burgwyn Clitherall, traveled in 1784 from the port of Wil-
mington, North Carolina, inland to her father's isolated estate near
the Great Smoky Mountains. She expressed a dread of "Wild Beas-
tees" that might be encountered along the way and feared to ride
through the "Piney Woods" alone on the journey. She had no
neighbors within walking distance of the estate and was not allowed
to make overnight visits away. Her "greatest relief in this solitude"

---

*Annette Kolodny, "To Render Home a Paradise: Women in the New World Landscapes,"
in *Women's Language and Style*, ed. by D. Butturff and E. L. Epstein (Studies in Contemporary Language, no. 1, Dept. of English, University of Akron, Ohio).

was "writing to, and receiving letters from England." Clearly Eliza's impression of wilderness was confining and fearful.

According to Kolodny, this sampling of early letters and diaries demonstrates that women were rejecting, in their minds at least, the popular male imaginings of adventure and promises of wealth and excitement, and thus the landscapes they implied.

It is important to remember that throughout history cultural conditioning and opinion had strongly centered women in the home. Consequently, they generally possessed none of the necessary skills to survive alone in the wilderness. In the era we are describing women were constantly told that they were weak, frail, uncoordinated, and less intelligent than men. Thus it is not surprising that they had little drive to be strong and capable out-of-doors. Most women did not have the mental attitude to look at wilderness as a different dimension, a fresh horizon, freedom, excitement, or a growth-producing experience. Moreover, with few exceptions, only men could legally hold title to land for most of the first two hundred years of our country's existence. Based on English law, this doctrine meant that women were denied the great pleasure and excitement of owning land and creating their own homes and livelihoods. Therefore, women had no incentive whatsoever to "carve a home in the wilderness." They would have seemed like misfits if they had yearned to do so. As Eliza Clitherall wrote in the 1770's (quoted by Kolodny), "The office of gentle Woman was to render Home a Paradise by the strict enactment of her several domestic duties."

Of course, as I said before, there were the exceptional few women who rejoiced in isolated, hard outdoor lifestyles—women such as the widowed Elinore Pruitt Stewart, a homesteader in her own right, and girls born in the wilderness who had no strong ties to people or places back East. But the vast majority of frontier women were there only passively. For these, let us examine what biological, psychological, cultural, and sociological factors kept them "imprisoned" and discontent in the wilderness.

In the most simple and direct terms, I would say the reason women did not live, work, and play in the wilderness *voluntarily* was that they had babies. Once a woman became a wife, and then a mother, she was normally trapped in a long cycle of childbearing and rearing that kept her close to home and at the constant call of young helpless human beings. Eventually she was either too old and tired to fare into the wilderness, or dead. In most eighteenth- and nineteenth-century homes, caring for children was a totally consuming task and being a housewife a full-time occupation, no matter where you lived, but particularly in the wilderness.

Women had virtually no way to limit their pregnancies nor any accurate knowledge about ovulation or birth control. Not until 1859 did the first medical article appear giving reliable information, and contraceptive measures were not even discussed or promoted until the very end of the nineteenth century. Until then doctors were subject to prosecution if they wrote about, lectured on, or disseminated birth-control methods to their patients. Thus women were biologically tied down—unable to simply pick up a rifle, saddle, and tent to go exploring, hunting, or trapping whenever they wished, as men did.

Nothing can describe this situation better than the terse, stoical words of Mrs. Mary Walker in her journal from the 1840's:

Rose about five. Had breakfast. Got my house work done about nine. Baked six loaves of bread. Made a kettle of mush and have now a suet pudding and beef boiling. I have managed to put my clothes away and set my house in order. May the merciful Lord be with me through the unexpected scene. Nine o'clock p.m. was delivered of another son. [She had eight children while homesteading in Oregon.]

The division of labor by strict biological function had deep roots in Pleistocene prehistory—women remaining near the home (or cave) and tending to child rearing, food gathering and preparing, and fashioning clothing, while men ventured forth to hunt, trade, defend territory, and so on. The same essential roles persisted up to and beyond the winning of the North American continent, and they were often reinforced in the West by the very rigors and dangers of wilderness conditions. From the beginning the discovery and exploration of our continent was considered an almost exclusively male occupation and a highly masculine adventure.

On the other hand, it has been pointed out that trail and frontier life might have been fertile ground for a breakdown in traditional biological roles. In their article "Women and Their Families on the

Overland Trail to California and Oregon, 1842 to 1867," J. Faragher and C. Stansell make this point and comment on why women were reluctant to take advantage of the opportunity:

The vicissitudes of the trail opened new possibilities for expanded work roles for women, and in the cooperative work of the family there exists a basis for a vigorous struggle for female-male equality. But most women did not see the experience in this way. They viewed it as a male enterprise from its very inception. Women experienced the breakdown of the sexual division of labor as a dissolution of their autonomous sphere.

Women's sphere provided them with companionship, a sense of self-worth, and most important, independence from men in a patriarchal world. Bereft of the footing which this independent base gave them, they lacked a cultural rationale for the work they did, and remained estranged from the possibilities of the enlarged scope and power of family life on the trail.

The Trail, in breaking down sexual segregation, offered women the opportunities of socially essential work. Yet this work was performed in a male arena, and many women saw themselves as draftees rather than partners. Instead, women fought *against* the forces of necessity to hold together a few fragments of female subculture left to them. . . .

The resistance of most women to taking a more active role deserves closer examination. First of all, I think the point must be made that it was not due to any "natural" inability. That women are at least the equals of men, both psychologically and biologically, has been demonstrated by several modern researchers. Ashley Montagu was perhaps the earliest well-known author to make a winning and straightforward documentation in *The Natural Superiority of Women* (1954); later followed Dr. Julia Sherman's *On the Psychology of Women* (1971), Dr. Juanita Williams's *Psychology of Women* (1977), and others, in a more thorough scientific coverage. These authors point out the various psychobiological advantages women have over men—fewer genetic flaws and sex-linked disorders; longer life; greater resistance to infection; better capacity to withstand adverse conditions; quicker recovery from stress; greater constitutional strength; keener auditory, olfactory, and taste senses; lower metabolism and therefore less need for food; faster maturation; a more loving and humane and less violent nature;

greater verbal ability, memory, and perception; and greater emotional resiliency. On the other hand, men generally possess a stronger musculature; exhibit greater physical aggression; are superior in spatial aptitudes; have a greater learning ability in science, mathematical reasoning, and informational subjects; and have faster reaction times and generally keener vision.

According to Dr. Julia Sherman, there is nothing in the current biological and psychological evidence which would prevent women from taking an equal role in the outdoors as elsewhere. In fact, if Paul Petzoldt, founder and former director of the National Outdoor Leadership School, is right, women do better than men in the wilderness. In a *Mariah* interview (June–July 1978) he said:

Women have been taught to think that they don't have as much endurance as men, but over the long haul, women will outdistance men time and time again. Women have *more* endurance; they adjust to the outdoors better than men. Women in this country have been brainwashed to think that they can't carry loads, but women are the load carriers all over the world.

Then what is the answer to why women did not take an equal role in the wilderness until very recently? While there are clearly fundamental sex differences apparent from the very beginning of life, most of the attributes we think of as sexual differences are cultural, not innately biological. They are acquired in early childhood training and in subsequent social indoctrination. There is no doubt that the North American wilderness was a setting of male dominance. Women were the silent sex, the forgotten sex, psychological nonpersons. They were simply prohibited to think or participate fully—not because of their psychological makeup or any specific male subjection, but because of the culture. In fact, their very omission in early American chronicles is, according to applied psychologist Ernest Groves, an indictment of our civilization itself, a lack of appreciation, and an evidence of an unbalanced appraisal of values. As Groves puts it succinctly:

It is the *mores* rather than persons that are responsible for the retardation of women in those cases where there clearly is discrimination. For the most part, we find our mores and systems of thought natural products of

the time and place, that assign women their responsibilities, and, therefore, . . . hamper the self-expression and self-determination of one sex
as compared with the other. The resistance met by ambitious and aggressive women who seek a freer life is not usually born of any disposition
on the part of men to keep women from going upward but rather from
the reluctance to accept social changes and to make the adjustments that
a new order demands.

Faragher and Stansell make this point well about the early pioneers:

Both sexes worked, both sexes suffered. Yet women lacked a sense of
inclusion and a cultural rationale to give meaning to the suffering and
work; no augmented sense of self or role emerged from augmented pri-
vation. Both women and men also complained, but women expanded their
caviling to a generalized critique of the whole enterprise.

At the start of the frontier era, as we have seen, the mores, or
cultural customs and beliefs, were extremely rigid and entrenched.
Some of these attitudes reach far back into the Old and New Tes-
taments, including, of course, the ancient belief that women
brought sin into the world—perhaps the most damaging of all, in
making women ashamed that they were even born female. A pro-
vocative comment on this point is offered by Dawn Lander in her
essay "Women and the Wilderness: Taboos in American Literature":

American tradition has regarded the white woman as an intruder into the
landscape and has treated the drama of the New World as the reenactment
of the myth of the Fall of Eden. . . .

The good women on the frontier stayed at home, psychologically if not
physically. The tradition of the American woman's submission to the wilderness experience has the same psychological overtones as the tradition
of her submission to sex: her husband has forced her into the wilderness,
but she needn't enjoy it, and because she transcends the experience, she
is celebrated for her sacrifice. The "wilderness" taboo denies feminine
wanderlust and has a dynamic similar to the sexual taboos which deny
feminine lust.

A factor that no doubt tended to reinforce the dependent position of women on the frontier was the protective way they were treated by men. It was often said by early wilderness women that men, especially Westerners, were extremely chivalrous, possibly because women were so rare, valued, and vital to survival in the wilderness. Indeed, women in the frontier communities were often the objects of intense rivalries by tough, even desperate, men, according to Erik Erikson in *Childhood and Society*. Probably frontier women derived feeings of self-worth by being bearers of culture to the raw wilderness, promoters of spirituality and religion, and teachers of the finer graces of life. As Dawn Lander comments, "The mere presence of a married white female is considered to be sufficiently potent to dispell the wilderness and constitute the establishment of civilization."

Two women of the period make the same point. Agnes Morley Cleveland, who ran a ranch in New Mexico in the late 1800's, wrote in her book *No Life for a Lady* that she never knew of a case of assault upon a white female by a white man: "A good woman was always safe." Nannie Tiffany Alderson, author of *A Bride Goes West*, lived on an isolated ranch with her husband and several cowboys in Montana in the late 1800's. She reported that "men *had* to be with the women for protection, but there was never a whisper of evil." Apparently men took their trust very seriously, and western men had complete faith in the chivalry of their fellows. Even strangers could stay alone with a wife and babies if they needed shelter. Near the end of her account Nannie wonders "if the splendid comradely attitudes of American men toward women originated in conditions such as then [prevailed] in Montana."

As an expression of concern for their fellow humans, the behavior of such men was commendable, but in its appeal to women's weaknesses rather than their strengths, it can be seen as a desperate but futile effort to maintain the status quo in an environment that encouraged change and growth. As Dawn Lander points out, the woman-on-a-pedestal image, though powerful, was often different from the reality:

The contemporary significance of the received tradition concerning white women in the American wilderness is that it denies feminine wanderlust, keeps women in the home, and reinforces contemporary racial taboos.

Nevertheless, neither fear of the landscape nor aversion to miscegenation are of necessity feminine traits. Both primary and secondary literature by women significantly modify the traditional image.

We will see this modification in the female characters described in Chapters 2 and 3; and we will see it in full force in the chapters on contemporary women in the wilderness.

Although, as Faragher and Stansell point out, most frontier women clung to traditional roles for security—at least at first—it is important to note that the wilderness itself had, in certain cases, a highly liberating effect. The wilderness opened the door to the "revolution" described in Chapter 4. In 1893 Frederick Jackson Turner, in one of the most famous and influential papers in American history writing, *"The Significance of the Frontier in American History,"* wrote that the cultural revolt against the East (hence also Europe) and its mores, coupled with the West's sense of self-consciousness, created American democracy and killed European aristocracy. The new land changed certain traditional aspects of human behavior and activities, leading to a vigorous individualism. It created a new man—and, I believe, a new woman. Although a few months of trail life was perhaps too short a time to effect a role change, a lifetime on a ranch, in a woodland cabin, prairie sod hut, gold-rush camp, or the like, could give rise to permanent new roles and foster concepts of self-reliance, inventiveness, and independence. It could also allow men to develop appreciation for women (in a way that was impossible before) as independent persons, not servile followers. In the long run, women became near equals to men on the frontier—and they also became far more enriched and self-expressing human beings.

And so, life on the frontier reinforced certain patterns of female behavior—the home, church, children, school, and social reform; while eventually it broke down others—the division of labor and conventional sex roles—and replaced them with intense individualism, expansion of work roles, and independence. The assumption of male superiority began to melt away as it was belied by new evidence of female capability. The mores of the time were restructured and reshaped, leading to a larger, freer life for women in the American wilderness.

Chapter 2

Frontier Women:
Case Studies

IN THE COURSE of my reading I found that women on the frontier seemed to separate naturally into five general categories: pioneers who headed west to homestead, farm, or ranch; women involved with gold rushes and mining booms; wives of army men who traveled with them; teachers and missionaries; and just plain adventurers (some fiercely independent, others the companions of mountain men and traders). A sixth category, American Indian women, will be considered separately.

While the majority of these women left no written record of their experiences, a few marvelous journals and collections of letters that have been passed down vividly describe the writers' reactions to this setting I shall draw on a few of these firsthand accounts here. In Chapter 3 we shall see the life of frontierswomen as it was interpreted by several novelists of that period and shortly thereafter.

The Pioneers and Homesteaders

Many of the pioneer women who traveled into the wilderness, moving across the continent to begin a new life as frontierswomen, were homesteaders. Other, usually wealthier, settlers had property

awaiting them, but their more favored circumstances did not necessarily guarantee an easier adjustment to wilderness life.

One woman who chronicled her journey west over plains, deserts, and mountains (and later, her experiences in a gold rush
mining camp) is Sarah Bayliss Royce, author of *A Frontier Lady*.
The trials and tribulations she and her family endured en route to
California were nothing short of horrendous, and Sarah described
them graphically. The Royces—Sarah, her husband, Josiah, and
her two-year-old, Mary—set off with their wagon from Iowa on the
last day of April, 1849. The refined and well-bred woman took with
her a Bible, her copy of Milton's works, and a tiny lap writing desk
because she had been brought up with an academy education in
New York State and loved to read and study. When it came time
to stop on the first night afield, she wrote:

I had for months anticipated this hour, yet, not till it came, did I realize
the blank dreariness of seeing night come on without house or home to
shelter us and our baby-girl. And this was to be the same for many weeks,
perhaps months. It was a chilling prospect, and there was a terrible
shrinking from it in my heart; but I kept it all to myself and we were
soon busy making things as comfortable as we could for the night. At first
the oppressive sense of homelessness, and an instinct of watchfulness,
kept me awake. Perhaps it was not to be wondered at in one whose life
had so far, been spent in city or town, surrounded by the accompaniments
of civilization and who was now, for the first time in her life . . . 'camping
out.' However, quiet sleep came at last, and in the morning, there was
a mildly exultant feeling which comes from having kept silent through
a cowardly fit, and finding the fit gone off.

Before arriving at Council Bluffs, Missouri, the Royces fell in
with other small groups of Forty-Niners, all of whom had discouraging news. Cholera was raging among the emigrants; supplies
were difficult to obtain; grass for stock was being eaten up by those
ahead; and the ferry crossing over the Missouri was crowded, ne-
cessitating a wait of several days. By the time the Royces left
Council Bluffs, it was already mid-June, really too late in the year
to be starting this long trek. Then came a number of severe thunder

and wind storms, a cattle stampede, and a hazardous river crossing which sent terror into Sarah's heart. She wrote:

> Now indeed a heavy gloom hung round us. The destroyer seemed let loose upon our camp. Who would go next? What if my husband should be taken and leave us alone in the wilderness? What if I should be taken and leave my little Mary motherless? Or, still more distracting thought— what if we both should be laid low, and she be left a destitute orphan, among strangers, in a land of savages?

On August 18 they reached Salt Lake City, where the wagon train broke up and each party decided to fend for itself. On August 30 the young family, one old man, and six oxen plus a wagon headed for the Great Salt Desert and the Sierra Nevada beyond. They made haste, for they still had far to go, and snow could block the mountain passes anytime after mid-October. Because of bad timing and overeagerness they missed the one meadow and water source available before the desert, and the Royces found themselves miles out on the burning sand and sagebrush with no food for the oxen and only two or three quarts of water. It was imperative to keep the animals alive, so they tore open straw mattresses to feed them and doled out mouthfuls of water. Everyone was near giving up. Sarah wrote:

> How still it was. Only the sound of a few feeble breaths. It would not take many hours of starvation to quiet them forever. But that calm strength, that certainty of One near and all sufficient hushed and cheered me. Only a woman who has been alone upon a desert with her helpless child can have any adequate idea of my experience for the next hour or two. But that consciousness of an unseen Presence still sustained me. I had now become so impressed with the danger of the cattle giving out, that I refused to ride except for occasional brief rests. I left the wagon and walked the remainder of the day. There was no alternative, however, the only thing to be done was to go steadily on, determined to do and endure to the utmost. When my little one, from the wagon behind me, called out, "Mamma I want a drink"—I stopped, gave her some, noted that there were but a few swallows left, then mechanically pressed onward again, alone, repeating, over and over, the words, "Let me not see the death of the child."

By afternoon they were saved, having backtracked fifteen miles and discovered the meadow and springs. Here they restocked and refreshed themselves, and on October 9 again set off across the desert. It must have been a grim trip, for they lost two oxen on this part of the trail.

The waning moon now gave us a little melancholy light, showing still the bodies of dead cattle, and the forms of forsaken wagons as our grim waymarks. In one or two instances they had been left in the very middle of the road; and we had to turn out into the untracked sand to pass them.

Fortunately they reached the Carson River in Nevada before thirsting to death, and they left the desert behind. The Sierra Nevada, their last great obstacle, now threatened the group with a new menace, for the trail was too steep for a wagon and team. Moreover, the high passes were already filling with snow. Providentially, they were met by two riders from the U.S. Government Relief Company, whose duty it was to help late emigrants over the mountains. The Royces had had to abandon their team, and without this unexpected aid and advice on how to pack and hike through the Sierra, they probably would have frozen to death.

Finally, on October 19, this courageous pioneer woman and her family crossed the highest ridge and began the descent into California.

I looked down, far over constantly descending hills, to where a soft haze sent up a warm, rosy glow that seemed to me a smile of welcome; while beyond, occasional faint outlines of other mountains appeared; and I knew I was looking across the Sacramento Valley. California, land of sunny skies—that was my first look into your smiling face. I loved you from that moment, for you seemed to welcome me with a loving look into rest and safety. However brave a face I might have put on most of the time, I knew my coward heart was yearning all the while for a home-nest and a welcome into it, and you seemed to promise me both. A short time I had on those rocks, sacred to thanksgiving and prayer.

Soon the Royces, like thousands of other eager pioneers who crossed the continent in that legendary year, were safely settled in a mining camp in California. Sarah's descriptions of her life there will come later in this chapter.

Sarah Royce seems to have come through her trials mainly because of her belief in God—and considerable luck. She simply committed herself and her family into the Almighty's hands and then carried on as loyally and strongly as she was able.

Several good accounts have been left by women homesteaders, who lived in sod houses on the prairies or in log cabins in the woods, almost always with husbands, fathers, or brothers. Many of these memoirs show courage and resoluteness in the face of exhaustion and despair, but only one that I know of portrays homesteading as an exciting and liberating experience for a woman alone. Elinore Pruitt Stewart's *Letters of a Woman Homesteader* is the cheerful, warm, humorous account of a young, orphaned, then widowed, mother of a two-year-old daughter. Elinore survived as a laundress and cleaning woman in Denver, but she hated city life and was intrigued by what she read of life in the country. Taking the advice of her minister, Elinore advertised to be a housekeeper to a rancher, hoping thereby to get situated in an area where she could eventually homestead. Her ad was answered by Clyde Stewart, an older Scottish cattle rancher, and she traveled to Burnt Fork, Wyoming, then sixty miles from the nearest railroad.

Even in 1909 this was still frontier land. At Stewart's ranch Elinore had her own saddle horse, a shotgun for hunting, and fishing gear to catch trout in nearby streams. In less than six weeks she had filed under the Homestead Act on 240 acres as her land claim (on a piece adjoining Stewart's ranch). She planned to build her own house amid a grove of twelve swamp pines, thinking "it would be very romantic to live on the peaks amid the whispering pines." She also noted, "A dandy thing is, I have all the nice snow-water I want; a small stream runs right through the center of my land and I am quite near wood." Apparently there was only one other house within sixty miles and little else but sage, sand, and sheep— which seems to have suited Elinore just fine.

Unlike most frontierswomen, Elinore was not afraid of wild animals, or isolation, and showed a keen eye for the natural beauty of the wilderness around her. She described what she saw on various trips to the county seat:

After driving all day over what seemed a level desert of sand, we came about sundown to a beautiful cañon. Suddenly a great wolf started from somewhere and galloped along the edge of the cañon, outlined black and clear by the setting sun. His curiosity overcame him at last, so he sat down and waited to see what manner of beast we were. I reckon he was disappointed for he howled most dismally. I thought of Jack London's "The Wolf."

It was too beautiful a night to sleep, so I put my head out to look and to think. I saw the moon come up and hang for a while over the mountain as if it were discouraged with the prospect, and the big white stars flirted shamelessly with the hills.

I saw a coyote come trotting along and I felt sorry for him, having to hunt food in so barren a place, but when presently I heard the whirr of wings I felt sorry for the sage chickens he had disturbed. At length a cloud came up and I went to sleep, and next morning was covered with several inches of snow. It didn't hurt us a bit.

On one occasion Elinore and her young daughter, Jerrine, rode up into the mountains to go trout fishing. After having caught "eight beauties," Elinore made a fire, dressed the trout, gathered some service berries, and fried the fish.

The sound of the dashing, roaring water kept inviting me to cast for trout, but I didn't want to carry them so far, so we rested until the sun was getting low and then started for home, with the song of the locusts in our ears warning us that the melancholy days are almost here. We would come up over the top of a hill into the glory of a beautiful sunset with its gorgeous colors, then down into the little valley already purpling with mysterious twilight.

Another such outing took Elinore and Jerrine high into the Rockies on a "camping-out expedition."

I wish you could once sleep on the kind of bed we enjoyed that night. It was both soft and firm, with the clean, spicy smell of the pine. The heat from our big fire came in and we were warm as toast. It was so good to stretch out and rest. I kept thinking how superior I was since I dared to take such an outing when so many poor women down in Denver were bent on making their twenty cents per hour in order that they could spare a quarter to go to the "show." I went to sleep with a powerfully self-satisfied feeling, but I awoke to realize that pride goeth before a fall.

Such a snowstorm I never saw! I scrambled out and poked up the fire; then, as it was only five o'clock, I went back to bed. And then I began to think how many kinds of idiot I was. Here I was thirty or forty miles from home, in the mountains where no one goes in the winter and where I knew the snow got to be ten or fifteen feet deep. But I could never see the good of moping, so I got up and got breakfast while Baby put her shoes on. We had our squirrels and more baked potatoes and I had delicious black coffee. After I had eaten I felt more hopeful.

Elinore had not been a housekeeper for more than six weeks when she and Stewart got married. Although she wished to be an independent homesteader and realized that becoming a wife "was such an inconsistent thing to do," she apparently believed it was a sensible thing to do. She wrote:

Ranch work seemed to require that we be married first and do our sparking afterwards. I should not have married if Clyde had not promised I should meet all my land difficulties unaided. I wanted the fun and experience myself. And I want to be able to speak from experience when I tell others what they can do. For this reason I want to earn every cent that goes into my own land and improvements myself . . . I know I shall succeed; other women have succeeded.

If she thought she had worked hard as a single and widowed woman, Elinore's labors had only begun when she married. She did all of the haymowing; helped with the planting of oats and other crops; milked seven or more cows every day; fed chickens; cooked for her little family (which soon grew to three more children), for hired men, and for guests; put up jellies and jams; kept Stewart's house; and oversaw the building of her own two-room cabin and the development of her own land. Her husband supported her independent efforts and helped out when asked to. Apparently homesteading agreed very well with Elinore Stewart, and she recommended it enthusiastically, as in this letter:

To me, homesteading is the solution of all poverty's problems, but I realize that temperament has much to do with success in any undertaking, and persons afraid of coyotes and work and loneliness had better let ranching alone. At the same time, any woman who can stand her own company, can see the beauty of the sunset, loves growing things, and is willing to put in as much time at careful labor as she does over the washtub, will certainly succeed; will have independence, plenty to eat all the time, and a home of her own in the end. I am only thinking of the troops of tired, worried women, sometimes even cold and hungry, scared to death of losing their places to work, who could have plenty to eat, who could have good fires by gathering the wood, and comfortable homes of their own, if they but had the courage and determination to get them.

I have tried every kind of work this ranch affords, and I can do any of it. Of course I *am* extra strong, but those who try know that strength and knowledge come with doing. I just love to experiment, to work, and to prove out things, so that ranch life and "roughing it" just suit me.

Apparently Elinore was blessed with superb stamina as well as a fortunate psychological makeup. Her unquenchable optimism, even more than her strength and vitality, is rare in wilderness women's memoirs. Whatever the reason for it, her letters are a joy and an inspiration to read, especially when she says, "I am the luckiest woman in finding really lovely people and having really happy experiences. Good things are constantly happening to me."

In marked contrast to Elinore Stewart's bracing letters is Mrs. Susanna Moodie's journal, *Roughing It in the Bush*, a chronicle of her seven-year (1832–1840) sojourn in the backwoods of Canada. I found the story of this English-born gentlewoman truly "moody," ambivalent, and filled with trials, tears, and fears.

Susanna's husband determined to leave the overpopulated British Isles and seek a better life in the New World, and, like so many other women, she had little choice but to acquiesce. The Moodies arrived safely at their isolated bush farmstead in Ontario. Susanna expressed great emotion and admiration at her first sight of the rugged beauty of the mountains and vast forest belt; however, she suffered from acute homesickness.

Dear, dear England! Why was I forced by a stern necessity to leave you? What heinous crime had I committed that I, who adored you, should be torn from your sacred bosom, to pine out my joyless existence in a foreign clime? Oh that I might be permitted to return and die upon your wave-encircled shores, and rest my weary head and heart beneath your daisy-covered sod at last! Ah, these are vain outbursts of feeling—melancholy relapses of the spring homesickness!

Susanna struggled with these feelings, trying to reconcile them with the loyalty she felt obliged to give to her new homeland.

Canada! thou art a noble, free, and rising country—the great fostering mother of the orphans of civilization. The offspring of Britain, thou must be great, and I will and do love thee, land of my adoption, and of my children's birth; and oh—dearer still to a mother's heart—land of their graves!

British mothers of Canadian sons! Teach them to love Canada—to look upon her as the first, the happiest, the most independent country in the world! You will soon learn to love Canada as I now love it, who once viewed it with hatred so intense that I longed to die, that death might effectually separate us forever.

During their first years in the new country, the Moodies endured a great many misfortunes. Susanna found most all her neighbors to be poor, uneducated, and unfriendly. They regarded the Moodies as wealthy gentry and borrowed and cheated from them unmercifully. Even when Susanna did not have a candle to light at night and was close to starvation, these neighbors would still not lend a hand. At times, too, the weather was just as unmerciful:

In spite of all my boasted fortitude—and I think my powers of endurance have been tried to the utmost since my sojourn in this country— the rigour of the climate subdued my proud, independent English spirit, and I actually shamed my womanhood, and cried with the cold. Yes, I ought to blush at confessing such unpardonable weakness; but I was foolish and inexperienced, and unaccustomed to the yoke.

The presence of wolves, bears, mice, fleas, bedbugs, mosquitoes, and black flies took an emotional toll, as did the ordeal of frequent illnesses. Susanna's account of the birth of her second child during an epidemic of fever is truly heart-rending.

Ague and lake fever had attacked our new settlement. The men in the shanty were all down with it, and my husband was confined to his bed on each alternate day, unable to raise hand or foot, and raving in the delirium of the fever.

After much difficulty, and only by offering enormous wages, I succeeded in procuring a nurse to attend upon me during my confinement. The woman had not been a day in the house before she was attacked by the same fever. In the midst of this confusion and with my precious little Addie lying insensible on a pillow at the foot of my bed—expected every moment to breathe her last—on the night of the 26th of August the boy I had so ardently coveted was born. I was left to struggle through, in the best manner I could, with a sick husband, a sick child, and a new-born babe. . . .

I was obliged to leave my bed and endeavour to attend to the wants of my young family long before I was really able. When I made my first attempt to reach the parlour I was so weak, that, at every step, I felt as if I should pitch forward to the ground, which seemed to undulate beneath my feet, like the floor of a cabin in a storm at sea. My husband continued to suffer for many weeks with the ague; and when he was convalescent, all the children, even the poor babe, were seized with it: nor did it leave us till late in the spring of 1835.

On several occasions Susanna found herself alone in her rustic home, a situation she found very hard to deal with.

For the first time in my life I found myself at night in a house entirely alone. Then I began to ask myself a thousand torturing questions as to the reason of their unusual absence. Had they lost their way in the woods? Could they have fallen in with wolves (one of my early bugbears)? Could any fatal accident have befallen them?

As it became later, my fears increased in proportion. . . . I had burnt out all my wood, and I dared not open the door to fetch in more. The candle was expiring in the socket, and I had not courage to go up into the loft and procure another before it went finally out. Cold, heart-weary, and faint, I sat and cried. Then I listened till the beating of my own heart excluded all other sounds. Oh, that unwearied brook! how it sobbed and moaned like a fretful child;—what unreal terrors and fanciful illusions my too active mind conjured up, whilst listening to its mysterious tones! That was the saddest and longest night I ever remember.

To make matters worse, Susanna, coming from a well-bred family, did not know how to milk cows, chop wood, walk through the woods, or do manual work. However, little by little she learned and even found some good in the hardships.

I had a hard struggle with my pride before I would consent to render the least assistance on the farm, but reflection convinced me that I was wrong—that Providence had placed me in a situation where I was called upon to work—that it was not only my duty to obey that call, but to exert myself to the utmost to assist my husband and help to maintain my family.

Ah, poverty! thou art a hard taskmaster, but in thy soul-ennobling school I have received more god-like lessons, have learned more sublime truths, than ever I acquired in the smooth highways of the world!

We found that manual toil, however distasteful to those unaccustomed to it, was not after all such a dreadful hardship; that the wilderness was not without its rose, the hard face of poverty without its smile. If we occasionally suffered severe pain, we as often experienced great pleasure, and I have contemplated a well-hoed ridge of potatoes on that bush farm with as much delight as in years long past I had experienced in examining a fine painting in some well-appointed drawing room.

Nevertheless, the combination of all their particular miseries— plus the added misfortune of poor crops, a house burned down, and tensions between the United States and Canada in the late 1830's stemming from the *Caroline* affair—forced a change in the Moodies' lives. Because they were destitute, Susanna started writing magazine articles and painting butterflies and birds on fungi (a folk art native to the North Woods) to sell. Her husband went to war, for which he got paid a small salary, and eventually was nominated sheriff of a district near Belleville, Ontario. Susanna called this "a heavensent gift to remove us from sorrow and poverty." Once she was living in town and out of the wilderness, Susanna Moodie summed up her experience in the woods this way:

For seven years I had lived out of the world entirely; my person had been rendered coarse by hard work and exposure to the weather. I looked double the age I really was, and my hair was already thickly sprinkled with grey. I clung to my solitude. I did not like to be dragged from it to mingle in gay scenes, in a busy town, and with gaily dressed people. I was no longer fit for the world; I had lost all relish for the pursuits and pleasures which are so essential to its votaries; I was contented to live and die in obscurity.

Every object had become endeared to me during my long exile from civilized life. I loved the lonely lake, with its magnificent belt of dark pines sighing in the breeze; the cedar swamp, the summer home of my dark Indian friends; my own dear little garden, with its rugged snake-fence which I had helped Jenny to place with my own hands, where I had so often braved the tormenting mosquitoes, black flies, and intense heat, to provide vegetables for the use of the family.

I have given you a faithful picture of a life in the backwoods of Canada, and I leave you to draw from it your own conclusions. To the poor, industrious working man it presents many advantages; to the poor gentleman, none! . . . Unaccustomed to manual labour, his services in the field are not of a nature to secure for him a profitable return. The task is new to him, he knows not how to perform it well; and, conscious of his deficiency, he expends his little means in hiring labour, which his bush-farm can never repay. Difficulties increase, debts grow upon him, he struggles in vain to extricate himself, and finally sees his family sink into hopeless ruin.

If these sketches should prove the means of deterring one family from sinking their property, and shipwrecking all their hopes, by going to reside in the backwoods of Canada, I shall consider myself amply repaid for revealing the secrets of the prisonhouse, and feel that I have not toiled and suffered in the wilderness in vain.

Susanna Moodie's book leaves the reader with a strong sense of melancholy and the realization that in many cases women could *not* adapt to the wilderness and, in fact, were ruined by it both physically and psychologically.

The Gold Rush Women

The great gold rushes and mining booms of the mid- to late 1800s called for a peripatetic lifestyle for both the men involved in this work and the women who traveled with them. One such woman was Sarah Royce, whose journey across the continent was already described. Suffice it to say that her troubles did not end once she saw the smiling face of California. She spent the next several years in a succession of mining camps, where the only hope of stability lay in finding gold and thus realizing one's dreams. At first, in Weaverville, where only one other woman lived, Sarah wrote, "I was willing, for awhile, to throw off anxiety; and, like a child fixing a playhouse, I sang as I arranged our few comforts in our tent. Indeed, part of the time it was [like] fixing a play-house. . . . Still, there was a lurking feeling of want of security

from having only a cloth wall between us and the outdoors." But
with her usual adaptability, she soon was able to write, " 'Ere long,
I felt as secure in my tent with the curtain tied in front, as I had
formerly felt with locked and bolted doors."

Illness ended the Royce's first quest for gold, and they set out
for Sacramento City. Again Sarah began housekeeping in a tent,
although she was not yet strong enough to sit up all day. But on
January 9, 1850, a great flood swept away their home, among many,
and the entire community had to take shelter on higher ground.
The Royces then spent several months in San Francisco, where
they lived in boarding and tenement houses. At this period Sarah
wrote, "The conveniences of civilized life, the comforts of home,
can not be keenly appreciated, or even fully seen, by those who
have never been, for a time, shut out from them. I had never
before realized the worth of quiet domestic life, unworried by ever-
threatening dangers."

Housekeeping in many other mining camps followed, where the
Royces usually lived in tents, occasionally in houses. At times she
was left alone all night when her husband was away. "It did seem
a little dangerous," she recounted. One hot afternoon two savage-
looking men passed by and asked for water. That night Sarah could
not keep one man's face out of her mind.

Every time I thought of it, a sense of the utter defenselessness of my
position would force itself upon me. I knew I was to be alone that night,
and as evening approached, I grew more and more wary and sensitive
to every sound; till by the time the children were in bed and asleep I felt
as if I should never be sleepy again. I had, before dusk, made everything
as snug as possible in our outdoor apartment and now, putting out my
light, that it might not attract notice I prepared to act as watchman for
the night.

It was bright moonlight and all looked so beautiful and peaceful that
I felt soothed, and pleasant, sacred thoughts relieved my anxiety; but I
did not feel at all sleepy. I hummed, very softly, some sweet verses, to
dear old tunes; and precious companionship seemed to gather about me.
I was losing all sense of fear when a shrill, loud, long bark, ending in a
prolonged howl, startled me. It was in the direction of the kitchen, and
I went softly to the slit on that side, and peeped out. After a few moments
of entire silence, there was a rustling in the bushes beyond the stove,

and soon there appeared out of the shadows a full sized coyote. He walked all about our little enclosure, smelt at every box and bag, tried with his nose to open the cupboard and seemed for some time bent on depredation: but failing in finding anything to suit him, by and by he trotted off into the woods again.

It was getting towards morning—I would rest. So I lay down and slept till the sun was shining full on the front of the house.

This incident gives us a sense of Sarah's abiding faith, as well as her sensitivity to the beauty of nature. In one lovely description of a village where she stayed, she wrote:

I first entered the most lovely village in California. . . . Every smoothly-rolling hill was dressed in bloom; and the flat land of the valley stretched like a gorgeous carpet from the center of the village far back toward the foot of a grand old mountain. The air was full of the songs of answering meadow-larks, occasionally enriched by a glee from the more retiring mocking-bird.

Later in her life, Sarah acquired a melodeon (the first one ever brought to California) and she delighted in "making the woods and the pretty hills ring with some of my favorite songs." Although the Royces never found much gold, Sarah seems to have grown content with her life in California:

As I look back . . . it always seems to me that there was then granted to me an extra installment of youth; so unexpectedly rich and fresh were the experiences that came to me during that time. Not that I was rich in worldly goods, nor in surroundings that are ordinarily supposed to make life happy. But there are spiritual treasures; experiences of heart and mind, the joy of having done good to some struggling soul, the gladness of witnessing and sharing victory over evil, the certainty of a Guiding Presence, always near; these things bring a delight to the spirit which never comes from mere outward prosperity.

The Army Wives

Still another group of frontierswomen were the wives of army men who followed their husbands from one lonely outpost to another all over the West. One who wrote eloquently of this life was

Martha Summerhayes, another well-educated, cultured young woman, from Nantucket, Massachusetts, who "cast my lot with a soldier and where he was was home to me." "Home," in this case, meant army forts at Prescott, Tucson, Fort Apache, and other locations in the wild Arizona Territory, where the young couple lived in the first years of their marriage, from 1874 to 1878. When Martha and her soldier husband moved on to other posts, she was still in love with "my hero," as she called him, but a far more seasoned army wife and mother. Her book *Vanished Arizona* is laced with the many difficulties she encountered—the stifling summer temperatures, sandstorms, black ants crawling over her baby, rattlesnakes, loneliness, dangerous Indians, jolting journeys in army wagons, sudden orders to change posts, primitive living, cactus thorns, uncertain mail, and the "ever hostile and dreary desert."

In the mid-nineteenth century Arizona had no railroad; it was connected by mule train to New Mexico, by steamer to San Francisco (via the Colorado River and the Gulf of California), and by telegraph to the rest of the United States. The territory boasted a population of 20,000 in 1874. Martha Summerhayes survived from post to post because she seemed to be forever entranced with military life, though she called it a "glittering misery," and because she continued to be in love with her husband, Jack. Even when she came close to death and was forced back to Nantucket to regain her health, she wrote:

In my summer in the East I had discovered that I was really a soldier's wife and I must go back to it all. To the army with its glitter and its misery, to the post with its discomforts, to the soldiers, to the drills, to the bugle-calls, to the monotony, to the heat of Southern Arizona, to the uniform and the stalwart Captains and gay Lieutenants who wore it, I felt the call and I must go.

Martha was alternately miserable or fairly content, depending on her circumstances. Witness her words on one bivouac:

I was worn out with fright and fatigue; my poor child cried piteously and incessantly. Nothing was of any avail to soothe him. After the tents were pitched and the camp-fires made . . . I was in despair. We were about as wretchedly off as two human beings could be, and live, it seemed to me. The disappointment at not getting across the river, combined with the fear that the Indians were still in the neighborhood, added to my nervousness and produced an exhaustion which, under other circumstances, would have meant collapse.

The mournful and demoniacal cries of the coyotes filled the night; they seemed to come close to the tent, and their number seemed to be legion. I lay with eyes wide open, watching for the day to come, and resolving each minute that if I ever escaped alive from that lonely river-bottom with its burning alkali and its millions of howling coyotes, I would never, *never* risk being placed in such a situation again.

Quite a contrast is this description of a pleasant riding party on some business to a Mormon settlement seventeen miles away: "A Mormon woman gave us a lunch of fried salt pork, potatoes, bread, and milk. How good it tasted after our long ride! And how we laughed about it all, and jollied, after the fashion of young people, all the way back to the post!"

Martha often pondered her life and wondered whether she had been wise to become an army wife. At times she concluded that, "My New England bringing up had been too serious and I wondered if I had made a dreadful mistake in marrying into the Army. Or, at least in following my husband to Arizona. I debated the question with myself from all sides, and decided then and there that young Army women should stay at home with their mothers and fathers, and not go into such wild and uncouth places. I thought my decision irrevocable." On the other hand, there were times when she was very glad to be with her husband. One winter at a remote fort, she wrote, "I was glad, in those days, that I had not stayed back East, for the life of an officer without his family, in those drear places, is indeed a blank and empty one."

But Martha's lively curiosity about her new world kept her from succumbing to depression. She apparently found the Indians particularly fascinating. At one time she had an Indian servant called Charley, whom she described in ways that we might find somewhat patronizing, if lyrical, now:

"Charley" appealed to my aesthetic sense in every way. Tall, and well-made, with clean-cut limbs and features, fine smooth copper-colored skin, handsome face, heavy black hair done up in pompadour fashion and plastered with Colorado mud, which was baked white by the sun, a small feather at the crown of his head, wide turquoise bead bracelets upon his upper arm, and a knife at his waist. . . .

Charley [often] wheeled the baby out along the river banks, for we had had a fine "perambulator." It was an incongruous sight, to be sure. There sat the fair-haired, six-months-old boy, with but one linen garment on, no cap, no stockings—and this wild man of the desert, his knife gleaming at his waist, and his gee-string floating out behind, wheeling and pushing the carriage along the sandy roads.

Over the years and the miles Martha's attitude toward the wilderness softened. Though she started with an extreme hatred of the desert, she later found herself missing it. In 1903 Jack Summerhays retired, and Martha wrote:

But that fatal spirit of unrest from which I thought to escape, and which ruled my life for so many years, sometimes asserts its power, and at those times my thoughts turn back to the days when we were all Lieutenants together, marching across the deserts and mountains of Arizona; back to the days at Camp MacDowell, where we slept under the stars, and watched the sun rise from behind the Four Peaks of the MacDowell Mountains: where we rode the big cavalry horses over the sands of the Maricopa desert, swung in our hammocks under the ramadas; swam in the red waters of the Verde River, ate canned peaches, pink butter and commissary hams, listened for the scratching of the centipedes as they scampered around the edges of our canvas-covered floors, found scorpions in our slippers, and rattlesnakes under our beds.

My early experiences were unusually rough. None of us seek such experiences, but possibly they bring with them a sort of recompense, in that simple comforts afterwards seem, by contrast, to be the greatest luxuries. I am glad to have known the Army.

Frances Roe, one other army wife who should be briefly mentioned, gave a rousing defense of the life. After seventeen years in the Montana Territory she wrote her personal justification of being an army wife:*

*Time-Life Books, The Women: Old West Series, vol. 23 (Alexandria, Va.: Time-Life Books, 1978).

We know, if the world does not, that the part we are to take on this march is most important. We will see that the tents are made comfortable and cheerful at every camp; that the little dinner after the weary march, the early breakfast, and the cold luncheon are each and all as dainty as camp cooking will permit. Yes, we are sometimes called camp followers, but we do not mind—it probably originated with some envious old bachelor officer. We know all about the comfort and cheer that goes with us, and then—we have not been left behind!

The Teachers

In this category, perhaps the smallest of those discussed here and the one least commonly encountered in the literature, I include the female missionaries who ventured into the wilder regions of America, often alone except for their God, and the hundreds of eastern women who headed west in the late 1800s to become "schoolmarms." Many were very young (as young as fifteen), single, and totally on their own in one-room schoolhouses far out on lonely prairies or in dense forests. Most were heeding the stirring words of Cathrine Beecher, who in 1845 wrote "The Duty of American Women to their Country." She claimed that "it is *woman* who is to come in at this emergency [the millions of children growing up uneducated on the expanding frontier] and meet the demand, woman, whom experience and testing has shown to be the best, as well as the cheapest, guardian and teacher of childhood, in the school as well as in the nursery."

Until then teaching had been largely a man's profession, for at that time ladies did not work for wages. Even when they started taking over as frontier teachers, their average salary might be only $25.00 a month, plus fuel and repairs for the schoolhouse!

In my opinion no one paints as enthusiastic, adventurous, and practical a picture of the frontier schoolteacher as Elaine Goodale Eastman, who was known as the "Little Sister to the Sioux." Elaine was a properly brought-up New England girl who decided to espouse the humanitarian cause of bringing our native tribes into the mainstream of American life. In 1885 she set out for the Great Sioux Reservation, where she taught in a small "camp school" at White River, Dakota.

During her three years there she studied about and lived with the Indians with wholehearted dedication and fascination. She bought an Indian pony and a small tent so that she could join Sioux families on their hunting and visiting trips. White Indian agents were shocked by her boldness, but Elaine knew she was safe and "entirely happy" with her red-skinned acquaintances. When well-meaning friends urged her never to travel with Indians unarmed, she announced: "They were poor psychologists and poorer realists. A revolver in my baggage would only have served to advertise lack of trust in my companions—and in the fact that I did trust them completely lay my sole and sufficient guarantee of safety."

During these wilderness trips Elaine slept either alone in her tent or in large tipis full of men, women, children, and dogs. She reports that each person's privacy here was inviolable, and there was never the slightest self-consciousness or indiscretion among the group. Fortunately, the then-prevalent superstition that a menstruating woman must never pass food to another person, especially a man, and hence must spend her period in a solitary lodge, never became a problem for Elaine on these trips.

On one four-hundred-mile ramble the young woman calmly accepted the rattlesnakes and the lack of food. She commented in her book *Sister to the Sioux*, "When plenty reigned we all feasted, and in times of scarcity we fasted together, nor would any other arrangement have been possible under those conditions. . . . Rattlesnakes were common and before going into camp near a prairie dog town, where they abounded, it was customary to beat the ground thoroughly. I saw many killed and was sometimes presented with the rattles."

Elaine delighted in her outdoor setting and garb, describing herself on one occasion this way: "I wore a calico frock and moccasins, with my sun-bleached hair in a long braid down my back, donning shoes and a hat only when going to town, and a naturally clear skin . . . deeply tanned from constant exposure."

Elaine returned to New England in the fall of 1889, with no money and no job, but, "ideas to spare and plenty of self-confidence." She believed that she knew a great deal about the Sioux and their needs. "I am amazed by such rashness on the part of a young woman," she wrote about herself later, "barely 26 years old without family or political backing and lacking even a college diploma!" Nevertheless, the "Sister to the Sioux" gave a series of excellent paid lectures and wrote many newspaper articles "straight from the heart."

For her persistence and devotion to her cause, Elaine was rewarded with a better position and salary. She returned to the Sioux Reservation as supervisor of education, complete with a team of horses, a wagon to live in, a camping outfit, and an Indian couple as cook and driver. Now she was in charge of a large territory, which necessitated the inspection and improvement of some sixty Indian schools, the largest number in any state or territory. Considerable criticism was leveled at this young unmarried woman working in wild Dakota country. But the U.S. Indian Commissioner, General T. J. Morgan, championed her, saying, "One who has already proved her mettle as Miss Goodale has, and whose training was so thorough in all directions, would make a more striking impression upon the Indians than a man."

Elaine proved a most successful inspector, speaking fluent Dakota, wearing moccasins, living in a Sioux lodge rather than a tent, making unannounced appearances at schools, and showing such obvious enjoyment with her Indian companions that everyone adored her.

Then in 1891 Elaine Goodale met an Indian physician (known to us only as Dr. Eastman) and agreed to marry him. She wrote: "When I promised to marry Dr. Eastman, it was with a thrilling sense of two-fold consecration. I gave myself wholly in that hour to the traditional duties of wife and mother, abruptly relinquishing all thought of an independent career for the making of a home. At the same time, I embraced with a new and deeper zeal the conception of life-long service to my husband's people."

The Eastmans led an eventful life, during which Elaine wrote four books for juveniles, handled all correspondence and publicity for her husband's lectures, and raised four children. After fifteen years of marriage she was to look back and say:

No, I won't say that the adjustment was easy or that I was never lonely, restless, and haunted by a secret sense of frustration. Every woman who has surrendered a congenial task and financial independence will understand. Saving the joys of motherhood, my pleasures must be vicarious ones. But I had always something of a one-track mind, and for many a year every early dream and ambition was wholly subordinated to the business of helping my talented husband express himself and interpret his people. Whether or not this was wise is perhaps an open question. Obviously, it was far from modern.

I count myself fortunate in my children—doubly blessed in my grandchildren— . . . . Nor am I ready to admit, with certain of my thoroughly disillusioned contemporaries, that God has left his heaven and all's wrong with the world.

The Wildest Women

A few women fit no definite category when it comes to wilderness living. They may best be called "adventurers"—defiant, freedom-loving, often eccentric women. Such characters as Calamity Jane, Lillie Hitchcock Coit, Isabella Bird, Nellie Cashman, Dr. Mary Sawtelle, and Pearl Hart were some of these gallant outdoorswomen who so astonished and startled the settlers of the late 1800s and the early 1900s. Several are described in Time-Life Books' *The Women* and in Fischer's *Let Them Speak For Themselves, Women in the American West, 1849–1900.*

It's hard to pick any two as examples, for they were all so different in character and calling. Yet Calamity Jane and Isabella Bird seem to be a well-matched pair—one a rough yet literate American "free spirit," the other a cultivated and genteel English world traveler. Both were courageous, excellent riders, and both were deeply concerned for sick and wounded people, either through nursing or by providing hospital care. The similarity ends there.

Calamity Jane, born Martha Jane Cannary in 1852, had a career (the details of which are questioned by some) that encompassed being a bartender, scout, gambler, drinker, cowgirl, sharp-shooter, prospector, stage driver, cook, stunt woman (in Bill Cody's Wild West Show), sometime prostitute, and wife (to Wild Bill Hickok). She was also the mother, by Hickok, of a daughter named Janey, whom she boarded with an old friend because of her own dubious reputation. In her ungrammatical, heart-rending, and often hilarious letters to her little girl, Calamity Jane displays her recalcitrant disposition, extremely generous and tender nature, and love of the outdoors. I've excerpted a few paragraphs from these letters (leaving Jane's grammar and spelling intact) as illustrative of this vivacious woman.

Writing to Janey on September 25, 1877, from Deadwood, "Territory Dakota," she says:

I am alone in my shack tonight and tired. I rode 60 miles yesterday to the post office and returned home tonight this is your birthday and you are four years old today. You are the dead spit of Meself at your age and as I gaze on your little photo tonight I stop as I kiss you and then remembering tears start and I ask God to let me make amend some how some day to your father and you. Without either of you the years ahead look like a lonely trail.

I am going down the Yellowstone Valley just for Adventure and excitement. I am sitting beside my campfire tonight. My horse Satan, is picketed nearby. . . . He looks an object of all beauty. I am so proud of him. I can hear coyotes and wolves and the staccato wail of Indian dogs near their camps—There are thousands of Sioux in this valley I am not afraid of them—They think I am a crazy woman and never molest me.

I went up stage to Cheyenne awhile back & had quite an exciting time. I dressed in mens pants & posed as Wild Bills partner, the Jack of Diamonds. Before we got away we had a shooting contest. I beat them all & it sure filled me full of hot air. Then the change driver was killed & i took his place. Your father dared me to drive the stage that trip after the killing. I did & found it was myself in one hell of a fix Janey.

You are destined never to have a mother to live with. I am looking after a little boy. His name is Jackie, he is five years older than you, his father & mother were killed by the indians. I found him the day your Father was killed. The Sioux indians are still troublesome. I went to the battlefield after Custor's battle & I never want to see such a sight again. In a house which had been dismantled was the carcass of a man apparently hidden there to escape the Indians seeking revenge. The squaws had cut legs and arms from the dead soldiers, then heads were chopped, then eyes probed out. You see, Custer had molested an Indian village, running the squaws & children from their camps, so one cant blame them for getting even in their own way. . . . Good night dear till next time.

In 1880 Jane wrote to her daughter again from Deadwood.

I am back here in Deadwood for a few weeks. I hate the women here. The majority of them are no better than I am but they cross the street rather than speak to me or pass me. If they only knew that I know about their fathers chukling over the notches of their shot guns that another of their daughters is married . . . . One smell under their arms would be enough for me were I a man.

Two years later she wrote:

"I am gambling these days to get enough money to give your Daddy Jim for yor education. [Janey's foster parent was named Jim O'Neil.] Easy come easy goes. I always find some poor damn fool worse off than me & help them to a grub stake or buy some God for saken Family of children clothing & food. I coudnt eat a mouthful if I saw some poor little brat hungry. I always think of you darling & away goes my money. Then I start all over again. I dont figure its any feather in my cap to act the way I do. I sometimes get a little tipsy Janey but I dont harm any one. I have to do something to forget you & your Father but I am not a Fancy Woman Janey if I were I wouldnt be nursing & scouting & driving stage."

Calamity Jane was so different from most women that she usually aroused feelings of disgust and hatred in them. Here she tells of a fracas she got into in Deadwood.

They came into the salloon with a horse whip & shears to cut off my hair. Well Janey I fixed them in my own way. I jumped off the bar into their midst & before They could say sickem I had them all howling. I cut off one of the bitches old black locks & thrashed the whip over their heads. You see, I wear pants so I can get around while these peticoted females yell for help. You should have seen her when I jumped off the bar. I grabbed her hoop skirt & 3 petticotes & flung them all up over her head. She couldnt fight back so I had her just where I wanted her. I tore off her long pantalets & left her standing there in her birthday bloomers for the men to get a treat. . . . I'll never live to be very old Janey. I cant stand this awful life very many years. I sometimes think I'll be married again & then the thought of being tied to one man's shirt tail sickens me. I wish things were different & I could live on through the years knowing I would someday have you with me.

In the seven years that followed Calamity Jane hooked up with Bill Cody's Wild West Show and traveled all over the United States and part of Europe. In July, 1898 she wrote:

I am tired & feel so old. I am nursing again. I can always fall back on that. I got so lonely for our old west & so disgusted with gadding all over the world—Lord! how I did hate England with its snobs its good for nothing women with their put on airs & brogue. They forgot they were thrashed by a handful of Americans not so long ago. I felt like shoutin it from the tree tops. I never saw so many human parasites as there are in England especially the women with their blokes.

After this long tour Calamity Jane seems to have started losing her good health and spirits. She wrote Janey in 1899:

This life is a long hideous night mare. This country is beautiful but I am growing to hate it because it has taken from me everything I ever loved. It took Bill from me, it was the cause of haveing to give you up. It has wrecked me, this country. I am not old Janey but I feel as though I had reached the end of my rope.

I guess my diary is just about finished. I am going blind—can still see to write this yet but I cant keep on to live an avaricious old age. All hope is dead forever Janey. What have I ever done except to make one blunder after another? All I have left are these little pictures of you and your Father. I cant go on blind & the doctor told me yesterday that in 2 months I would be absolutely blind. O how I wish I had my life to live over—

Calamity Jane died in 1903 and was buried next to Wild Bill Hickok's grave, as she had desired. Though she left a fantastic reputation for wild exploits, this small book of letters reveals the tenderness and affection of a mother and wife which persisted beneath her prickly outer nature. Jane's love for Janey and Wild Bill Hickok was the one stable and steadfast element in her life as she trekked from frontier town to frontier town engaged in a variety of work, and camped in wild places.

By including Isabella Bird, an Englishwoman, in this chapter, I have broken my rule of discussing only North American women. But I feel the exception is justified, for in addition to her well-documented travels in the Himalayas and Tibet, her account of the period she spent in Colorado in the fall and winter of 1873, *A Lady's Life in the Rocky Mountains,* is as vivid, perceptive, and eloquent a portrayal of the western wilderness as any early female writer has bequeathed us.

Unlike Calamity Jane, Isabella Bird was every inch a lady, as well as a lover of the outdoors and an excellent writer. She seldom complained of loneliness or revealed her personal feelings. Ironically, she never intended any of her letters to her sister, which now make up *A Lady's Life*, to be published; journalism was not the purpose of her journey. Isabella had been delicate as a young woman and hoped to improve her health by travel. And although she often rode alone for miles in the wildest country, she did not consider herself an explorer or a geographer. Her sole purpose was "for recreation and interest." Nevertheless, she was the first woman ever elected (1892) as a fellow of the Royal Geographical Society of England.

The unbeaten paths she trod and the unusual people she encountered impressed and appealed to Isabella. She was never molested; on the contrary, she was well treated.

I saw a lumberer taking his dinner on a rock in the river, who "touched his hat" and brought me a draught of ice-cold water, which I could hardly drink owing to the fractiousness of the horse, and gathered me some mountain pinks, which I admired. I mention these little incidents to indicate the habit of respectful courtesy to women which prevails in that region. These men might have been excused for speaking in a somewhat free-and-easy tone to a lady riding alone, and in an unwonted fashion. Womanly dignity and manly respect for women are the salt of society in this wild West. There's nothing Western folk admire so much as pluck in a woman.

Isabella was quite accurate in her descriptions of tree species, wildlife, elevations, and dimensions of natural objects and places. And only once in her book did she show any dislike or fear of animal life:

I killed a rattlesnake this morning close to the cabin, and have taken its rattle, which has eleven joints. My life is embittered by the abundance of these reptiles—rattlesnakes and moccasin snakes, both deadly, carpet snakes and "green racers," reputed dangerous, water snakes, tree snakes, and mouse snakes, harmless but abominable. Seven rattlesnakes have been killed just outside the cabin since I came. A snake, three feet long, was coiled under the pillow of the sick woman. I see snakes in all withered twigs, and am ready to flee at "the sound of a shaken leaf." And besides snakes, the earth and air are alive and noisy with forms of insect life, large and small, stinging, humming, buzzing, striking, rasping, devouring!

Time after time she gloried in the magnificent landscapes of Colorado.

The scenery up here is glorious, combining sublimity with beauty, and in the elastic air fatigue has dropped off from me. This is no region for tourists and women, only for a few elk and bear hunters at times, and its unprofaned freshness gives me new life. . . .

This is truly the "lodge in some vast wilderness" for which one often sighs when in the midst of "a bustle at once sordid and trivial." This scenery satisfies my soul. Now, the Rocky Mountains realize—nay, exceed—the dream of my childhood. It is magnificent, and the air is life giving.

While staying in Estes Park, Isabella managed to climb Long's Peak—a mere five years after it had first been scaled. Her guide was Mountain Jim, "as awful looking a ruffian as one could see." He proved to be extremely fond and careful of Isabella, despite being known as a notorious desperado. In a gentlemanly, courteous, and stubborn fashion, he dragged the forty-two-year-old woman, "slipping, faltering, gasping from the exhausting toil in the rarified air, with throbbing heart and panting lungs, and tongue so dry that articulation was difficult," up the peak. Isabella finally stood atop the 14,700-foot mountain, which she described rapturously:

From the summit were seen in unrivalled combination all the views which had rejoiced our eyes during the ascent. It was something at last to stand upon the stormrent crown of this lonely sentinel of the Rocky Range, on one of the mightiest of the vertebrae of the backbone of the North American continent, and to see the waters start for both oceans. Uplifted above love and hate and storms of passion, calm amidst the eternal silences, fanned by zephyrs and bathed in living blue, peace rested for that one bright day on the Peak.

We reached Estes Park at noon of the following day. A more successful ascent of the Peak was never made, and I would not now exchange my memories of its perfect beauty and extraordinary sublimity for any other experience of mountaineering in any part of the world. Yesterday snow fell on the summit, and it will be inaccessible for eight months to come.

Some of Isabella's wilderness rides would have tried any but
the toughest adventurers. It seems it was nothing for her to ride
thirty miles over a span of fourteen hours, having eaten nothing
but raisins. One of her most harrowing trips came when she left
Estes Park, rode down to Golden City, and got lost in a blizzard
on the track to Denver. She described the experience thus:

It soon became so dark that I could not even see Birdie's ears, and was
lost and benighted. I rode on, hour after hour, in the darkness and
solitude, the prairie all round and a firmament of frosty stars overhead.
The prairie wolf howled now and then, and occasionally the lowing of
cattle gave me hope of human proximity. But there was nothing but the
lone wild plain. You can hardly imagine the longing to see a light, to hear
a voice, the intensely eerie feeling of being alone in that vast solitude.
It was freezing very sharply and was very cold, and I was making up my
mind to steer all night for the pole-star. When I heard the undertoned
bellowing of a bull, and a dog bark and a man swear; then I saw a light,
and in another minute found myself at a large house, where I knew the
people, only eleven miles from Denver!

She found an adventure in a snowstorm on the way to Longmount
more of an ordeal, but she persevered:

By that time I had reached the prairie, only eight miles from Longmount, and pushed on. It was simply fearful. It was twilight from the
thick snow, and I faced a furious east wind loaded with fine, hard-frozen
crystals, which literally made my face bleed. I could only see a very short
distance anywhere; the drifts were often two feet deep.
Reaching a wild place, I lost it, and still cantered on, trusting to the
pony's sagacity. It failed for once, for she took me on a lake and we fell
through the ice into the water, 100 yards from land, and had a hard fight
back again. It grew worse and worse. I had wrapped up my face, but the
sharp, hard snow beat on my eyes—the only exposed part—bringing tears
into them, which froze and closed up in my eyelids at once. You cannot
imagine what that was. I had to take off one glove to pick one eye open,
for as to the other, the storm beat so savagely against it that I left it frozen,
and drew over it the double piece of flannel which protected my face. I
could hardly keep the other open by picking the ice from it constantly
with my numb fingers, in doing which I got the back of my hand slightly
frostbitten. It was truly awful at the time.

I calculated that if I did not reach Longmount in half an hour it would be quite dark, and that I should be so frozen or paralyzed with cold that I should fall off. When I reached the hotel I was so benumbed that I could not get off, and the worthy host lifted me off and carried me in.

All told, Isabella Bird covered 800 miles in Colorado, mostly alone, on her beloved mare Birdie. It was an extraordinary feat for a woman in those days, and an accomplishment worthy of any skilled explorer.

American Indian Women

It would be wrong to overlook the role that women from many Indian tribes played in the exploration and settlement of the western wilderness. From the advent of white explorers and adventurers, there were Indian women who chose to accompany these men as interpreters, peacemakers, or guides. The fact that the whole culture of these women was deeply rooted in the wilderness must be kept in mind when drawing comparisons. It should also be noted that my purpose is to describe not their normal lives and roles within the tribal structure, but only their involvement with the settlement process.

Besides Sacajawea, who will be discussed at length below, we know of at least two or three other Indian women who played important roles in this process. An Indian woman was reported to have manned a large canoe for the well-known Scotch trader, MacKenzie, in Canada. The Indian wife of the geographer David Thompson helped find a pass through the Rockies and walked three thousand miles with her husband. And then there is Malinché (Doña Marina), a stolen Aztec chieftain's daughter, who became Cortés's mistress and the main interpreter and secretary in his dealings with the Aztecs of Mexico. In addition, hundreds, if not thousands, of Indian women became the temporary companions of trappers, traders, voyagers, and mountain men. Some of these unions were as casual and short-lived as "the tightening of a pack-horse cinch or the dip of a canoe paddle" (to quote Walter O'Meara). Other alliances proved deep and lasting, resulting in real marriages which spanned several years. O'Meara writes of Shagowashcoda-woqua, who married John Johnson, a trader in the settlement of

Sault Ste. Marie, Michigan, in the mid-1800's. She lived with him for thirty-seven years, had eight children, and kept a huge house and library at Sault Ste. Marie. As a widow, she continued to manage his extensive maple sugar plantation and his fishing fleet on Lake Superior. Another Indian woman married Donald Smith, Governor of Hudson Bay Company, in 1835; this marriage lasted forty-three years.

Whatever the relationship, Indian women were indispensable to their white male companions, since they could cut wood; make maple syrup; gather wild rice, roots, and berries; scrape skins; fashion moccasins; dry meat and fish; put up and take down shelters; pack horses; pull sleds; tend fields; sew, pitch, and portage canoes; net snowshoes; bear and care for children; clean; and cook. Many a wilderness man and wilderness trading post owed their very existence to the manual skills and endurance of Indian women. Furthermore, the qualities cultivated by Indian women—bravery, patience, generosity, and truthfulness—helped to make them congenial and suitable living companions under the hard and dangerous conditions of the wilderness.

Despite the fact that few Indian women actually found security, prestige, or financial reward in their relationships and wilderness homes with white men, they normally stayed with their new lives and worked hard for years. Occasionally they were deserted, beaten, or even murdered by their white male consorts; and sometimes they were disowned by their own people.

They had no legal rights in their nonmarital unions with white men, and the attitude of the white men toward them seems to have been ambivalent. On one hand, they were appreciated for their skills and virtues, and in some cases no doubt sincerely loved. But racial taboos were strong, as was the urge to bring civilization to the wild. Only the presence of the virtuous, white female could bring about this goal. As Dawn Lander commented (see Chapter 1),

White women who refuse to restrict their behavior to what society intends for them find the wilderness a natural habitat for a forbidden sexuality. . . .

The only women who are permitted in the wilderness are of subordinated class and race: blacks, Indians and white whores.

Nevertheless, the willingness and steadfastness of these Indian women contributed an enormous amount to the early exploration and exploitation of the North American continent.

The best-known example of an Indian woman acting as guide, interpreter, and peacemaker is Sacajawea. Contrary to popular belief, this young (sixteen-year-old) Shoshoni girl did not assist in the direct exploration and daily route-finding of Lewis and Clark's advance party. Though occasionally she was able to point out the best passes through the mountains, she functioned chiefly as the expedition's interpreter and token symbol of peaceful intent when the party met strange Indian tribes along the way. Sacajawea was the first woman, as far as is known, to cross the North American continent from the Missouri River to the Pacific Ocean, a distance of some 2,000 miles. The young squaw, who had been captured and bartered off by French Canadian traders a few years earlier, was the wife of Toussaint Charbonneau, a French Canadian trapper living at Fort Mandan in North Dakota. When Lewis and Clark stopped to spend the winter of 1804–1805 here, they hired Toussaint because he had lived with Indians and could communicate by sign language with the river tribes. By good fortune his wife, Sacajawea, wanted to accompany him on the trek. The explorers quickly realized that when they reached the mountain tribes an Indian who spoke Shoshoni would be invaluable in order to negotiate for pack horses and mounts.

Sacajawea gave birth to a baby boy on February 11, 1805, and six weeks later left with the expedition. The thirty-three people (thirty-two of them men) went up the Missouri in six small canoes and two large pirogues. Sacajawea soon showed the value of her wilderness and survival skills. She was able to gather roots, nuts, and berries to supplement the expedition's food supplies. When one of the large boats containing the bulk of the party's valuable cargo capsized, she caught and saved many of the lighter articles which were irreplaceable. Captain Meriwether Lewis was impressed and described Sacajawea in his journal as "the Indian woman to whom I ascribe equal fortitude and resolution with any person on board. . ."

As time passed, the small, seemingly frail girl won a place of respect and love in the hearts of the entire group. She proved her greatest value when they met a Shoshoni band in the Bitterroot Mountains of Idaho, who turned out to be the long-lost friends and relatives from whom she had been wrested years before. She was instrumental in negotiating with these Shoshoni for horses to take Lewis and Clark across the Rockies, thus saving them an arduous trip.

Rather than stay with her own people, Sacajawea went on with her husband and the expedition. Thanks to this young mother and her child, the potentially aggressive tribes of Indians along the way let the group pass in peace. Clark wrote of her presence: "[She] reconciles all the Indians as to our friendly intentions. A woman with a party of men is a token of peace."

They reached the Pacific on November 8, 1805, having walked, ridden, and paddled over four thousand miles. Sacajawea and Toussaint overwintered with the explorers and returned east with them the following spring. They arrived at Fort Mandan in August 1806, sixteen months after starting out. Toussaint was paid with a horse and lodge worth $500.33⅓ cents. As for Sacajawea, Clark wrote to Toussaint: "Your woman who accompanied you this long and dangerous and fatiguing route to the Pacific Ocean and back, deserved a greater reward for her attention and service than we had in our power to give her. . . ." (Although Clark paid her nothing, he later raised and educated her little boy as a token of his esteem and gratitude.)

Apparently Sacajawea died of a fever along the upper Missouri River when she was about twenty-five years old. However, her wilderness training, her quiet matter-of-fact and resilient nature, and her adaptability to rough conditions contributed greatly to the first white crossing of this continent and set an example for others— both men and women—to follow.

Now that we have followed the stories of a number of white frontierswomen whose backgrounds and experiences are quite diverse, we can ask what general attitudes about the wilderness they share. Almost all speak, if not complain bitterly, of the hardships, the primitive conditions, the loneliness and social deprivations due to the isolated living conditions. Still, almost all these women (and many others not presented here) show an enormous fortitude and resourcefulness. They accept and handle situations, such as giving birth under a wagon or being flooded out of a tent, which might render most modern white civilized women helpless or terror-stricken. The women also show great physical strength and endurance, in their riding, wagon driving, and reaction to cold and heat, wind and snow, and drought. Because in those days women were supposed to be weak and fragile, these writers do not draw attention to their hardiness.

The women's reactions to wildlife vary. Some writers wax eloquent over birds and big game; others relate fear of wolves and bears; all are repulsed by snakes. The wilderness beauty, even though stark and strange to their eyes, is evident to most of them. Even if they hate it at first, be it desert or forest, with time and distance they often come to appreciate and yearn for their surroundings.

A feeling that comes through in many of these writings (though it is not often stated explicitly) is the women's dependence on the men in their party or family for sheer survival. Many ask what would become of them if they were widowed or left alone in the wilderness with their children. Only Calamity Jane and Isabella Bird were calmly independent and did not seem to need a man, although both had close friendships with men and relied upon them for logistical support and livelihood at times.

Except for Calamity Jane, most of these women also seem to have had a faith in some kind of God and drew amazing strength from their religious convictions. It often seems that the main way they got through their incredible hardships was by clinging to this staunch belief and leaving their fate entirely in the hands of Providence. Whatever their sources of strength, the women of the frontier era were proving that they could make their way in the wilderness.

Chapter 3

Frontier Women in Fiction

LIFE ON THE frontier was a popular subject with American novelists of the late nineteenth and early twentieth centuries, and the staunch pioneer woman is often cast as a heroine. Indeed, in the fiction of western America we find perhaps more strong and self-reliant female characters than in any previous period in literature. This was also the era of realism in fiction; many of the best novels were carefully researched by their authors, and their depictions of the wilderness and the people who came to live there are for the most part quite accurate.

I have chosen to survey here the work of four writers whose detailed portraits of frontier women I greatly admire: Conrad Richter's trilogy *The Trees, The Fields,* and *The Town;* A. B. Guthrie's classic *The Way West;* Ole Rölvaag's *Giants in the Earth;* and Willa Cather's *My Ántonia* and *O, Pioneers!.* The four novelists come from fairly different backgrounds, but all share an enthusiasm for this period in American history and a commitment to describing people, places, and events honestly, sensitively, and realistically. As Ole Rölvaag declared: "The only unforgiveable sin is to write about life untruthfully."

Conrad Richter was born in 1890 in a small Pennsylvania mountain community, the descendent of tradesmen and preachers. He was an avid collector of folk tales and historical documents, from which he distilled the authentic details that abound in his work. His writing is characterized by restraint, attentive description, and tight narrative structure. His epic trilogy of the Ohio pioneers, spanning the eighteenth century and on into the post-Civil War era, has been called the truest picture we have of frontier life.

Sayward, Richter's heroine, is, to my mind, the best literary depiction of a strong wilderness woman. The trilogy traces her life as she grows from a young girl moving with her family into the vast wild forest that covered the Midwest in the early 1800's, to a vigorous, busy mother of ten children and the keeper of corn and cattle, and finally becomes an eighty-year-old rich and respected matriarch of her town. It subtly relates how Sayward went from hating trees—to her the symbol of the wilderness—to cherishing them when they were all gone from her property. Early in the saga she states that she

always was against the vast blanket of trees which she felt imprisoned them and was full of vermin and varmints. . . . Why, all her life she had hugged herself to see a tree come down. It meant you could see the sun and stars a little better. A mite more light and air could come in. A few more stalks of corn could grow and give meal to hungry young mouths. Why, back in the woods, she and every other settler woman hated the trees like poison. They were your mortal enemy. All your life you had to fight them, chop, split, nigger them off till nothing was left and then their wild sprouts kept coming up to plague you. Even now long after the trees were gone, the big butts still lived on in your joints. Heavy lifting and rolling had thickened them till you sometimes felt like an old tree walking.

In her old age Sayward looks out over the city and is distressed to see hardly a tree.

All winter she looked at the naked city and square. When the ground first thawed in the early spring she put a mattox, shovel and old axe in the chariot and had Chancey drive her into the country. She picked out three young maples, a buckeye, a basswood, and a white wood poplar. They drove back to town with the long whips sticking out of the back of the chariot. Until she finished planting them, a small crowd of folk had gathered to watch. Where did she get them? Did she think they would grow in the city? Where did she get the idea—from her hometown back east?

All Sayward will reply to these people or to her family is, "The town doesn't look right to me without any trees, especially not the square." Thus her sentiments come full circle as the wilderness disappears.

The first book, *The Trees*, presents a very interesting picture of the roles of men and women on the frontier, and the way the women feel about their position. After her mother dies and her father deserts the family, Sayward thinks:

She knew well enough he was running off. God Almighty had made a man free that way. When things got out of kilter at home, he could take his gun and go to the woods. But a woman had to stay home and mind the big kettle and the little kettle. It wasn't likely she'd get away far as a whoop and a holler till the littlest one, was he son or brother, got big enough to take off by himself. And by that time she'd have forgot all about that mess of troubles and have plenty new ones.

"But it's no use a cryin' you ain't a man," Sayward told herself calmly. "God Almighty done it this way and you kain't change it."

Sayward's sisters, Genny and Achsa, also feel these differences.

Genny could hear the bound [indentured] boy calling to her now. It came over her she was a deer, too. The bound boy was hunting her like men always hunted women and wild things. Never would they let them be to live their own lives. No, men always came after, smelling and tracking them down. But the bound boy would never find her. She was a young doe. A delicious wildness came up in her. The woods looked different now. The trees and bushes, even the poison sumach, were friendly. They stood over and bent down at her and tried to hide her. You had to be a deer to know how the wild things felt when a man was after you.

This comparison of a woman to a wild creature is fascinating to me. Evidently Sayward and her sisters had a good deal of wilderness in them, struggling to get out. Yet sometimes it seemed a losing battle. When Achsa's little sister runs away and gets lost, the following passage appears:

You could see Achsa hankered to go along [to search]. Every last man and boy, Louie told her. But not women and girls. They were no good in the woods. They only made it harder.

Achsa's black eyes burned back at him. You could tell she reckoned it easy enough to be a man and go out in the woods whooping to keep in line and beating the bushes for a little tyke in a red dress that by this time the brush must have whipped halfways off her back. You did no whooping at women's work. No, you stooped by the fire till your face singed and your leg muscles ached so folks got enough to eat. And you heard no horn. All you listened to was women's talk from daylight to dark.

Sayward marries an educated but unkempt lawyer who mysteriously came from Maine to live in a remote cabin. After they have settled down and she has become a mother, she spends long hard days carving a farm out of the wilderness so her family could survive while her husband does his legal work. Richter describes her life in vivid detail:

She had a big wheel now for wool and a little wheel for flax, and Will Beagle had set her up a loom by the wall. Her crops did well among the stumps. She had a small bunch of ewes toward wool, geese toward down, cows toward milk and leather, and a patch in flax. But it was a "tejus" crop. You had to plow it, drag it, sow it, weed and pull it. And that was only the start, for then it took spreading, bundling, stocking, flailing, sweating, rotting, braking, swingling and hatcheling, one after the other.

But Sayward was a hustler, ever clearing more ground and mauling rails to fence it in, her three boys a'helping. This was in fall and winter. Spring and summer they worked with her in the fields. Always were they behind in their work. Making a farm out of the wilderness is a backbreaking job. In spare time Sayward sent them out scouring the woods for sang to trade, and teas and herbs for home. They had to gather linn for rope and hickory bark for light wood when candles ran low. After dark they shelled and ground corn in the chimney corner, filled the weaver's quills, whittled pegs and gluts and plaited straw. Then, the minute supper was done, his weaving and her spinning started.

After eight children (one of whom died) and an illness, Sayward begins to practice the only birth control she knows: abstinence. Again, Richter's metaphorical use of a wild creature, the squirrel,

is very effective and shows his close observation of the natural
setting.

Oh, she couldn't expect Portius to fall in line with her. . . . The woman
was the one that had to pay the fiddler. She had to give her flesh and
blood before her babe was born, and her milk and tending afterward.
You might as well say she was mammy and pappy both. The man was
just the one who didn't know what he was doing when he dropped the
seed, like a squirrel hiding a nut or acorn in the ground. That squirrel
had no notion of raising a stand of oaks or a chestnut orchard. Truth to
tell, you could almost do without the man, but you hadn't dare tell him
so, or he'd be miffed. The way Portius acted, he must have reckoned it
a terrible thing, this going against her vow to freely be his wife. But he'd
get used to it in time.

Apparently Portius did not "get used to it," for he reacts to Sayward's stubborn refusal by having an affair with a young school
teacher, which results in an illegitimate child. When Sayward learns
of this, she returns to his bed, thinking:

She was broke to the yoke now. She had fought against it. She had
yawed around and fouled it. But it did no good in the end. It only got
her under the whip and the harrow. She better go along quiet as she
could now in her . . . yoke and bear her load.

She also bows to his wishes to move into an elegant brick house
in town. By this time she has come to love her log cabin, and like
a fish out of water, she roams about the huge house, remembering
how this very land had once held huge trees, then her own corn
fields. She ponders:

What was the world coming to and what hearty pleasures folks today
missed out of life! . . . Was that the way this great new country of hers
was going to go? The easier they made life, the weaker and sicker the
race had to get? Her pap's generation could get down on their knees and
thank the Almighty they lived and died when they did. How would they
ever have come and settled this wild country if they said to each other,
"Ain't you afeard?" How would her pappy have fetched them the long
way out here on foot if he'd kept asking all the time, "Are ye all right!
How do ye feel? Do ye reckon ye kin make it?" No, those old time folks

she knew were scared of nothing, or if they were, they didn't say so. They knew they ran bad risks moving into Indian country, but they had to die some time. They might as well live as they pleased and let others bury them when the time came.

Sayward's is the classic story of a pioneer woman and a true reflection of the character that this experience most often developed: fearful of her wild surroundings at first but gradually growing to love their beauty and freedom, resigned to the "God-given" role that women were meant to occupy yet inwardly rebelling against it.

Though he spent his early years in Montana, A. B. Guthrie (1901–) had probably the least firsthand experience with pioneers or their descendents of the four writers discussed here. The main influence on his work seems to have been his father, a newspaper editor from whom he inherited a fascination for Western Americana as well as his profession. After working at odd jobs in many states, Guthrie practiced journalism for twenty years, though he did not begin to write his chronicles of the West until he was thirty-eight. His novels are fast-paced, colloquial, grittily realistic, and sometimes sentimental; they give a faithful if sometimes romanticized view of frontier life.

Rebecca, the motherly female figure in Guthrie's novel *The Way West*, is very reminiscent of Sayward, though less reflective. Yet some of her thoughts are wonderfully perceptive, showing both the liberating and disquieting effects that wilderness can have on women, and the vastly different positions of men and women in that era. She comments acutely on the tendency of men, especially in the uncivilized West, to put women on a pedestal:

> Some of the others stuck to queer ideas of women, not liking to think of them as flesh and blood and stomach and guts but as something different, something a cut above earthy things, so that no one should let on to them that critters had hindends. Women had harder heads than men liked to believe.

Rebecca and her husband travel west from Missouri on the Oregon Trail in 1846, encountering many of the same perils de-

scribed by real pioneer women in Chapter 2. Guthrie sees clearly
the contrast between men and women in their ability to regard
pioneering as an adventure. Rebecca says:

Men were queer, taking such a real and simple pleasure in the work
of muscles and the roll of wheels. The more miles they made, the better
spirited they were, as if there wasn't any aim in life but to leave tracks,
no time in it but for go. They didn't mind eating mush with blowing sand
in it. But women worked at the purposeful fret of living—the little drain-
ing businesses of rubbing and scuffing and ringing out and hanging on
a line. Did they feel the load of things, the day by day doing of chores
that would just have to be done again? The wet, red hands that dry air
would chap worse, the dark disquiet, the wordless apprehension that
made all troubles big?

Guthrie apparently believes that life on the trail *was* liberating
for women in some ways. He describes in the following passage
how the experience changed them—and their menfolk's view of
them as well.

Raw or not, the women did their part and more. They travelled head to
head with men, showing no more fear and asking no favor. They had a
kind of toughness in them that you might not think, seeing them in a
parlor. So, on a trail, women came to speak, and men to listen, almost
as if to other men. It was lucky for the pride of men that few travelled
with their wives to Oregon. They'd never quite believe again a woman
was to look at but not to listen to.

So it was with Rebecca's husband, who, as quoted in Chapter
1, had earlier dismissed her opinion about heading West with the
comment: "God knows women have aplenty to say, but no say-so."
    Ole Rölvaag's *Giants in the Earth* is perhaps the most powerful
and somber of the novels mentioned here. The novel graphically
conveys the loneliness and depression of an immigrant family's life
on an isolated prairie homestead in the Dakota Territory during
the late 1800's. Born in 1876, Rölvaag himself emigrated from
Norway when he was twenty, winding up at an uncle's farm in
South Dakota. An excellent, mainly self-taught, student, he eventually became head of the Norwegian Department at St. Olaf's

College in Minnesota. Rölvaag dedicated his writing to his fellow
Scandinavians who settled the northern woods and plains; certainly
his own background enabled him to describe their situation per-
ceptively and compassionately.

The tale of Beret, wife of Per Hansa, runs through *Giants in the
Earth* like a bitter thread. Beret is simply not cut out to be a
pioneer, "not built to wrestle with fortune." She cannot adapt or
root herself in the new soil. She is continually homesick for Norway
and uneasy in America. It strikes her from the very beginning that
out on the plains, "something was about to go wrong. How will
human beings be able to endure this place? Why, there isn't even
a thing that one can hide behind!" Beret seldom goes walking
outdoors, and her only refuge from the vast empty prairie is their
homesteader's sod house. Typically dark and claustrophobic, it was
at first even bare of the comforts of curtains, rugs, or whitewash.
Her uneasiness soon increases to dread. She lies awake at night
in tears, wrestling with fearsome thoughts. "What would happen
if something suddenly should befall them—attack or sickness or
fire—yes, what could they do?" With the advent of winter, her
despair deepens.

Beret had grown more sober as the autumn came, more locked up
within herself; a heavy heart lay all the time in her bosom, but she tried
her best to hide it from her husband. Her face wore that weary, abandoned
expression which had now become habitual to it. Whenever she was left
alone, a sense of such deep melancholy lay upon her, that her whole
appearance seemed to reflect a never-ending struggle with unreality.

The more Per Hansa and his sons grow to love their land, the
deeper Beret is driven into her private darkness. She eats less and
less, suffers from insomnia, loses things, becomes unkempt, cries
frequently, and can barely communicate. Per Hansa tries to talk
about the future but fails completely to draw her out of herself;
ultimately her husband and her children are dragged down with
her.

Beret begins to see giants in the clouds, feels an evil power
looming over the plains. She hides in a great chest which she
fancies will be her casket. The little Norwegian community fears

that she might do harm to herself or her family. Like Richter, Rölvaag uses metaphors from nature to powerful effect. As a result of Beret's illness, he says, her husband's "whole figure seemed fearfully ravaged and broken, like a forest maple shattered by a storm."

Through the ministrations of a circuit-riding minister, Beret regains some mental health, only to become a religious fanatic. Her new personality and beliefs eventually drive Per Hansa to his death.

For me, the whole message of Rölvaag's book was of the cruel costs that some women, and men as well, had to pay for seeking new lives in the wilderness. The hardships Beret faced were much the same as those which thousands of other frontier women had to deal with, regardless of where they settled. Many overcame these difficulties, but many others whose characters were not so strong succumbed to them.

Willa Cather's works contain some of the greatest description of the American prairie wilderness ever written, and her feeling for its people is equally strong. Her family settled on a ranch in Nebraska when she was a child in the 1880's, and Cather absorbed with fascination the speech patterns and customs of neighboring immigrant families. She later portrayed them in her novels with precise detail and great sensitivity.

After *Giants in the Earth* I turned to the two Cather novels with relief. Her heroines, Ántonia and Alexandra (the latter in *O, Pioneers!*), are, like Beret Hansa, foreign immigrants. They are eking out an existence on the wild Nebraska prairie. But in sharp contrast with Beret, both of Cather's women love the land and are as self-reliant and strong as oxen. They know no other life and want no other. The heroine of *O, Pioneers!*, far from feeling oppressed or disoriented by wild nature, finds in it reassurance and stability:

Alexandra drew her shawl closer about her and stood leaning against the frame of the mill, looking at the stars which glittered so keenly through the frosty autumn air. She always loved to watch them, to think of their vastness and distance, and of their ordered march. It fortified her to reflect upon the great operations of nature, and when she thought of the law that lay behind them, she felt a sense of personal security.

This is not to intimate that life was easy for Alexandra or Ántonia—particularly the former, who had no husband with whom to share the farm work until late in life. Yet their struggles built character and beauty in both women:

Ántonia had always been one to leave images in the mind that did not fade—that grew stronger with time. She lent herself to immemorial human attitudes which we recognize by instinct as universal and true. I had not been mistaken. She was a battered woman now, not a lovely girl; but she still had that something which fires the imagination, could still stop one's breath for a moment by a look or gesture that somehow revealed the meaning in common things. She had only to stand in the orchard, to put her hand on a little crab tree and look up at the apples, to make you feel the goodness of planting and tending and harvesting at last. All the strong things of her heart came out in her body, that had been so tireless in serving generous emotions.

Both Alexandra and Ántonia are deeply rooted in the soil of their adopted land, and through it they express themselves. They have no fear of this prairie wilderness nor of its trials and tribulations. They are truly part of this new land. In the character of Ántonia we see a woman whose spirit and physical being are fully in tune, who expresses through her body a sense of communion with the natural world.

For the first time, perhaps, since that land emerged from the waters of geologic ages, a human face was set toward it with love and yearning. It seemed beautiful to her, rich and strong and glorious. Her eyes drank in the breadth of it, until her tears blinded her. Then the Genius of the Divide, the great, free spirit which breathes across it, must have bent lower than it ever bent to a human will before. The history of every country begins in the heart of a man or a woman.

I believe that Willa Cather is the only writer who could have portrayed these two women so intimately and warmly—perhaps because she, too, was a woman who had grown up on the prairies.

In the fictional portraits of frontier women by these four authors, as in the real women of the last chapter, we see a wide range of reactions to wilderness life, with Rölvaag's Beret and Cather's

Ántonia and Alexandra at opposite extremes. Surely the personal experience of the writers had much to do with how they drew their characters in each case. Though I have read of no specific woman close to Rölvaag who was as disturbed as Beret, he must have known or known of women who shared her unhappiness. Willa Cather, by all accounts, was as indomitable as her heroines.

The three male novelists show much compassion for the situations of the women they portray and considerable insight into their feelings. Nevertheless, the strongest female characters were created by the only female writer of the group.

We might end our look at real and fictional early wilderness women by noting that in spite of their individual differences, one factor is common to all: the frontier experience was for them a matter of endurance and survival. Not until somewhat later did the wilderness cease to be a battleground and begin to become a place of personal or professional fulfillment. In the next chapter we will see how this transformation came about.

Chapter 4

Changing Times

As WE HAVE SEEN, with few exceptions the women who came to live on the North American frontier during the early period of settlement did so only passively, accompanying their menfolk because they had little or no choice in the matter. Some adapted well to their new surroundings; others did not. However, it seems fair to say that their collective experience, viewed as a whole, did eventually encourage them to develop greater strength and resourcefulness and new skills, and fostered an attitude of independence and pride in their accomplishments. So it may be regarded as the first step toward bringing out the wilderness in women.

Now we will begin to consider the phenomenon of women entering wilderness work and life by their own choice. Although the presence of women in wilderness-oriented careers has become significant only in the last fifteen or twenty years (this virtual revolution will be examined in the next chapter), the factors leading to it began to exert their influence in the latter part of the nineteenth century. In this chapter I shall survey these diverse factors, not necessarily in any chronological or historical order, and attempt to build a total picture of the circumstances that have made it possible for women in recent years to find personal and professional fulfillment in the wilderness.

The influence of the American wilderness on the women who

came in contact with it has been profound, on both the individual and the cultural level. From the start its toughness and rugged beauty, and the isolation it imposed, began to change women psychologically and physically. Gradually it alienated them from European traditions and even from the customs of eastern America. It molded new personalities and strengths: frontier women became self-reliant, courageous, self-confident, and strong through handling wilderness crises. Their judgment sharpened. Their muscles toughened. Their manner became more straightforward and natural and their views more democratic than would have been possible in the socially stratified communities of Europe and the East. In the far West, particularly, women could be nonconformists. A Calamity Jane could wear pants, round up Indians, and drive a stage, even though she might occasionally be forced to bear the censure of critical female neighbors.

From the mid-nineteenth century on, the heroic efforts of early feminists, combined with those of social progressives in general, and spurred by the pressures of increased industrialization in America, began opening various doors and letting in the light upon women. From having little future except in marriage, a nunnery, or prostitution, women came to assume new working roles. In *American Women: Images and Realities* Ernest Groves describes how tavern- and inn-keeper, school teacher, type setter, photographer, journalist, store- and ferry-keeper, and many other jobs gradually became socially acceptable work for women. Country women managed entire estates, ranches, plantations, and farms single-handed or with daughters or sisters. Out West there were even a few cowgirls, such as Lucille Mulhall, who could ride, rope, and shoot as well as any man. Other females went into business for themselves in more traditional female occupations such as midwifery, laundering, millinery and seamstress trades, cooking, or the entertainment world. (It should be mentioned, however, that, after domestics, prostitutes were still the second-largest group of working women in the West.) Although women were always instrumental in the care of the sick and wounded, and in concocting healing potions, the first real educated and licensed female medical doctors did not appear until after 1850. And it has taken a century for them to be truly accepted and encouraged in their practice.

Both the Revolutionary War and the Civil War were definite

catalysts in making women more independent and enlightened. Without men around to take care of them, women took over traditionally male tasks and became wonderfully resourceful. Whether they were minding isolated plantations and farms and keeping them self-sufficient and productive, or tending wounded soldiers and making bullets in the cities, women played significant new roles during these wars. An estimated four hundred women enlisted in male disguise to serve as soldiers, spies, saboteurs, and scouts in the Civil War.

Growing industrialization, especially in the Northeast and Midwest, also helped release women from their traditional confinement to the home and encouraged their participation in the outdoors. Not only did women find new work and economic opportunities, but they now had more time for self-growth, exploration of new horizons, and recreation. Refrigeration, household sanitation, factory-made clothing, gas and electric lights and kitchen appliances, steam heat, the typewriter, the telephone, and various modes of transportation brought dramatic changes to women's lives. Industrialization and mechanization vastly decreased the amount of time and energy spent on sheer human survival. Think what a difference these inventions would have made in the life of Sayward, Conrad Richter's heroine. And, certainly, the important role that women played in the trade union movement since its beginnings was a major factor contributing to their increased political power and self-respect.

It is not necessary to belabor the advances which medicine, education, and psychology brought to women. For the first time in the New World—where the average colonial family had nine children—females could control pregnancy and not be tied to a string of youngsters. Thanks to birth-control methods and education, no longer could it be said of a woman that "she is a fruitful vessel, and seldom fails in her annual tribute to the honours of the family."

When women began to learn that they were *not* frail, dumb, faint-hearted, and flighty creatures who should never be subjected to the strain of "brain work," yet another aspect of the revolution emerged. According to one early theory, as stated by Dr. Edward Clarke of the Harvard Medical School in the mid-1800's, women aged eleven to twenty would be susceptible to neuralgia, uterine

disease, hysteria, and bearing deformed children if they were allowed education equal to that of men. It took a long time to break
down these archaic beliefs, but gradually women proved they were
the intellectual equals of men.

Once the first colleges and universities began admitting wom-
en—Oberlin and Mt. Holyoke in 1837; Elmira and Iowa State in
1855; Vassar in 1865; and Cornell in 1872—it quickly became clear
that the "weaker sex" would not collapse or become sterile by using
their brains. Nor was education solely for the sake of pleasing men
any longer the proper rationale for learning. Gone was Jean Jacques
Rousseau's eighteenth-century mandate from *Emile:*

A woman's education must therefore be planned in relation to man.
To be pleasing to his sight, to win his respect, and love, to train him in
childhood, to tend him in manhood, to counsel and console, to make his
life pleasant and happy, these are the duties of women for all time, and
this is what she should be taught while she is young.

So much for the great philosopher's theories of education!

As these shibboleths began to fall, women found more and more
work at a professional level. For example, Cornell University, during its first half century of existence (1850-1900), produced a distinguished and varied group of women graduates who excelled in
the fields of science, education, medicine, and other professions.*

At the same time as these changes in education and the professions, women were gaining new legal rights. Early American law
had placed severe disabilities upon both single and married females. Although colonial authority usually upheld premarital con-
tracts between husband and wife in relation to the wife's property,
and protected a wife's rights in her husband's property, allowing
her a share of it and her personal clothing if they separated, married
women still had no civil rights, no hope of guardianship over their
children, and no political power. Men had absolute authority over
the home, and women owed them absolute obedience. Further-

*An excellent overview of the position and dilemma of women in science between 1830
and 1880 can be found in Sally Gregory Kohlstedt's paper titled "In from the Periphery:
American Women in Science, 1830–1880" (*Signs: Journal of Women in Culture and Society,*
1978, vol. 4, no. 1).

more, women had no elective franchise and no voice in the country's politics. All this changed gradually, thanks in good part to the suffrage movement, to the labor and trade union movement, and to the many women's social reform and welfare organizations which sprang up in the early 1900's. Women's laws and rights today are a far cry from the 1875 Wisconsin Supreme Court ruling which stated:

The Law of Nature destines and qualifies the female sex for the bearing and nurturing of the children of our race and for the custody of the homes of the world—in love and honor. And all life-long callings of women, inconsistent with these radical and sacred duties of their sex—are—when *voluntary* [my emphasis]—treason against it. (Reports of Cases Argued and Determined in the Supreme Court of the State of Wisconsin, 1876, as quoted in R. W. Smuts, *Women and Work in America*.)

The Revolution in Dress

All the changes discussed above had indirect ramifications in preparing women for and pushing them into wilderness activity. In my opinion, two smaller but extremely significant changes did more than anything else to release women for outdoor life. One was the change in feminine fashions from tight corsets of whale-bone, long dragging skirts, hoops, bustles, and tight sleeves (the whole costume could weigh as much as fifteen pounds per lady), plus fragile shoes or boots, to simpler, looser, lighter, shorter, and more practical vestments and footwear. Amelia Bloomer, a feminist and a postmistress in Seneca Falls, New York, did a tremendous service to womankind by popularizing her "Turkish costume," a short skirt worn over loose trousers gathered at the ankles. Despite the *New York Herald's* prediction that "the attempt to introduce pantaloons . . . will not succeed," the "bloomer costume" soon reformed women's dress.

Men's sensible clothing appealed to many women. One unusual testimonial comes from Elsa Jane Forest Guerin, who masqueraded as a man for thirteen years (1850–1863), working as a cabin boy, waiter, brakeman, inspector, trader, and saloon owner—all the time dressed as a man. She wrote: "I began to rather like the freedom of my new character. The change from the cumbersome, unhealthy attire of women, to the more conventional, healthful habiliments of man, was in itself almost sufficient to compensate for its unwomanly character." Elsa Jane often returned home to visit her two children attired in conventional ladies' clothing, but she always grew bored by the inactivity and restrictions imposed upon her as a woman, so she would resume a man's role. Although she was eventually exposed and admitted her true identity, she remained in men's attire for the rest of her life, even after marrying for a second time.

Another advocate of dress reform was Dr. Mary Walker. In spite of great protest, this female graduate of the Syracuse Medical College also wore men's clothing. A surgeon during the Civil War, she was captured behind Confederate lines and spent four months in prison before she was finally freed. She was later awarded the Congressional Medal of Honor—the first woman ever to be so honored.

In 1896 a group of men and women ascended Mount Rainier in the state of Washington. George G. Cantrell described the journey in a magazine story, which included this comment:

That half of the party composed of the gentler sex, in becoming short skirts and leggings, found their new attire such an improvement over the cumbersome long dresses that they preferred footing it along the road with gentlemen to riding in the wagon.

Clearly the die was cast for women to start wearing more practical clothing.

The Changing Outlook on the Wilderness

The second key factor in bringing women into the wilderness professionally was the profound change in attitudes toward nature. The turning toward nature that took shape in the mid-nineteenth century, and later gave rise to the conservation ethic, was strongly influenced by the Romantic movement in literature and art, with its often sentimental, even religious, appreciation of the outdoors. As the vast American wilderness was being explored and settled, it was no longer seen as a hostile force to be conquered; rather it was becoming a place to go for healthy, beneficial recreation and perhaps even to find a closer connection with God. According to

Hans Huth, author of *Nature and the American,* the "howling wilderness" became "the wilderness pleases." Or as Roderick Nash has said, "it was ultimately civilization that made possible the appreciation of wilderness."

This whole turnabout in the way of looking at nature can be seen in a number of respected male nature writers—Emerson, Thoreau, John Burroughs, Longfellow, and John Muir—and also in the work of a very few early women nature poets and novelists. We must, of course, mention Emily Dickinson, who, although not a "nature poet" per se, showed an acute observation of the natural world. Then there were novelists: Willa Cather, who was discussed in Chapter 3; Sarah Orne Jewett, who wrote about rural Maine; Mary Austin, who described the deserts of Southern California; and Mary Anna Hallock, who described life in rough mining towns. By the 1930's women were firmly established as writers on nature, and since then they have produced their share of influential books—for instance, Rachel Carson's *Silent Spring,* Anne Morrow Lindbergh's *Gift from the Sea,* and Sally Carrighar's *One Day at Beetle Rock.*

In the fine arts almost all the interpreters of nature were men until the 1860's. Often, in fact, a painting signed by a woman could not be exhibited or sold. This lack of a significant women's presence in the fine arts generally led Germaine Greer to write in her 1979 book, *The Obstacle Race:*

There is then no female Leonardo, no female Titian, no female Poussin, but the reason does not lie in the fact that women have wombs, that they can have babies, that their brains are smaller, that they lack vigor, that they are not sensual. The reason is simply that you cannot make great artists out of egos that have been damaged, with wills that are defective, with libidos that have been driven out of reach and energy diverted into neurotic channels. Western art is in large measure neurotic, for the concept of personality which it demonstrates is in many ways antisocial, even psychotic, but the neurosis of the artist is of a very different kind from the carefully cultured self-destruction of women.

In spite of the obstacles a few female artists persisted and gave us some wonderful scenes depicting wilderness beauty, Indians, and primitive western life. Among these we might mention Grace Carpenter Hudson (1880's), Mary H. Foote (1800's), Mary Eliza-

beth Achey (1860–1885), and Eliza Barchus (1885-?). Today the
Arts and Humanities Committee of the National Committee on
the Observance of International Women's Year states in a recent
publication: ". . . nearly 300,000 American women are molding
sculpture, writing poetry and history, painting canvasses, teaching
languages, music, drama and art, singing, dancing, and acting."
Though few of these women specialize in natural subjects, this
number clearly shows the dramatic upswing in women entering
the arts in recent years.

Women and the Natural Sciences

The natural sciences—botany, zoology, forestry, wildlife management, ecology, marine biology, and so on—were practically
untouched by women until very recently. The earliest record I
could find of a woman naturalist was in South America: a Dutch
naturalist-artist, Maria Sibylla Merian. She arrived in Surinam in
1699 to spend three years collecting and sketching insects, plants,
and other natural objects, and produced a large portfolio in Latin.
The earliest female naturalist in North America was Jane Colden
(1724–1766), an unschooled but well-trained botanist who worked
with her father, a well-known botanist. Living in Newburgh, New
York, she began her studies when she was twenty-five and was
soon able to describe and sketch over 340 local plants. She cor-
responded with Linneaus, the great Swedish taxonomist and botanist; discovered the gardenia; and found a new plant species.
When she was presented by her father to an international circle
of scholars and botanical collectors, their reactions were compli-
mentary, to say the least. For example, ". . . As this accomplished
lady is the only one of the fair sex that I have heard of who is
scientifically skillful in the Linnaean system, you no doubt will
distinguish her merits and recommend her example to the ladies
of every country." Jane Colden's plates and plant descriptions are
still considered valuable museum pieces, though her scientific
achievement is now outdated.

The woman who became a leader in the nature study movement,
in fact the "mother" of it, was Anna Botsford Comstock (1854–1930).
Although she started out by doing wood engravings to illustrate

her husband's books on entomology, she soon became an entomologist in her own right. Educated at Cornell University, she later became its first female professor and one of the four original women admitted to Sigma Xi, the national honorary society of the sciences. As a professor, she founded and for several years headed the Department of Nature Study at Cornell. There she wrote the classic *Handbook on Nature Study,* which has been published in eight languages.

Preceeding Anna Comstock by a few years, though on a slightly less professional level, was Martha Maxwell, a home-grown naturalist, expert taxidermist, and skilled markswoman. She and her husband lived in Colorado during the 1860's and 1870's, and it was there that Martha began her careful observations of birds and mammals in the wild as a means of reconstructing them later as authentic mounts. In 1873 the town of Boulder offered her a hall in which to display her specimens; this became the Rocky Mountain Museum, which was later moved to Denver. She achieved such realism and artistry in her settings and stances that one visitor to her Centennial Exhibition in Denver declared, "I don't believe them critters was shot. I've looked 'em all over and I can't see any holes."

Women at Play

Around the turn of the century, a number of factors—such as the establishment of the first national parks and the U.S. Forest Service, the growth of the Women's Garden Club movement, and the writings of John Muir and other popular naturalists—encouraged people to look upon wilderness as a place to enjoy themselves. More and more women at this time began to fare forth, often on their own and sensibly dressed, to explore the outdoors for the sheer pleasure of it.

Those who took up mountain climbing had some notable female pioneers to emulate. We have already read, for example, about Isabella Bird's climbing exploits in 1873 in the Colorado Rockies; her accomplishments in the Himalayas are even more impressive. Another intrepid soul was Fay Fuller, the first woman to conquer Mount Rainier (14,370 feet). She went up in 1890, clad in bloomers and stout boy's shoes. Annie Smith Peck (1850–1935) did Fay a few better. In 1885 this tiny woman, who was born and bred in Rhode Island and taught classics at Purdue University and Smith College, went to Switzerland. The Matterhorn made a strong impression on Annie, and she began climbing lesser mountains in Europe. In 1888 she scaled California's Mount Shasta (14,380 feet), wearing knickers, a tunic, and boots. Not content to stop there, some ten years later she went up the volcano Popocatepetl and Mount Orizaba in Mexico, at that time the highest peak (18,314 feet) ever reached by a woman.

Annie had said, "Being in all this from earliest years a firm believer in the equality of the sexes, I felt that any great achievement in any line of endeavor would be of advantage to my sex." And so at the age of fifty she climbed 21,300-foot Mount Sorata in Bolivia. Shortly thereafter she scaled Huscaran, in Peru, at 22,205 feet—standing higher than any other American man or woman had ever been!

Although mountaineering had started as a pastime, this intrepid woman became a lecturer, earning her income from speaking and writing on her climbing experiences. She was a fellow of the Royal Geographical Society in England and an early member of the Society of Woman Geographers in the United States. Annie Peck was considered one of the world's greatest alpinists. Still going strong, she climbed Mount Madison (5,380 feet) in New Hampshire at the age of 82.

Also around the turn of the century a number of women became "outdoor sports," as the term is used in connection with hunting and fishing. Usually they were accompanied by their husbands, boyfriends, or guides. The early issues of various outdoor magazines offered stories about, or by, these "modern Dianas." The October, 1908, issue of *Field and Stream* contained an article by B. W. Mitchell called "A Woman in the Selkirk Wilderness," in which she says:

Nights in the silent places have a charm all their own. The idea of fear is an absurdity. No where is one so safe. True, she may be awakened by the "whoof!" of a surprised bear as he ambles by to feast on berries; or she may turn uneasily as a porcupine walks across her feet; or she may even have to pull a pretty little woodmouse by the tail out of her hair. These are nothings. Far worse intruders creep the sheets in many a pretentious inn.

One other woman in particular took my fancy. In 1912 Mrs. Shirley C. Hulse wrote about snowshoeing in *Field and Stream*. Apparently she was a natural at the sport, for the first time she put showshoes on, she walked fifteen miles and climbed over the top of a three-thousand-foot mountain. She described it thus:

Have you travelled miles through the aisles of the green timbers where the snow was so deep and nothing could exist without wings or snowshoes? Have you melted a hole in the snow, kicked the fire to one end, rolled yourself in your blanket on a pile of boughs on the other end, and listened to the wolves running while you went to sleep? Snowshoes can take you where you cannot possibly go without them—perhaps you wouldn't want to go anyway, and if you feel that way about it, I hope that you may someday weigh 250 pounds and have dyspepsia and a tobacco heart.

Then there was an intrepid female hunter and New York City newspaper woman who courageously tackled my own Adirondack Mountain wilderness in the late 1880's. Mrs. Fannie Buss Merrill suffered from a lingering cough and was advised to leave New York City and go to "the Woods," where she should sleep outdoors in an effort to cure herself. Not knowing exactly where she should head, Fannie got on a train at Grand Central Station and arrived (after several inquiries) at Fourth Lake. There she stopped at the Cy Wood camp and set up a tent near a log cabin for hunters, where she stayed for several weeks, hunting with a guide in the Adirondack forest, trekking for miles on the cold November days, and camping in a lean-to. Fannie was quite a markswoman. She boasted to her daughter, Serena, that she had once challenged Annie Oakley to a shooting match and bested the famous sharpshooter.

The Intrepid Explorers

The late 1800's and early 1900's were the golden age of American scientific exploration, and many large expeditions were sent out by museums of natural history and anthropology in those decades. A number of women joined their husbands on these adventurous and dangerous expeditions. Many wrote books about their experiences, books which have inspired innumerable young girls to take up outdoor activities and perhaps even to become professional wilderness women. Unfortunately, these early women were all too often relegated to the role of helpmate and did not receive recognition for their contributions to the team's effort.

One such explorer was Elizabeth Agassiz, who accompanied her husband, the famous Harvard zoologist Dr. Louis Agassiz, on his scientific expeditions, taking notes and helping in his research and publicity. Elizabeth coauthored with him *A Journey to Brazil* (1867), observations about a trip down the Amazon River.

Some of the women who went exploring with their husbands in the early 1900's were founders or early members of the Society of Woman Geographers. Among these were Grace Barstow Murphy, whose book *There's Always Adventure* describes her voyages to the southern Atlantic and other little-traveled parts of the oceans with her ornithologist husband, Robert Cushman Murphy; and Delia Ackley, who went with her husband, Carl, on several trips to Africa over a twenty-year period to collect big game animals for museums. Delia wrote *All True* and *Jungle Portraits*, and during one of these trips she became the first white woman to cross Africa accompanied only by native bearers.

The Society was formed in 1925 because women, no matter how qualified, were not admitted to the Explorers Club—the most prestigious group of world travelers in this country—and *still* are not. Many of its early members, described in the booklet "Vignettes of Some Early Members of the Society of Woman Geographers" (see Chapter 7), lived and worked in wilderness conditions before the 1920's. Yet the hardships imposed by this kind of life seem not to have bothered them unduly, probably because most of them possessed a positive and cheerful outlook and were stimulated by their work and surroundings. Making reputations for themselves did not appear to be their primary motivation, nor did trying to prove themselves equal to or better than male explorers and adventurers. Rather, they were fascinated with a particular aspect of nature and curious to unfold its mysteries.

Today membership in the Society of Woman Geographers is restricted to those traveling women who have done distinctive work in geography or allied sciences. They must have added to the world's store of knowledge and have published or produced some permanent record of their work.

Among other husband-wife teams from the first part of this century were Sally and James Clark, who gathered specimens in Africa, the American West, and Alaska for museum exhibitions. In addition to being a big game hunter, Sally was a dress designer and sculptor. The American Museum of Natural History is filled with the Clarks' specimens.

Osa and Martin Johnson were another adventurous couple who recorded exotic cultures and animal life on film. They worked in Borneo, Malekula, Kenya, and the Congo. While photographing for weeks at a time, Osa often provided meat for the table by hunting wild animals.

Florence Page Jacques, a prolific writer and artist, and the wife of the painter Francis Lee Jacques, wrote fine nature books about their wilderness experiences in the North Woods, many of which were illustrated by her husband. *Canoe Country* is just one of her many volumes.

A host of other wife-husband teams may have had a less scientific purpose, but they produced descriptions of nature that were equally authentic and just as inspiring. I will cite a few of my favorites here. Theodora C. Stanwell-Fletcher's *Driftwood Valley* is the story of a young couple who built their log cabin and spent three eventful years in a remote part of British Columbia, over two hundred miles from the nearest road, railroad, or telephone. Both people used this experience to study wildlife throughout the seasons and to collect plant and animal species for a Canadian museum. Dana and Ginger Lamb coauthored *Enchanted Vagabonds* and *Quest for a Lost City*. The former narrates their canoe trip from San Diego, California, to the Panama Canal (sixteen hundred miles); the latter chronicles a walking trip through Mexico searching for a lost Mayan ruin. Jean and Frank Shor followed the exact route of Marco Polo through Asia and wrote *After You, Marco Polo*.

Of course, there are many more, but these are the ones who stand out in my mind and whose writings and examples gave me and many other women courage and inspiration to do something unusual in the out-of-doors. Clearly, these couples and their books provided role models to many people who craved the excitement and the stimulation of some kind of wilderness activity or profession.

It is probably safe to say that, since the beginning of the twentieth century, women have begun participating in almost every field of scientific endeavor, although the natural sciences were probably the last ones to be attempted. As mentioned before, professional women working in the outdoors and living in the wilderness are a very new social phenomenon. As late as the 1950's there were practically no female wildlife or marine biologists, foresters, timber cruisers, geologists, ethologists, ecologists, or the like. The main thrust of women to enter these professions really came in the 1960's and even more in the 1970's, when time and circumstances had finally given women the opportunities to make a choice and take advantage of it, limited only by their individual abilities.

Chapter 5

The Making of Professionals

As I MENTIONED in Chapter 4, it has been far from easy for women to break into any of the wilderness-oriented professions. For decades women bent on pursuing a scientific education and career, especially one that involves working in the outdoors, have encountered subtle manipulation and sometimes outright discouragement. Most men felt that women were not suited for such work, and many even clung to the old saw that woman's destiny was solely biological. Moreover, remnants of the early belief that intellectual achievement was not a female virtue still held many women back from using their minds. Both our culture and our educational system were almost totally unsupportive of women who wanted to follow unconventional paths.

The story of my own career, I think, well illustrates the problems that women have faced. I always loved the outdoors and was fascinated by biology. But my mother refused to let me go camping because I was a girl, and until I was nineteen she even refused to let me learn to drive a car. Thus I was a complete novice about the skills and independence required for any outdoor career.

When I left suburban New Jersey to attend the University of Miami, Florida, I planned to major in marine biology, though I knew nothing about diving, boats, motors, or Florida fish and wildlife. To my surprise, my instructors took apparent pleasure in showing me the rudiments of this outdoor profession and the skills associated with it. My marine biology professor encouraged the boys and the girls equally to dive and collect on field trips, so I was able to learn the basics of snorkeling and scuba diving, and even to go underwater with a diving helmet. My zoology instructor invited me into the field on an archeological dig for Indian artifacts. I worked part time in a National Audubon Society office, and one of the wildlife tour leaders bought me a pair of binoculars and took me bird watching in Florida Bay. I felt I was peeking into an exciting new world and being tenderly introduced—by men—to natural history and outdoor skills. However, when I decided that the thing I wanted most in life was to be an Audubon tour leader myself, I was firmly told that no woman would be permitted to hold such a responsible position, driving clients through the Everglades and taking them out in boats.

My professor advised me that it would take six years to earn both bachelor's and master's degrees in marine biology, and that then jobs were difficult to find, especially for women. To a freshman that seemed quite a long time to stay in school, especially when there seemed to be little professional future. I decided to pursue only a bachelor's degree for the time being, and, since I had become interested in terrestrial biology, to major in wildlife conservation. So I transferred to Cornell University, one of the few schools offering this specialty to undergraduates.

In my Introduction to Wildlife Conservation class I turned out to be the only woman out of thirty students majoring in this subject. In the woodland management and surveying courses I was the only female among two dozen students. Fortunately, no one gave me any flak when I insisted on learning to handle a chainsaw and ax, run a small mammal trapline, and carry my own surveying transit. These skills were all part of the classwork, and I was eager to learn them at last. It should be pointed out that Cornell has had perhaps the most liberal attitude toward women students of all the land grant and Ivy League universities in the United States. As we saw in Chapter 4, it was one of the first universities to admit women. The generally open and even-handed attitude of its professors fosters independence among the students. Heaven knows what kind of response I might have received if I had sought this type of course work at a more conservative institution. I doubt I could have learned things such as snowshoeing, censusing wildlife, chainsawing, timber cruising, trapping, nature photography, or collecting and preparing specimens. At Cornell the only deterrents I found were occasional chiding for wearing jeans and other practical outdoor clothing and, of course, the rigid and totally inequitable hours and dormitory regulations imposed on women students.

Once I had become somewhat accomplished and set in my career choice, I began to meet more resistance. It seemed like the more advanced my course work became, the harder it was to convince professors that I seriously wanted to do outdoor work. When I expressed the desire to conduct a short field study during my senior year, most of my professors suggested some type of literature review or museum work instead. I was adamant that I wanted to study animals *in the field*. Finally one instructor reluctantly agreed to let me conduct a deer browse survey on a wildlife refuge area thirty miles away. The day I drove off to set up my vegetation plots, I felt as if I were going on an expedition to some remote region.

Occasionally I did receive discouraging or even rude remarks from professors. One famous scientist warned me not to make a career out of ornithology or ethology, like Margaret Nice and Jocelyn Crane. (Nice was an ethologist who wrote a classic work on bird behavior; Crane a tropical biologist and long-time assistant of the renowned biologist, Dr. William Beebe. Both were active in the thirties and forties.) If I did, he prophesied, I would end up a neurotic old maid. Those were fighting words!

Between the time I graduated with a bachelor of science degree in wildlife conservation and my marriage to a resort hotel owner in the Adirondacks, I diligently applied to every state conservation department in the United States for a job as a wildlife technician, wildlife biologist, or conservation officer (game warden). I was turned down by all of them, with the sole exception of the State of Wyoming, where a kind-hearted official offered me a "job," learning without pay. At that time there were no female game wardens, and to my knowledge there never had been. The only role models that I could look to for inspiration were Dr. Lucille Stickel, a wildlife statistician working for a U.S. Fish and Wildlife Service office near Washington, D.C., and Dr. Brina Kessel, a professor of wildlife and zoology at the University of Alaska. Two female marine biologists were just beginning to be recognized at

that time—Dr. Eugenie Clark (profiled in Chapter 11) and Rachel
Carson.

And so, with my husband's blessing, I went on to get a master's
degree. We agreed that I could go to school during the winter and
help run our resort in the summer. I applied to about a dozen
universities, most of them in the West. Only Colorado State
University, thanks again to a wonderful professor, was willing to
let me do field work. I was offered a scholarship *if* I would devote
my research to a library problem, but when I insisted that I wanted
to do field work and study animals, the offer of financial aid was
withdrawn. Various male students looked askance at my research
and asked why I wanted to climb mountains in the winter to study
mule deer when I really should stay at home and raise a family.
In one sense, I found westerners more conservative in their views
of female roles, but at the same time they were more spontaneous
and open to letting women do what they wanted if they had the
pluck. In this phase of my schooling, clothing was never a problem.
I simply dressed like everyone else—that is, like a cowboy.

During my doctoral program, back at Cornell, I found the same
strange mix of support and discouragement. A few professors and
students thought I was crazy to be so determined to study wildlife
ecology and to promote conservation in developing countries,
which had become another of my goals. Others just took it for
granted. I was fortunate to have three professors who championed
my ambition and goals and became wonderful friends and mentors.
Interestingly, the class in which I had been the lone female only
a few years earlier—Introduction to Wildlife Conservation—now
was pulling in an enrollment of over five hundred students, one-
third of them women. Clearly, the burgeoning environmental and
feminist movements were largely responsible for this change.

It was during this period, 1965 to 1970, that the prejudice against
women in formerly all-male fields such as wildlife and forestry
began to disappear. It was being replaced by a far more honest
and challenging hurdle, that of holding one's own as a capable
scientist among others. These were years of turbulence and change,
of strong emphasis on individual freedoms, and of testing rigid
traditions and institutions. There were other changes, small but
significant: for example, I was never chided for wearing boots,
levis, and hunting shirts to class, as I had once been.

When I look back on these years of my college and postgraduate education, I recall few, if any, overt denials in my chosen field. But I did endure many subtle expressions of displeasure and disapproval. I was encouraged to learn, and then to become a teacher or a research assistant, but seldom a peer of the men around me. Encouragement came mainly from professors who had become friends and mentors and who were either liberal or generous by nature. Perhaps they enjoyed dealing with a stubborn female student in an unorthodox field, to see if she could "cut the mustard." Perhaps what made the difference was simply their personal interest in me as a budding professional. And again I must emphasize that my choice of college was of the greatest importance. If Ezra Cornell had not long ago decided to found a school in which men and women could be equally educated, I might never have reached my professional goals.

I think that my innate stubborness and independence, and my insistence on fair treatment, were also important ingredients in my becoming a wilderness woman. Paradoxically, discouragement only strengthened my professional ambition and drive.

A colleague, Dr. Barbara W. Gerber, associate dean in the division of professional studies at the State University of New York, Oswego, commented on women in nontraditional professions succinctly, but strongly, in a letter to me:

I think that the issue of independence is vital—women are not encouraged to strike out on their own—and most of the women in traditional roles would not feel free to go off on their own, nor would they gain much encouragement from those near to them, such as family, friends, or mentors. Maybe that makes it quite understandable why it is only the very best professionals are found to be women. There are practically no mediocre women in *non*-traditional careers.

Our whole culture was such that women were indoctrinated against work outside the standard female role, so it is little wonder that anyone at all transcended those role expectations. To a lesser degree, but with real general impact, this still is prevailing today. Fewer women are encouraged to go into areas of study that lead to professions you could practice in the wilderness than are encouraged to go into traditional occupations. The majority of women are slated/slotted into teaching, social work, secretarial work, and nursing. Not exactly the best training for making a living in the wilderness. And so, the basic argument is that women were kept out of everything—in a culture that emphasized the notion that biology is their destiny. Everybody knew that women were not suited for wilderness or other unusual types of work, and that they are forever different.

My experience was not unique. Two other wilderness women who have Ph.D.s, Dr. Eugenie Clark and Dr. Margaret Stewart, tell similar stories of early prejudice in their profiles (see Chapters 11 and 15).

My interpretation of the treatment we all received is that when a woman is inexperienced, young, and eager, men professionals are pleased to help her learn basic skills and knowledge, almost as if she were a little sister or a protegé. But once she demonstrates her competence and determination to succeed in an all-male domain, she meets resistance and even jealousy. This may continue all through the rigorous training period (graduate school, early field work, and first jobs) and during her early professional career. Only after a woman has incontestably proven herself in any number of ways—scientific publications, exceptional field work, new discoveries, job promotions, or frequent conference contributions—is she "accepted" into the professional clique or organization.

The statistics on women in science, in wilderness-related or other areas, clearly indicate that it has been, and still is, difficult to succeed. Social, cultural, and institutional constraints continue to limit females in both their education and their subsequent employment.

According to *American Men of Science,* in 1920 there were 185 women in agriculture, botany, geology, and zoology out of a total of 3,011 scientists in these fields and a grand total of 9,486 in all scientific professions. In 1938, there were 7,525 men and 597 women in the subjects named, out of a grand total of 27,287 professional scientists. (I was unable to locate more recent statistics to compare with these, but it is at least encouraging to note that the title of this publication is now *American Men and Women of Science.*)

A 1977 survey of doctoral recipients prepared by the National Research Council, Committee on Human Resources, shows 295,800 scientists and engineers in the United States who received their Ph.D. degrees between January 1934 and July 1976. Only 10 percent of these were women, of which approximately 330 women were in the earth sciences; 7,500 were in the biological sciences.

Under *Characteristics of Experienced Scientists and Engineers, 1976,* from the Surveys of Science Resources Series prepared by the National Science Foundation, 26,999 "environmental scientists" (atmospheric and earth scientists, oceanographers, foresters, and conservationists) were listed; 860 were females.

Further inequalities are evident in salary levels. The 1977 survey of doctoral recipients revealed that the median annual salary for full-time employed Ph.D.s was $25,600. However, the average for men was $26,000, whereas for women it was $20,700.

I would like to give one more example to strengthen my argument. A matter close to my heart is the status of female environmental conservation officers, once known as game wardens—the officers who specialize in enforcement of environmental law, including fish and wildlife laws for both federal and state governments. As far as I have been able to learn, even as recently as 1975 only two or three women had ever been so employed in the United States. Two began as temporary trainee candidates in Colorado, the first state in the nation actually to train and hire females for this type of work in its department of fish and game. One of these women, Joan Bass, moved to New Mexico, where she was employed as a game warden and wildlife researcher. The other married and quit. More recently, a young woman named Deborah Palman became Maine's first woman fish and game warden.

There are also six women working as special federal wildlife agents for the Fish and Wildlife Service of the U.S. Department of the Interior. But as of 1980 only one, Cindy Schroeder, works totally in the field. She is responsible for protection of domestic and international fish and wildlife resources, and control of human activities to ensure the appropriate management of these resources. Cindy works in Utah, catching poachers and nest robbers (often in covert operations); she also gives talks to schools and clubs, and conducts investigations on violations of conservation laws. In the course of her work, Cindy operates many different types of equipment, including air boat, snowmobile, all-terrain vehicle, and four-wheel-drive trucks and jeeps. She says of her position (in a letter to me):

I've worked hard to establish my credibility as a wildlife officer and I feel like I have a good reputation. Yet each time I start in a new place I'm faced with a familiar negative response from others, and a "Gee, does she really carry a gun?" type of attitude. I feel that I work and am committed to excellence in this important field of wildlife conservation. I discover more every day, that a woman has to be twice as good to be considered half as good! I am especially discouraged when I think that my agency (as well as society in general) readily accepts any man in a wildlife field, but with a woman it's considered an automatic negative fit. I find myself constantly trying to demonstrate that for me this job is a good fit. All in all, I can't say that I have a difficult time in terms of acceptance because I am very interested in this line of work and expect to be allowed to do my job. I ask to be judged on my individual merits whether I am successful or a failure.

Even New York State, considered to be one of the most advanced in equal employment opportunities for women and with the highest level of education in general, did not hire its first woman environmental conservation officer—among 250 men—until the fall of 1979. The commissioner of the New York State Department of Environmental Conservation, Robert F. Flacke, announced: "Women in conservation law enforcement are a new phenomenon. But they have already been successful in other law enforcement roles in New York State and I am confident that [they] will make a significant contribution to our Environmental Law Enforcement efforts."

In its 1978 publication *Doors to the Future,* the U.S. Department of the Interior lists some other state and federal outdoor-related positions. The National Wildlife Refuge System, within the U.S. Fish and Wildlife Service, was begun in 1903 by Teddy Roosevelt. The system now comprises 34 million acres in 390 refuges— the world's largest network of lands managed for the benefit of wildlife. The first woman manager of a refuge was appointed in the early 1970's; today there are sixteen women working as refuge managers or assistant managers. Karen Smith is one of the shining examples, having worked at the Lost Wood National Wildlife Refuge in northwestern North Dakota for over two years now. Her story is related in an article in *Fish and Wildlife News:*

When she arrived at the 27,000-acre refuge in 1977, Smith encountered some of the same attitudes toward a woman professional that she had experienced previously. There was a matter of supervising two middle-aged maintenance men who had worked on the refuge for a number of years. And there were the attitudes of nearby landowners and locals in the two neighboring towns, both about 20 miles distant.

There was a bit of apprehension at first about having a female supervisor, but it slowly but surely resolved itself in four or five months. Smith says, "I have a crew here that's super. They're two tremendous people.

"My whole life has basically been in a man's world of fish and wildlife. I've faced the 'quit competing and get married' attitude through most of my life and am constantly confronted with these things. When it doesn't happen it surprises me more than when it does.

"When I first arrived I think the community was more startled than anything else. But I have not run into any problems. People are probably more open-minded out here. People listen. And when I don't have the answer, I'll admit it."

Within the National Park Service, a division of the Department of the Interior, a number of women are now employed as both seasonal and full-time park rangers, naturalists, and interpreters. The only black woman I've run across in my survey of professional wilderness women works in this federal agency. She is Martha Aikens, a staff interpretive specialist in the Everglades National Park. Besides inspecting and operating interpretive facilities and devices such as dioramas, slide shows, educational trail signs, etc., Martha's job involves considerable hiking, canoeing, wading, and operating a boat in the Everglades.

Years ago I also worked as a seasonal park ranger in this same park. I recall vividly the uniform we were required to wear: knee-length tight skirt, pumps, white blouse, and a cute little cap—all quite inappropriate for walking boardwalks and trails, bushwacking through hammocks, wading in swamps, or standing in the blazing sun. It took me weeks of cajoling to win permission to add a pair of pants and flat-heeled shoes to this uniform. Nowadays, Martha and other female park rangers dress sensibly in trousers, wide belts, boots, khaki shirts, and broad-brimmed sombreros.

Women are also working outdoors in many state conservation departments, nature centers, and wildlife research labs; and as scientists within the Interior Department's Bureau of Land Management, the U.S. Geological Survey, the National Oceanic and

Atmospheric Agency, the Soil Conservation Service, the Heritage
Conservation and Recreational Service, and the Marine Mammal
Commission, to name a few other federal organizations. They probably constitute 10-20 percent of the current total. Of course, there
are others working for universities, private conservation organizations, and museums, but I have no figures available.

Now let us turn to some real professional wilderness women to
see what their experiences were and how they began their professional lives. I have included in each of the fifteen profiles that
follow something of their early childhood experiences and outdoor
training. Thirteen of the fifteen women I interviewed grew up to
follow specialized careers in the wilderness or related to the wilderness, and the obstacles and aids they encountered along their
way are described in their profiles. The other two live in the
wilderness and have hobbies or interests directly related to the
outdoors and natural history. In general, most of the women reported positive support and exposure to the outdoors when they
were young. Most mentioned mothers with strong interests in
natural history, or fathers who included their daughters in their
sporting and outdoor activities. If the parents were not outdoors-
oriented, they still encouraged their daughters to be independent,
to read and explore, and to care for animals.

Three women reported that their husbands were instrumental
in promoting their wilderness education and appreciation. In two
cases—Margaret Murie and Diana Cohen—the women joined
their husbands as helpmates and from this beginning learned the
skills and knowledge to make them wilderness women in their own
right. The third, Maggie Nichols, says that she "dragged her husband along, kicking and screaming at times, in an odd reversal of
the stereotyped roles." They then went on to experience "so many
fantastic times in the outdoors that I can hardly imagine what life
would have been like without them."

Only one woman stated that her outdoor appreciation and skills
were largely self-taught, although she admitted to being nurtured
by professional outdoor groups later in her career.

Now it's time to let these remarkable women speak for themselves. I hope that, after meeting them through these profiles,
readers who have been drawn to the wilderness will find in them
the example and inspiration that were lacking for so many years.

Part II

THE WILDERNESS WOMEN

Chapter 6

Elaine Rhode

Freelancer in the Aleutians

A GROUP OF wildlife biologists were forcing their way through the five-foot tangles of rank grass on Buldir Island, one of the wildest and most inaccessible islands in the Aleutian chain. They moved as fast as possible, trying to avoid holes or sharp, slippery rocks hidden by the thick vegetation. They teetered and wavered for balance on the fifty- to sixty-degree slopes which plunged straight to the Bering Sea. Wooly skeins of fog drifted down from the shrouded peak above them, obscuring vision. From time to time a shout would ring out, and the ragged line of scientists would rush toward the caller, skirmish with the quarry, and disappear into the grass. Then either a triumphant yell would rise, or the drive line would spread out again and move on in silent determination.

Finally, after a successful encounter, they stopped, converged, and flopped in exhaustion on the grassy bank of a creek.

"Quite a wild goose chase we're having today," sighed a bearded young biologist from inside his rain hood. "This makes only two nonbreeders all day. We've got to find some family groups to-morrow, gang." He pulled out pliers and a ring of brightly colored plastic leg bands from his day pack and gently soothed the squawking five-pound bird. Then he clamped an orange ring and a coded Fish and Wildlife Service metal band around its leg.

"Those darn birds can run faster through this grass than greased pigs," grumbled another man, cheeks and nose flushed from wind-burn.

"Maybe they have better traction when it's foggy and wet like this." The only female in the group, a slight, fair-haired woman of twenty-eight, spoke up cheerfully. She began to nurse the raw, red blisters on her forearms caused by contact with the stalks of wild cow-parsnips.

Elaine Rhode was part of a U.S. Fish and Wildlife Service team capturing and banding the endangered Aleutian Canada goose on Buldir Island. It was her first trip to the Aleutian Islands and only the second time a white woman had ever set foot on Buldir. Elaine had come there for two purposes. One, to get firsthand information on the ongoing wildlife studies, the weather, and scenery to authenticate a script she would eventually write for a film. The second and main reason was to help biologist G. Vernon Byrd and his team catch the elusive geese.

To reach Buldir, fourteen hundred miles from Anchorage and seven hundred miles from the Soviet Union, she had flown to the island of Shemya, then taken the Fish and Wildlife Service vessel *R/V Aleutian Tern* across sixty miles of open ocean to Buldir. Luckily, though the fog thickened as the boat neared Buldir, the sea was relatively calm, so mail, fresh supplies, and Elaine could make a fairly dry landing by inflatable rubber craft on that rugged, unsheltered shoreline.

Buldir: "birthplace of storms" . . . "cradle of the wind" . . . so Elaine would write in her movie script. "An island which sits astride two major subterranean plates and is subject to frequent quakes, faulting, and volcanic eruptions." She gained indelible impressions on her expeditions to the Aleutians. The most remote of Alaska's great wilderness regions, the islands start at False Pass, near Unimak Island, and arch west and south between the Bering Sea and the North Pacific Ocean for eleven hundred miles. Over ninety of the islands are named, and all but seven private ones comprise the Aleutian Islands National Wildlife Refuge. The chain includes Attu and Kiska, notorious battlegrounds from World War II. No more than eight thousand people live permanently in the Aleutians, for their weather is perhaps the worst in North America. Rainstorms,

Elaine Rhode at work on one of her freelance writing projects. Photo by Anne LaBastille.

gale-force winds, huge waves, and winter blizzards batter the tree-less islands. A woman—or anyone, for that matter—could hardly pick a more difficult place to work in the whole world.

However, "my greatest worry in first going to the Aleutians," confides Elaine, "wasn't the weather or the isolation of being the only female with several men. No, I was afraid of failing—of not being able to keep up with the guys. I'm only five foot six and 125 pounds, and though I had been canoeing, hiking, and bicycling on weekends, the rest of the team had been trekking Buldir for two months. During our first day of chasing geese, I was delighted to find I could hold my own and stay up with the drive line. Apparently the guys noticed, too, and word got around—'she's O.K.'

But I was also wary of being caught in the stereotyped female role in camp. So I overreacted and at first avoided any traditionally female work like cooking and scrubbing pots. Soon I discovered that some men loved to cook, while others pleaded they'd only poison us if they were permitted in the kitchen. And we all had to keep camp clean. So I relaxed and pitched in and enjoyed surprising them one rainy morning with coffee cake. Duties rotated in comfortable agreement.

"As for our work with the geese, Vern Byrd inspired us all. We all swore he worked thirty hours a day with a smile on his face, and we had a hell of a time trying to follow in his path. Vern also set the pace for my treatment: the guys respected my independence while still often giving loving care. My ego would have swelled if I hadn't been so high on all the new sights and experiences of the Aleutians. After all, we had a job to do!"

The Aleutian goose is one of eleven races of Canadian geese— a smaller, darker, white-neck-ringed version of the common Canada species. It is also the least known and most mysterious race. No one had ever discovered, for instance, where the geese migrated in wintertime.

Although these geese were once numerous throughout the island chain, until quite recently most biologists thought the birds had become extinct. In the early 1900's fur farmers released Arctic foxes on almost every Aleutian island except Buldir. Like the Russians who had started the practice earlier, they hoped to reap rich rewards in the inflated fur market of that era and never realized the ecological repercussions of such an introduction. The foxes took over on islands which had never known a mammalian land predator, exterminating, or severely decimating, many ground-nesting birds—seabirds, ducks, ptarmigan, and the Aleutian geese. On just one island, Agattu, Olaus Murie—the pioneering wildlife biologist who made numerous field studies in Alaska in the 1920's and '30's—reported a mere handful of Aleutian geese only fourteen years after the release of the foxes, whereas earlier there had been thousands of breeding birds.

Meanwhile a few geese found sanctuary on fox-free Buldir, although no more than about four hundred adults survived even here. They were discovered there in 1962, and in 1963 eighteen goslings were captured and shipped to Patuxent Wildlife Research Center in Maryland to begin a captive breeding program. The first chicks were successfully hatched in 1966, and as the captive flock grew, Fish and Wildlife Service scientists prepared to reintroduce geese to Amchitka Island, which had been rid of Arctic foxes. It didn't work; the birds disappeared within a week.

The habits and habitat needs of the birds in their wild state were still unknown. So in 1974 the Service began a banding program and study on Buldir. The overall goals were to determine where the geese wintered, so as to afford them protection during that vulnerable period of their life, and to gather knowledge for the release of enough captive geese to repopulate three more Aleutian islands. If these things could be accomplished, the species would no longer be in danger of extinction.

A great many obstacles stood in the way of these well-meaning biologists who were trying to make amends for the mistakes wrought on the ecosystem years before. For one thing, the wild birds behaved in a most ungooselike fashion. They completely shunned the one fresh-water lake on Buldir, even during their molt when they were unable to fly. They preferred to hide, nest, and roost on the precipitous, green-swarded mountainsides. Therefore, the researchers were forced to struggle through tall grasses to catch them. Once one of them smashed his knee on a sharp rock, and his companions had to rig a stretcher from burlap bags and two poles to carry him back to camp and eventually to the boat. Elaine's part in the rescue was to break trail—even to the extent of lying down and rolling to smash the grass flat so the carriers could see their footing better.

Elaine joined the team in its second summer, and her reaction to Buldir was overpowering. "I fell totally in love with this wild, wet environment and the band of devoted biologists who clung determinedly to its shores. To me the Aleutian Islands are absolute wilderness, and I felt highly privileged to get to know them. Weather there is so fierce and forbidding that most people are scared away. But after living for a month on that eastern-hemisphere island amid auklets, petrels, puffins, kittiwakes, and sea lions—not to mention the geese—I resolved to go back again and again."

Elaine's resolve may have been further strengthened by the

beginnings of a romance with one of the Buldir wildlife biologists. "Our friendship started without pretenses or social trappings on the island," she reminisces. "It seemed ideal, but we both had some growing to do. Distance and our busy, independent schedules popped that bubble. I regret the pain but treasure the good times, and even more, I value what I've done on my own since then."

She did manage to return the next summer, this time on assignment for the U.S. Fish and Wildlife Service to photograph the newly established holding facility for the captive Aleutian Canada geese on Amchitka Island. The first birds were flown in from Maryland early in 1976 to give them time to adapt to cold and gales, as well as to adjust their biological clocks. The scientists had correctly deduced that this period of acclimatization was the key to enabling the geese to survive after their release. Also, some eggs were taken from nests on Buldir and rushed by boat to Amchitka, where they were put in incubators and tended carefully until hatching. Since Amchitka had historically held large populations of breeding geese, it was hoped that two hundred goslings per year could be produced there, raised, and later released to other islands.

At the end of her two-week stint on Amchitka, Elaine reluctantly sailed away toward Shemya Island to catch the twice-weekly plane. By the time the boat was passing Buldir, the captain knew she had missed the last flight of the week, so he dropped her off there for the weekend. To her absolute delight a storm blew up and she was weathered in on Buldir for ten days. During this enforced stay she helped Byrd and his biologists on seabird studies. By day they recorded the comings and goings of auklets on the talus slope; by lantern light they caught and banded forked-tailed and Leach's petrels as they flew back to their burrows. They observed the nocturnal departure to sea of the downy ancient murrelets; and they measured, weighed, and photographed any bird they could get their hands on.

Elaine was popular with everyone. All the men wanted to spend some time with her and show her favorite places like South Marsh, the petrel plots, the caves in the auklet colony. "I was wary about repeating good things, but that return to Buldir was an exceptional experience. Vern knows how to make a person feel wanted, and his attitude just rubs off on everyone around him. I have lasting, extra-strong friendships from the time when I was part of that special Aleutian family."

All too soon it was time to leave Buldir and return to her job on the mainland with the Fish and Wildlife Service public information office: writing scripts, newsletters, brochures, and portfolios on work being done throughout Alaska. As a further spin-off Elaine wrote articles for *National Wildlife* and *Ducks Unlimited* magazines on the remarkable Aleutian Canada goose program.

By this time the geese had been tracked to wintering grounds in Sacramento and Castle Rock, California. The number of wild geese on Buldir had increased to fourteen hundred, and the second attempt to start new populations on other islands had begun. So Elaine's stories had happy endings. Money had also suddenly appeared for a film from the raw footage taken earlier on Buldir and nearby islands. Elaine wrote the script and collaborated with the original filmmakers. Their labor of love was called "Chain of Life— the Aleutian Islands"; it earned the Conservation Film of the Year award from the Outdoor Writers' Association of America and was named Runner-up Best Film at the University of Montana's International Wildlife Film Festival.

The Aleutian film and articles, unusual products for the Fish and Wildlife Service, climaxed Elaine Rhode's years of work with the agency. Now the self-aware and self-directed Capricorn woman took assessment. She realized that from here on her job would probably become more and more deskbound with less and less intriguing field work. She recalls, "Maybe it was the seven-year itch, the thirty-year-old passage, whatever . . . I knew it was time for a change, a challenge, and I wanted the assurance of staying in Alaska. So I decided to go freelance and be my own boss. I gained confidence from reading of another woman's independent pursuits and determination in Anne LaBastille's *Woodswoman*."

Thus began a new period in Elaine's career of combining her background in wildlife biology with her writing and photography talents, working out of her tiny wood A-frame house in southern Alaska. She had come far, both physically and mentally, from her childhood in east-central Wisconsin, her college days at the University of Wisconsin in Madison, her first jobs as reporter and editor of hometown papers, and her initial appointment with the Bureau of Sport Fisheries and Wildlife in Minnesota.

As a child in Wisconsin, Elaine liked to play in wild places— the bluffs, lowlands, ravines, rolling hills, open fields, and woods near her home. She hiked the railroad rights-of-way with her father, a chemical engineer for a paper company, and explored marshes and creek channels by rowboat with both parents. Her horizons expanded in 1959 when the family began to realize a dream of spending one month each summer traveling and tent camping throughout the United States, Canada, and Mexico. Elaine fell in love with the high mountains, seashores, and other noncity places they visited.

The event that decided her on a wilderness career, she believes, was a college geology field trip to the Yukon Territory in the summer of 1967. Her professor admitted that the geology "would just sink in naturally," and that he was really teaching his class wilderness skills.

"I remember being astounded when I first saw a down sleeping bag being stuffed into its sack," laughs Elaine. "I had to try it myself, just to prove it wasn't a trick."

Thus from others Elaine picked up tips and techniques. She went on more field trips, not so much for the geology as for the backcountry outdoors experience. She feels that the experience of living and working with a small group of peers in a tent camp of their own creation, hundreds of miles from the nearest town, fostered a confidence in nature and a self-reliance that has directed her path, subconsciously as well as consciously, ever since that time.

"The next year, when a summer job plan fell through, I headed out West with my college roommate. She and I traveled for six weeks, following the sun to bare spaces on the maps, hiking, exploring, and camping in wilderness areas and national forests because at that time they were so empty of people. Next vacation we went to Big Bend National Park in Texas and roamed the backlands. We just reveled in the freedom of being women on our own in wild places."

Elaine got her B.S. and went on to graduate study in environmental communications. During one summer break she had her first experience hiking alone on a week-long trip to Isle Royale, a large and wild island in Lake Superior. She was dropped off by boat at the end of May, practically the first visitor of the year. In the course of the week she came face-to-face with a moose on the trail, was almost stepped on in her sleeping bag by another moose, blistered her feet with wet boots, and gorged on gorp and sunshine. The only problem was her blisters, which caused great discomfort, but she didn't let them slow her down. "At first I sang to myself to forget the pain," she remembers. "Then I began taking Excedrins because it got so bad. But by the time the boat picked me up the blisters were better, and everything in my life seemed clearer and brighter."

Postponing her graduate studies for a while, Elaine accepted a temporary position with the refuge division of the Fish and Wildlife Service in Minneapolis, where she developed interpretive materials for the prairie wetlands in the Dakotas and Minnesota. Before this appointment ran out, another division hired her; this time she designed interpretive materials such as slide shows, trail markers, and brochures for refuges in Nebraska and Wyoming. She also accompanied the noted wolf authority Dr. Dave Mech to northern Minnesota and helped him radio-collar three timber wolves. Mech taught Elaine to howl like a wolf—the "soul of the wilderness"— and she still howls in lonely areas just for the joy of it. "It often has a disconcerting effect on my male field companions," she acknowledges with a grin.

After getting her master's degree in 1971, she went back to work in Minneapolis, writing interpretive concepts for Alaska. By July, 1972, she was headed to the "Great Land," on detail for two months with a new team charged with carrying out Fish and Wildlife Service responsibilities under the 1971 Alaska Native Claims Settlement Act. The new refuges called for by the Act had to be explained to the Eskimo and other tribes in simple language, as well as in environmental-impact-statement jargon. Elaine could write well in both styles.

"I insisted I had to personally see and feel the country I was

writing about," she explains. "So I flew in small aircraft over
hundreds of miles of unpeopled land. Whenever we stopped at
remote villages, the Fish and Wildlife Service pilot usually knew
several native residents, so I got to listen to many stories."

The prototypes that resulted from this short assignment were
approved, and by November, to Elaine's jubilation, she was packed
and headed up the snowy Alaska Highway in her Volkswagen en
route to a permanent job in Alaska.

During the next two years the *cheechako* (outsider) got an intimate look at more of Alaska than most "sourdoughs" (native Alas-
kans) do in a lifetime. She traveled by small aircraft, canoe, sea-
going vessel, and foot, from one end of Alaska to the other: places
such as Togiak, Barter Island, the Wrangell Mountains, and the
Noatak River. These trips produced ten beautifully illustrated
booklets about proposed Alaska national wildlife refuges and a
movie script entitled "On the Threshold: Refuges—Alaska."

Elaine then joined the public affairs office of the Fish and Wildlife Service, and her involvement with the Aleutians began. "It
was funny," she remembers, "how throughout my career, male
work associates have raised their eyebrows in surprise at the in-
novations and feminine perspective I brought to my projects. Little
things that the men had never thought of themselves. However,
most of the males I have worked with have treated me with respect
and on an equal basis. The ones who had problems or misunder-
stood a woman's entry into the field were forty-five or older."

One woman seems to have played an important role in inspiring
Elaine in her outdoor work—Margaret Murie, the widow of Olaus
Murie, who did some of the original surveys of fauna in the Aleutian
Islands for the Fish and Wildlife Service (see Chapter 17).

Elaine recalls that she met Mardy about ten years ago, "and had
my first sourdough pancakes in her woodstove kitchen at Moose,
Wyoming. While eating, we watched a pine marten try to steal a
meat bone from the bird feeder on the windowsill. ("Sorry you
can't see the bears," Mardy said, "but they have already cleaned
up the moose that died in my front yard.") I had read her books,
Two in the Far North and *Wapiti Wilderness*, and secretly dreamed
about a life like hers. Now here I am, living in Alaska and working
in some of the wild places she and Olaus studied and helped to

save. And I'm still using the sourdough recipe Mardy shared with me way back in Wyoming."

One of Elaine's first jobs as a freelancer took her back to the Aleutians as a temporary biological technician, observing sea otters on Amchitka and Attu islands under the direction of Dr. James Estes. Attu is the westernmost point on the North America land mass and still carries vestiges of early Aleut villages, the first *promyshlennik* (Russian fur hunters) camp of the mid-1700's, and Japanese and American war bases of 1942–1943. The island of Amchitka, also war-torn, still holds thousands of rusting quonset huts in addition to buildings used during three underground nuclear tests from 1965 to 1971. As usual, Elaine was the only woman among several men on one of the islands. She often worked alone for days at a stretch. Her research activities consisted of making half-hour scans of otter study areas to record the number of animals resting, feeding, traveling, interacting, and grooming. She also made stopwatch records of diving and feeding sequences and observed the otters' eating habits and food items.

One of her shoreline study areas on Attu was at Holtz's Bay, an isolated harbor accessible only by foot from the main camp twelve miles away, where four other biologists were staying. Elaine decided to spend a week making observations at Holtz's Bay. By the time she had assembled her food, binoculars, camera, wool pants and shirts, sleeping bag, tent, Quester telescope, flashlight, cooking pots, and boots, her pack weighed seventy-five pounds. "I took off in fog and rain, forded two rising rivers, and backpacked that long, long way to Holtz's Bay. By the time I got to a sheltered camping place I was exhausted, but there were ten otters resting in the kelp beds right at my doorstep. That made the whole day look brighter. I stayed there alone for six days. It was wonderful. There were waterfalls and rainbows. The bay was pristine, rugged, and quiet. The weather was occasionally sunny and glorious, and I even walked barefoot on the tundra. I felt as though it was my private paradise, with only the birds, otters, seals, and foxes as my neighbors.

"I never tire of the land and the wildlife," Elaine says simply. "They are always satisfying, whereas people vary."

The study Elaine worked on that summer of 1977 is part of a

classic piece of wildlife research, in which Dr. Estes and his colleagues proved that sea otters play an extremely important role in
maintaining shallow algal communities in their habitat.

At and around Attu Island, where otters were scarce or absent,
researchers found sparse kelp beds, a dense carpet of sea urchins,
and greatly reduced community diversity. In contrast, Amchitka
Island, 250 miles away, had dense kelp and sea grass beds, a rich
associated community, and about sixty otters per square mile. The
conclusion was that when otters were absent or reduced, sea urchin
populations increase and eat up much of the kelp. Consequently,
many sea organisms that normally feed and live in or around the
kelp beds, such as fish, harbor seals, and bald eagles, are reduced.
Sea otters prey on sea urchins, and thus this single mammalian
population determines the structure, dynamic relations, and stability of the near-shore marine ecosystem. And not just in the
Aleutians, but all along the northern Pacific coast down to California. This finding corroborates studies that Margaret Owings
arranged in the Big Sur–Monterey area of California (see
Chapter 9).

By summer of 1978, after a quiet winter of writing and editorial
consulting, Elaine was eager to get back into the field. Again she
was hired by the Fish and Wildlife Service as a biological technician, this time joining a team surveying the western Aleutians
for marine mammal and bird populations. It was her best look yet
at the Aleutians and at the paradise of birdlife which summers
there. The team cruised the entire eleven-hundred-mile chain,
following in the footsteps of Olaus Murie and Victor Scheffer,
Murie's expedition cohort and another general biologist. Elaine's
team was the second survey effort in almost forty-five years.

The long days were filled with activity, whether on board the
Aleutian Tern or ashore. The team would stay busy until midnight
or 1:00 A.M. if the ancient murrelet chicks were going to sea, or
they might start at 5:00 A.M. if cliff-nesting murres needed counting.
At the end of the day they would gather in the galley or use
flashlights in their tents to write up the day's notes. Elaine carried
field guides to birds of Europe, Asia, and North America everywhere she went because the species have such mixed distributions
in the Aleutians.

Their studies included sighting cetaceans to help determine the distribution and abundance of these marine mammals; making counts of pelagic birds; observing murre activity patterns; setting up permanent monitoring plots on islands to document long-term population changes of nesting marine birds; cataloguing the enormous auklet colonies on Kiska Island; and checking the effects of Arctic foxes on ground-bird communities.

One morning, Elaine recalls, the cook aboard the boat was in great consternation at having found a fledgling auklet splashing around in the head. Instead of flying away from its island nest to the sea, the young bird apparently was attracted by the ship's lights and tumbled into his own "big world of ocean." The cook, however, thought it was one of the freeze-dried auklet specimens, miraculously come back to life. "We all laughed for days over that!"

Expedition life had its far more serious moments, however. The team was camped on Kiska Island, between Buldir and Amchitka, where 41 percent of all the crested and least auklets nest while breeding in the Aleutian Islands National Wildlife Refuge. These enormous colonies contain more than 1.3 million birds. One of the chief concerns of the Fish and Wildlife Service is the potential disaster that an oil spill might wreak upon these birds. Conceivably an oil tanker accident could wipe out a million birds, and no one could do anything about it. Given the absence of planes and airstrips, the islands' lack of permanent human habitation, bad weather, and lack of communication, such a spill could even occur and never be discovered.

On August 2 the biologists awoke to a *williwa*—a warm, wet wind. Rain and warm winds were sweeping furiously down Kiska volcano. The smell of sulphur hung heavily in the air, and the ocean was steely gray. As Elaine wrote in her journal, "Every so often the waves committed suicide by leaping up into a waterspout. The tents looked as if they might take off any second, so we all dove back inside. We only went outside that day to pee, grab munchies, and radio the ship. That night we had some limited radio reception warning us of a typhoon's approach."

By the following day the *williwa* had calmed down, and by August 5 the air was strangely still. Nothing stirred till 11:00 A.M.; then mist and rain began, and swells started rising on the sea. A lone fox crept near the camp and stared at the humans from a ridge where foxes had never been seen before. The barometer fell to 28.96. And then the typhoon's edge was upon them. Elaine's journal describes it vividly:

The wind must have risen to sixty miles per hour in gusts. My tent leaned right over onto my face. I just lay on my back and braced the poles with my feet. Outside the cook tent was being shredded to bits. We were in danger of losing our only shelters, getting soaked, and ending up crowded in a heap under tent scraps, trying to avoid hypothermia.

The ocean was smoking white, noisy, and covered with wind devils. Sheets of water were blowing into my tent. The walls sank way in, and the wind was white with streaming mist. At 2:00 P.M. the barometer hit 28.86. One by one my tent's fiberglass poles shattered. About 5:00 P.M. an eerie calm told us the 'eye of the storm' was passing overhead. I could look right up at a blue hole above. The guys, who had been helplessly watching my tent flatten during the blow, now came to the rescue with strapping tape. We shuttled more supplies from the remnants of the cook tent into our sleeping tents before the next blow forced us inside again. At the next lull we fixed supper and sat down to play cards. Radio transmission was so feeble that we could only manage to ask that a message of our predicament be relayed to the *Tern*.

At 2:15 A.M. Elaine's journal read: "It's getting seriouser. I had to tie down the zipper to keep the tent from billowing open. Finally I just hid in my sleeping bag and tried not to think. It stinks of sulphur again. It's spooky being so close to an active volcano."

Seven o'clock the next morning showed the barometer at 28.82 and the sky ominous. Some of the biologists were beginning to show the strain. One just stayed in his tent and played a harmonica, a forlorn sound accompanied by wind whipping the tent flaps. Until the storm passed and the ocean settled, there was no way the ship could rescue them.

A pod of killer whales swam by at evening time, lifting the team's spirits a bit. All five biologists finally squeezed into one tent that night to play cards and try to forget the typhoon. They'd already swapped books and read them all. Elaine wrote: "In adversity I find myself becoming extra cheerful. I think women can take rotten weather as well or better than men. Of course, writing in my journal helps a lot."

Two days later the winds had lessened to fifteen miles per hour, the temperature had dropped to 46°F, and the sun peeked out between squalls. Everyone felt better and they decided to move all the gear down to the beach in anticipation of rescue. Even the fox had reappeared and played in the outhouse hole, strewing toilet paper about like confetti. At 5:00 P.M. the ship suddenly appeared, and by nine o'clock the team and all their equipment were safely aboard. "We took showers and ate salads," Elaine's journal notes. "Boy, for once we were really glad to be off an island!"

Will the plucky freelancer ever go back to the Aleutians after such an experience?

"I hope so," she exclaims buoyantly. "If things go right, I'm planning to return to Amchitka to do a photo story on the changes over the ten years since the atomic blasts. There was quite a stir back then, yet people have almost forgotten about it now. I'd love to spend another summer anywhere in the Aleutians." Then she adds, with a characteristically adventurous gleam in her eye, "And someday I want to study seabirds in Antarctica—that's about as wild as you can get on this planet."

Chapter 7

Jeanne Gurnee

Explorer Underground

THE UNDERGROUND CAVERN was stifling and humid. Headlamps and flashlights threw erratic beams of light on the cave walls, creating grotesque shadows behind the group of explorers. A dank, musty smell pervaded the air, and a nervous rustling of bats hanging from the ceiling whispered down. Ahead, the limestone floor seemed to pitch off into total blackness, sloping steeply to a narrow "choke," barring further passage. A small tunnel led off sideways toward a cliff. Sweating and panting, the speleologists turned and scrambled up this slippery wall, found a hidden pass, and walked forward into a new cave room. Their startled eyes stared down at hundreds of pieces of pottery, burned altar sites, and the remains of a human skeleton stretched out on the floor.

There was absolutely no sign of human disturbance, vandalism, or exploration. Suddenly it dawned on them that this was the first entry by human beings in hundreds of years. Among the first party to discover this Mayan ceremonial cave—not used since about 800 to 1000 A.D.—was one woman, Jeanne Gurnee, a tall, attractive brunette about forty years old. "It was like standing inside a newly opened Egyptian tomb," she recalls. "I'm still awestruck by the total silence and the visual experience. The floor and its ancient footprints were coated with a patina that forms on clay and mud only when they're not trampled or discolored by any live creature

Jeanne Gurnee examines a travertine cave formation in Samay Cave, Guatemala, during the 1968 expedition co-sponsored by ABC and the Explorers Club. Photo by Roy Davis.

for centuries. There beside them lay *my* footprints—made one thousand years later!"

The cave, named *Sejul* (Kekchí Mayan language for cave), was the extraordinary climax to several weeks of exploration in the mountains of Alta Verapaz, Guatemala, in the winter of 1968. Jeanne and her husband, Russell Gurnee, had made several trips to this interesting country over the years; however, this expedition was the high point of them all. Sponsored by The Explorers Club and the American Broadcasting Company, it hoped to determine how ancient and modern Mayan Indians used the caves of this high limestone country. Eleven explorer-scientists, four support members, and a television camera crew of nine made up the team. Jeanne acted as logistical planner, log keeper, and writer; her husband, Russell, an engineer and the past president of the National Speleological Society (NSS) was the leader. The purpose of the trip was also to produce a one-hour documentary film on serious scientific exploratory work plus a series of reports. (The film, entitled "Riddle of a Mayan Cave," was shown on television late in 1968. The reports were printed as "Mayan Cave Discoveries" in the *Explorers Journal*, September, 1968.)

Why would a woman like Jeanne Gurnee, trained as an art teacher and lecturer, want to, in fact thrill to, explore caves? To cope with dense jungle growth, rugged roads and trails, hours of horseback and jeep travel, slippery ascents in the dark, tricky rope work, pouring rains, and health hazards seldom heard of by the general public? In other words, to be a speleologist (cave scientist)?

Jeanne's answer is that caves represent one of the last great frontiers for pioneers and some of the rare remaining wilderness on earth. "When you step into a virgin cave," she explains dramatically, "you know you are in a place that's never been seen, stepped on, mapped, or explored. Caves are uncultivated and uninhabited by human beings. And the underground is just about the only part of our world that's never been photographed—even by satellite," she emphasizes. "This underground wilderness is an area I need to seek out again and again—to learn from, to prove myself in, to respect, to preserve, and to deeply enjoy."

The dangers Jeanne faces when caving in remote places are considerable. She knows the ever-present possibility of bumps and bruises, falls and fractures, while exploring underground tunnels, cliffs, and caverns. Then there are two diseases which can be contracted within or near caves. One is "cave sickness," or histoplasmosis. Humans and animals alike are affected by this fungus, usually through inhaling spores in the air or touching those which reside in the dung deposits of bats and birds on cave floors. Mild infections resemble a chest cold, but severe cases may cause pneumonialike symptoms, with chest pains as excruciating as a broken rib, and mortality as high as 90 percent if the disease is not treated. Jeanne and Russell have been exposed many times and now seem to bear a natural immunity.

Rabies is the other cave disease; it can be contracted through the bite of a rabid bat, including the vampire. Bats are the only warmblooded mammals known to harbor the disease and not always die; it's 100 percent fatal in all other species. In Latin America, bat-transmitted rabies is a major concern. Thousands of domestic animals die yearly following the bites of vampire bats. Few humans succumb, but cavers, coming into contact with bats roosting in caves, run higher than average risks of an unexpected attack.

It might seem strange that a girl raised in suburban New Jersey would take to caving with such intense interest. As a child, Jeanne played in rural woodlots, farm fields, swamps, and lakes, but she never set foot in a cave. "There wasn't a twig or creature in our area that I didn't learn about early in life," reminisces Jeanne. "My mother was the chief source of encouragement and knowledge for my outdoor experiences. Although Mother worked mostly as a librarian, historian, musician, and community leader, she was keenly interested in natural history and horticulture. If she didn't know an answer, she'd refer me to books or to people who could help me." Jeanne's father, a consultant in color and pigment technology, was the more active parent. He taught his daughter tennis and many other outdoor activities.

Jeanne's varied educational background likewise gives little hint of her subsequent career in caves. She graduated from the Katherine Gibbs School in New York and the New York School of Interior Decoration, then went on to do extension work in graphic arts and typography at Columbia University and New York University, and in environmental law and municipal land use and planning at Rutgers University and Bergen Community College, both in New Jersey. She went to work in an art studio in New York under the tutelage of a well-known artist and graphic designer, and soon began to take over some lecturing assignments for her employer.

When she was twenty-five, Jeanne entered her first cave and took the first step toward becoming a caver. She had just married Russell Gurnee, also from New Jersey, and the couple had gone to Mexico on their wedding trip. Along the Pan American Highway north of Mexico City, they were intrigued by black holes in the hillsides. Finally in Monterrey they stopped at Garcia Caverns.

"Just like a couple of tourists, we rented burros and rode up a steep switchback trail to reach the mouth of the cave." Jeanne smiles in remembrance. "I recall feeling and hearing a whoosh of cold air as we timidly entered the mouth. Then we saw the mag-

nificent formations of stalagmites and stalactites, and the huge
rooms. We got hooked then and there!" Jeanne and Russell visited
all the commercial, tourist-oriented caves they could find on the
way home. And every February since then they've spent a 'caving'
vacation in some foreign country.

The second breakthrough in becoming speleologists came when
Jeanne was giving an art lecture at a college in New Jersey. Also
appearing was James Fowler of the Academy of Sciences in Philadelphia. She stayed to listen and heard about the National Speleological Society. "I went home that night incredulous and asked
Russ, "Do you know there's an organization of people who explore
caves?"

Together they decided to attend a meeting. The NSS was quite
small in the 1950's, composed of about nineteen hundred members.
The Gurnees began going on local field trips with the New York
chapter. Soon they were spending most every weekend crawling,
climbing, and slogging through caves. Jeanne laughs, remembering. "At first my friends considered me an oddity. They certainly
thought it was a strange way to spend Saturday and Sunday. But
either you're interested in caves, or you're not. Sooner or later
some specific area gets to you—studying geological formations and
archeological remains, censusing bats, exploring and mapping new
passageways, observing blind cave creatures, and photographing
caverns. I've done a bit of all. Actually, I like everything about the
cave experience."

The NSS affiliation brought Jeanne and Russell together with
other cave lovers, widened their knowledge, and offered them
companionship. Most of all, it showed what a good combination
the Gurnees made in cave work.

"Russ is a Virgo and he has a meticulous nature, whereas I'm
a Sagittarius with plenty of drive and spontaneity. Put those traits
together and they work well. On top of that," Jeanne grins, "it
helps to have had thirty years of caving experience with the world's
top speleologists. So far, I've participated in six expeditions on
three continents and visited approximately a thousand caves around
the world."

One of the Gurnees' earliest and most exciting adventures was
exploring a cave inhabited by *guacharos (Steatornis caripensis)* in

northwestern Venezuela. These strange hawklike birds, with a wingspan of up to four feet and eyes that glow like rubies when reflecting light, are found only in Venezuela, Colombia, Ecuador, Peru, and Trinidad. *Guacharos* are the only avian species which roosts and nests in dark caves by day, then flies out to feed at night. Like bats, the reddish brown birds use an echolocation system similar to sonar to navigate in the dark, emitting sounds which bounce back from walls and other obstacles and warn the birds. But whereas bats' sonar is practically inaudible to humans, the *guacharos* give off a typewriterlike ticking noise, sounding, in Jeanne's words, like "flying geigers looking for something to count."

The young of the *guacharos* are unusual also. Chicks are fed the wild fruits of oil palms and other trees, and they grow extremely fat before they learn to fly and leave their cave home. People have harvested them for centuries, catching them while young and help-less and rendering their fat for cooking—hence the popular name "oilbirds."

To study and photograph these odd creatures meant combining caving with birdwatching. The Gurnees flew to Caracas and then drove seventeen hours by jeep with a Venezuelan speleologist, Dr. Eugenio de Bellard Pietri, to reach the *guacharo* cave in the remote valley of Caripe. Jeanne describes their entry in one of her first publications, "The Cave of the Guacharos" (*Natural History*, December, 1956), as follows:

We approached the cavern of the birds. Large stalactites near the entrance were covered with green growth, a strange bridging between the lush vegetation outside and the cool grey sterility within. A clear stream issued from one side of the opening and tumbled over the rocks outside. We were excited.

After checking our flashlights, we lit carbide lamps and snapped them on our helmets. Presently we were splashing our way up a wide stream. Mineral-laden moisture, slowly dripping from the ceiling through the ages, had created fabulous formations in this mile-long tunnel, turning what might have been a barren subway into one of the most fascinating caves we had ever seen.

We came to what seemed to be the end of the long entrance room. The passageway closed down considerably, and as we contemplated the complete blackness ahead, we began to hear odd but distinct sounds. It was particularly strange, because most caves, in addition to being completely black, are silent. As we passed to the next room, a shocking series of cries issued from the darkness, and we knew that unseen creatures were all around us. Here, finally, were the *guacharos*.

Thousands of rattling voices filled the air with such a continuity that they became a sea of earsplitting noise. We shined our lights upward. The ceiling was so high (120 to 150 feet) that a flashlight beam was lost in the blackness. We knew that the birds were looking down from the ledges near the ceiling with a sensitivity beyond man's powers.

We turned out our lights, then, and stood in a thick blackness more complete than anything experienced above ground. Time, space, and sound were deceiving, and the clacking sounds continued to echo everywhere from the vaulted galleries.

While the birds were what we had come more than 3,000 miles to see, we were not prepared for the singular beauty of the cavern itself, and we decided to explore it further. Climbing up and over a slippery mound of guano (bird droppings), we entered Precious Hall. Its name gives only an inadequate idea of the magnificent and colorful formations. The room was estimated to be 600 feet long and 60 feet wide.

We located a pit at one end. Flashing a light down, it seemed to be a 30-foot free drop to the floor. Securing a cable ladder to the top, we descended to a small passageway. We crawled along and came to another pit. Jeanne chimneyed down another 15 feet into a hole lined on all sides with beautiful, translucent orange crystals. Along one side our lights reflected against some almost four inches long. Crawling on again, we climbed up a tight passageway through a low-hanging curtain of stalactites to another black pit. About it were some of the most weird and erratic formations we had ever seen. Having done this exploring, we climbed out of the pits and returned again to the noisy room of the Guacharos.

In some places oilbird populations have been endangered and even exterminated due to the taking of young oilbirds. For this reason, and because of mutilation of cave walls and ceilings by visitors, in 1949 the Venezuelan government established the cavern at Caripe as the Humboldt Natural Monument, named after the famous explorer-scientist, Baron Alexander von Humboldt, who first visited this cave in 1799. The Natural Monument protects these improbable birds and their home. The newer (1975) El Guacharo National Park encompasses both the cavern and 37,500 acres of surrounding mountains and forests.

Not all the caves Jeanne studies are inhabited by bats and birds. Some contain water—rivers, streams, waterfalls, and pools. The Tanamá River in Puerto Rico is her most fascinating and frightening underground exploration to date. She describes it as "the only river-cave I know of in the world like this. The river starts high in the Central Cordillera and flows right down to the north coast of the island, shooting through nine uncharted caves enroute."

On their first scientific exploration of the Tanamá, Russ rented a small plane and the team flew over the supposed course, but the vegetation was too dense for them to predict what lay below. Some help regarding the water level of the river was obtained from gauges the United States Geological Survey (USGS) had installed along the river.

"Any trip down the Tanamá is like our very first time," Jeanne says. "If the water happens to be too low, we scrape bottom and can't navigate; if it's too high, we are within head-lopping distance of the roof of the river-cave. Even after we check the gauges, there are many surprises. That first time we were washed along down the river in the two-man rubber boats and could see it would be a one-way trip. The sides are steep canyons and huge boulders, so there is no way to walk out. The water flows so fast that there is no way to paddle back upstream again."

Jeanne continues describing her first trip on the Tanamá. "When we hit the first cave mouth, we had no idea what lay ahead! All we could see was a pinpoint of light ahead, about eight hundred feet away. Debris—floating trees, branches, leaves, and garbage— were choked inside the entry. But we forced our way on and then shot swiftly through the tunnel."

Luckily they were able to portage around the roaring waterfalls by picking their way around giant rocks. The boats were extremely difficult to maneuver, however. If they hit a rock or shoal, the rubber rafts, unlike a canoe or kayak, just spun around and around.

"I learned you have to go with the motion," Jeanne reflects, "not fight it. You take advantage of the fast water pushing you along. The whole idea becomes to work *with* nature, not against it. In fact, that's a good mental attitude to have whether you're in the wilderness of a cave or anywhere. Occasionally I find men who want to pit themselves against the natural conditions, but no one should ever foolishly act this way in caving. It inevitably leads to problems. Caves can be too tricky, too dangerous. Cavers must always remember that they have to go back out the same way they got in, so it doesn't pay to try fancy rope work or to strike off alone."

The Tanamá has been run three times by speleologists and hydrologists. Jeanne Gurnee has made two of these daring trips. As a result of this exploration, the scientists discovered two invaluable facts. First, histoplasmosis danger exists in some of the caves along the Tanamá. Even more important, water samples indicated that the river is the main water supply for Arecibo. The tailings from a proposed copper mining project in the area were going to be dumped into the Tanamá and might have caused serious pollution and contamination of drinking water downstream. Thanks to the findings from the exploration, the mining project was discouraged.

Between such exciting ventures Jeanne has been active in both the NSS and the Society of Woman Geographers (SWG). The NSS serves as a central agency for the collection, preservation, and publication of information relating to speleology. It also seeks to preserve caverns through proper conservation practices. Jeanne has done correspondence and editing for NSS, and as director of its internal organizations chartered over thirty new chapters and was responsible for coordination among chapters and regions. She writes grant proposals for new trips and prepares reports afterward. She was the first woman to address the annual congress banquet of NSS in 1977. (Women compose 20 percent of the group.) She was awarded fellow status in 1969.

As a member and executive officer of the Society of Woman Geographers, Jeanne has played an active role in its operation, too. One of Jeanne's contributions was to publish a booklet, *Vignettes of Some Early Members of the Society of Woman Geographers in New York*, by Gertrude Dole (1978). It highlights famous women explorers such as Harriet Chalmers Adams, Delia Akeley, Osa Johnson, Amelia Earhart, Annie Smith Peck, Pearl Buck, and Margaret Mead.

Often, as in Jeanne's exploration of the Mayan ceremonial caves in Alta Verapaz, Guatemala, members of the society have worked in wild places where no woman has even been before. "The Geogs

have given me a lot of emotional support," she claims. "Just knowing that other women were pioneering the unknown long before
me, and then consorting with fellow explorers at our meetings, is
inspiring and encouraging. We all seem to have the same approach
to our work—whatever the job, do it and do it well. We tend to
be positive women who are doing something we like."

Over the years Jeanne has found her caving interests focusing
more and more on conservation and the wise use of caves. She
feels it's no longer enough just to explore a cave; she prefers to
have a particular objective. "I enjoy the wilderness experience of
getting to, in, and out of them so much that conserving the cave
and its surroundings is almost an obligation now."

"Fortunately," she adds, "God put most caves in limestone and
volcanic rock regions where population density is low, so often
there's still a chance to preserve the environment."

On a reconnaissance trip to Puerto Rico in 1958, the Gurnees
and some caving friends were traveling through the contorted karst,
or limestone, hills in the western part of the island. On a standard
road map they noticed the blue line of a river which disappeared
at one point and reappeared about three miles later. They stopped
near the spot where the river was supposed to disappear, and
Jeanne inquired of some workers nearby whether they knew where
the river came out. The workmen slashed through the underbrush
with machetes and guided the group to a huge sinkhole which
exposed the Rio Camuy three hundred feet below. The discovery
that no one had previously navigated the river led to a series of
expeditions over the next ten years, sponsored by the National
Geographic Society, The Explorers Club, the National Speleological Society, and the Commonwealth of Puerto Rico. Some seven
miles of subterranean river were eventually explored and mapped,
and an underground river route which could potentially be developed for tourists was charted.

The area is one of few pristine sites on the heavily populated
island which has not been cut, burned, farmed, grazed, or built
up with houses, and in 1960 the Gurnees made a proposal to the
Puerto Rican government that the area be protected as a park. No
action was forthcoming, so they bought a small farm which encompasses the three main entrances to the Rio Camuy. Finally, in

1965, the Land Administration of the Commonwealth began buying up land and transferring it to the Department of Parks. The following year the NSS made another expedition, and in 1967 it prepared a master plan for the development and protection of this cave system, "Conservation through Commercialization—Rio Camuy Development Proposal." The report spurred the government to buy a total of five hundred acres, but park status is still 'in a holding action,' so Jeanne and Russ continue to keep their farm and pay taxes on it. "When the government is ready, they can have it," says Jeanne simply. "We have no profit motive—only a perpetuation motive. I guess it has been an aim of many people, but some day I'd love to be able to give land for a park or preserve, especially one like Rio Camuy, with its gigantic entrances, vaulted chambers, remarkable formations, sense of mystery, untamed rushing river, and overwhelming impact.

"Russ and I believe that private ownership of superb land is not the best answer. A human life span is so short. And what happens when we're gone? Others might not feel the same way and unknowingly destroy this great natural phenomenon. We feel that governments can better assure perpetuity of a major natural wonder. But we want to be sure that the Camuy is developed sensitively. This would include proper, but discreet, lighting, easy and safe trails, well-trained guides, and good design of surface facilities. In short, the public should be given an educational as well as enjoyable experience, and see an aesthetically developed and well-maintained phenomenon."

Jeanne consistently promotes this idea now in speeches and consulting jobs. In 1975 she presented a paper at a speleological congress on Cuba's Isle of Pines, and more recently to the U.S. National Cave Association, a national organization of commercial cave owners. The Gurnees stress mixing good business with sound environmental use of caves. This would include developing part of a suitable cave for public visitation and conserving the rest for study and future exploration. In short, conservation through commercialization.

Jeanne made another contribution to cave conservation in Barbados in 1978. The government had called in a team of consultants to advise on the development of Harrison's Cave, a small limestone cavern, and nearby Welchman's Hall (a gully). This time Jeanne worked with her husband, as well as a cartographer, a hydrologist, an engineer, and a park planner. Manmade enlargements of existing narrow tunnels had already begun; and the threat of ceiling collapse and rockfall, the amount of natural ventilation available for large groups of people, water pollution potential from sewage leaking down from houses above, and disposal of trash were all valid concerns. "It's important to bring in consultants before opening up a cave to the public," explains Jeanne, "otherwise it may be damaged beyond repair." On the initial exploration the Gurnees had to crawl on their bellies up the shallow main stream, which cascades through Harrison's Cave. Fortunately, the cavern's elevation, about 850 feet, is considerably higher than most of this low, cane-covered Caribbean island, so there is no danger of flash flooding such as occurs during rainy season in caves located lower down.

While Harrison's Cave is not quite as spectacular as Rio Camuy or the Mayan ceremonial caverns, the team decided it is well-suited to tourist use and will give visitors a unique natural history experience in a region where very few caves are known.

Jeanne is the first environmental commissioner for her home town in the New Jersey woodlands and an officer on the municipal zoning board. She feels that *wilderness* has a particular meaning for those who live in heavily populated areas. "Our small town has 3.2 square miles and nine thousand inhabitants. Recently a small parcel of three acres was made available to our borough by sale. It had a fine stand of trees, a meandering brook, and thick untouched native vegetation. In such a suburban area this may be the only wilderness some of our residents may know in years to come. These places put us in touch with nature and bring us back to the reality of our unembellished environment after being surrounded by manmade things day after day."

When I met Jeanne in the city, she was dressed in high boots, white skirt, and trim burgundy blazer. During my acquaintance with her, I had formed the impression of a well-organized, confident, and happy woman who showed no bitterness, competitiveness, or resentment against men or life. I passed these observations along to her now.

"That's pretty accurate." Jeanne replied. "Mostly I've been able to do what I wanted to do if it has been helpful and useful. I believe that if a woman has an idea worthy of exploration, is capable of accomplishing it, and can present herself in a valid and proper manner, she can do it."

"But would you have gone to explore all those caves and promote their conservation without your husband?" I asked.

"Who knows if I would have gone in all those caves without Russell. . . . In life it always takes someone or some situation to introduce us to what we later choose to do. Probably if I had been exposed to mountain climbing or birdwatching instead, and Russ had been excited about it, too, we would have gone in that direction. We both happened to like caves.

"Whatever the particular out-of-doors interest, I eventually would have moved toward conservation—not in the unreal sense which means don't use it, but in such a way that human beings can exist in nature without misusing it.

"When women have the proper exposure to outdoor pursuits or professions and learn the techniques well, they can accomplish them as well as men. Those women I know who have been taught ing techniques, exploring procedures, boat handling in white-water, and so on are as adroit and professional as men. Interestingly, wives of men who are tops in rope climbing, for example, are also tops."

I asked Jeanne how she felt about feminism as a political movement.

"It's quite parallel to the black movement," she replied. "I don't quite believe in making an issue about either. Too often women make too much of the fact that they're women and, therefore, something is supposed to happen. If she goes ahead and creates her own aura, and is as well-informed as possible in her field, a woman is likely to be accepted no matter what she's doing. In a way, maybe that's how I got appointed environmental commissioner. I saw the need for land-use mapping in my town, studied up on it, and carefully presented the project to our mayor."

Jeanne has tried to pass on these attitudes and her love of the wilderness to her two daughters, who are now in their mid-twenties. She began taking them out on trips when they were six weeks and five months old, respectively. "A friend made me an Indian papoose carrier, so I just strapped the baby in and set the board against a cave wall or tree. My daughters were always exposed to the outdoors. They feel it's the natural condition, that there's nothing alien about it. Both girls have been to survival school and can manage well alone with just a fish hook, tarp, and matches. They also accompanied me on a 1973 European tour which included exploring ice caves, salt mines, and other natural phenomena from Belgium to Czechoslovakia.

"My girls have come away from their wilderness experiences more happy, healthy, and self-assured than I ever knew them to be," says their mother. "I don't think they'll ever live or work in the outdoors full-time, but they'll return to it again and again. As for me," she went on, "I see women being in the wilderness as a natural state.

"Beyond the personal benefit, I know wilderness is valuable for many public reasons. For instance, right here in New Jersey preserving fresh-water wetlands (one kind of wilderness) is vital to the preservation of the quality of our drinking water because these wetlands filter the waters from streams which empty into reservoirs in one of the most densely populated areas in the United States. Some scientists say that we should preserve the New Jersey Pine Barrens (wetlands) and other areas like it because we still do not fully understand the complexities of the ecology of these areas. Wilderness can also teach us about our survival. People need it to return to, to reaffirm their animal relationship with the natural environment. I do not know of anyone who has not learned and benefited from this exposure."

Chapter 8

Krissa Johnson

Architect with a Chainsaw

KRISSA STEPPED OUT on the frozen lake. A pale November sun rose above the dense forest, glinting off her axe and metal bucket. Out on the ice she stopped, looking down at the light dusting of snow over her water hole, which had skimmed shut with an inch of new ice. Raising her axe to chop it open, she stopped it abruptly in midair. A pack of wolves was running toward her across the lake. She lowered her axe and stood stock still. To her surprise the wolves paid her not the slightest attention, but jumped, feinted, nipped, and dashed about, looking for all the world like a bunch of German shepherds. Krissa was so fascinated that she stood motionless despite the cold. The vibrant spectacle lasted about ten minutes on that sparkling British Columbia morning.

Suddenly the wolves picked up the sound of a moose crashing through the spruce forest. They paused in their play, poised for a signal from the leader, and then broke into a run. All that was left behind were a jumble of footprints on the snow and the echoes of their howls in the air. Krissa recalled later that she never felt the slightest fear, only wonderment—and two very cold feet from standing still so long. Still bemused by the wolves' antics, she axed open the hole, picked up her pail, and filled it with clear lake water. Then she hurried back to her log cabin. As soon as she had eaten breakfast, Krissa made the rounds of several other log build-

Krissa Johnson making a cut in a foot-diameter spruce log for the side of a cabin in the Adirondacks. Her face shield and ear protectors are essential equipment. Photo by Anne LaBastille.

ings, some finished, some partly done, standing here and there in the forest. In each one she built a fire to warm the interior. Stopping at the largest, she put a huge pot of coffee on a wood stove, then sat down with her books to wait for the class of students to arrive from Prince George, a town twenty-six miles away. These caretaker chores were her way of paying for use of the little log cabin beside the lake.

What had brought Krissa Johnson to the B. Allan Mackie School of Log Building was one of those twists of fate that change the entire course of one's life. She had been studying design at Bennington College, planning to work in the theater in New York City. While she was at college, Krissa lived in a small cabin in the Vermont woods to save on expenses. She led an almost schizoid life, rushing to the city to see plays and mingle with actors and other designers, then coming back to the rustic serenity of her woodland cottage. As her senior year drew to a close, it became harder and harder to switch back and forth. She found it difficult to decide which lifestyle was best, or whether she should abandon both and go to graduate school.

She was sitting in her cabin reading the Canadian back-to-the-land magazine *Harrowsmith* when she saw an article entitled "Log Building Renaissance" and an ad for the B. Allan Mackie School of Log Building in British Columbia. The school offered a nine-week course in the fall for $1,000. Krissa wanted to learn log building so that someday she could build her own log home. This challenging skill would make her more self-sufficient and independent. But would they accept women? Krissa decided to apply and see.

She was accepted, and subsequent events seemed to support her decision to attend. A close friend gave her a chainsaw for her college graduation present. Spending the entire summer after graduation at her family's Adirondack home on her beloved Big Moose Lake cured her of any ideas of ever living in the city. She found a local waitressing job which earned her the price of tuition. An Adirondack acquaintance happened to be driving out to British Columbia in September and offered her a ride. Without hesitation Krissa headed west with her chainsaw.

The course was being offered for contractors, not novices, and Krissa worried that she wouldn't be able to hold her own, although she had grown up in a family which was always building things. Her father was a construction engineer, and she had spent hours with him on various jobs. Besides that, she had helped many friends with building. Nevertheless, she felt sure she would be less qualified than any of the other students. She prepared for the challenge by reading everything on log building available, and she stopped to inspect famous log buildings all along her route across Canada. She hoped that memorizing the species of trees in Canada and bringing a big box of tools with her to the school would ease her acceptance, too.

Despite her careful preparations the first day of school was traumatic. Thirty-one men arrived on the scene and saw Krissa standing there with her long blond hair, green-gray eyes, and orange Husquavarna chainsaw. First they thought she might be Mackie's daughter (she was twenty-one at the time) or one of the students' wives. Finally they realized she was single, alone, and a student like themselves. There were awkward introductions and stares of disbelief. Victor Janzen, the head instructor, lectured awhile and then instructed the students to start up their saws and take turns cutting down a forty-inch DBH (trunk diameter measured at breast height) Western cedar. The first day's lesson was to split up the cedar into roofing shakes. Krissa tugged on the starting rope of her saw, and it sputtered into life—then literally fell apart in her hands. On the long, bouncy ride out from Big Moose to British Columbia, some parts of the chainsaw had jiggled loose. Krissa received several belittling looks but no offers of help. Finally she put the saw back together and started working on the tree.

Next she volunteered along with others to split twenty-four-inch shakes from the wooden bolts with a froe (a cleaving tool used for splitting shingles from a block of wood). She was busy with her work when she looked up and saw all the men staring at her in amazement; apparently they had never seen a woman handle a froe before. When lunchtime came, no one ate with Krissa or talked to her. Later that afternoon it came time to carry the new shakes up onto the roof of an unfinished log building and start nailing them down. Krissa had never shaked a roof but she had shingled at least two, and was used to working high on scaffolding, so she casually climbed up the ladder and went nimbly right on to the ridgepole. Several men stopped dead in their tracks to watch. A few even stayed down on the ground and handed the shakes up to her. "I think they were glad to be at the bottom," she recalled. "Actually, the best place to be is at the very top. Nobody drops anything on your head that way."

After the first day Krissa figured out that "we were all a bunch of turkeys. No one really knew what they were doing, but I was certainly holding my own. The men just couldn't believe my energy and that I really wanted to learn about log building."

Gradually things evened out. Victor Janzen accepted Krissa at once, and one by one the students became her friends, although a few men still pushed her out of the way from cutting notches or acted as if she couldn't handle some of the jobs. As she found out, there is a very strong strain of machismo in the north country. Krissa didn't fit in, and she never would. But being a strong feminist, she didn't try to.

The course was extremely thorough. After starting at the top of the building and finishing the roof, the students worked their way down. They learned about roof support systems, trusses, foundations, log aesthetics, R (thermal) values, different species of trees to be used, fire insurance, various kinds of notches, and log shrinkage. Everyone began to see the responsibility of being a log builder. Vic Janzen impressed on them that they were custodians, preserving the best of logs from an era: "Good log buildings may, in the next century, be all that's left of our vanished forests."

Krissa discovered that Allan Mackie and his wife Mary had created not only a log building school, but a lesson in lifestyles and a course in conservation and history. Using the several hundred acres of land they own near Prince George, they have constructed a dozen log buildings and hope to use them eventually as an environmental center. Mary Mackie runs Canadian Log House Publications, Inc., and has published two books on log building plus a yearly magazine, *The Canadian Log House*. Allan Mackie is considered the foremost log builder and instructor in Canada at present. He tells his students, "Log construction is the only contemporary construction method that enables an individual to exchange his own labor and ingenuity, rather than cash or a mortgage debt, for a home to be proud of." And now, he adds, "women are beginning to assert their interest in building with logs."

One of the first and most important points Mackie makes to all his classes is avoiding the "lawg caybun" mentality. Too many people, Mackie says, think of a log cabin either as a makeshift shelter built in some far-off swamp by a gnarled old man wearing buckskin underwear, or as a one-room shanty. He stresses that a log house can be one of the most aesthetically satisfying dwellings in which to live; logs bring the natural world back into our lives in a way that is becoming more necessary than ever to our survival as thoughtful human beings. There is a deep sense of peace, he maintains, living in a house made of hand-hewn wood. Furthermore, the log building has an amazing durability that will rival concrete and timeless good taste. The tree as it exists naturally is already an almost perfect building material—the successful product of millions of years of trial. It only remains for the builder to accord the tree the respect it deserves.

Assistant instructor Ron Strutt teaches with pride that log buildings are adapted from centuries-old techniques used in Russia and Europe. Some homes there are still lived in after five hundred years. Krissa and her companions learned that the first log towns probably were built by a southern Russian people who emigrated north in the sixteenth century under fear of religious persecution. In the vast coniferous forests of Siberia, they "cut a town," that is, cut the forest down and built a town. Everything they constructed—graineries, homes, stables, windmills, and outbuildings—was of logs; and everything was built to last a lifetime. The Russians worked only with broadaxes, chisels, and knives. Each master builder had his own mark, and it was possible to tell by a glance at a timber who had cut and hewn it. They actually were fine cabinetmakers working on a grand scale. Some buildings were very ornate, with carvings, bell towers, balconies, and railings. The master builders were accorded great respect in their culture.

As Krissa absorbed this history lesson, she was reminded of an Adirondack craftsman who had been a major influence on her life. Earl Covey, a master cabinet maker and builder, grew up in Big Moose and built many beautiful camps, cottages, boathouses, hotels, and an outstanding community chapel in that area. Although he had no more than a fourth-grade education and only paper bags on which to draw his "blueprints," Covey had a genius's knack of using the innate qualities and characteristics of local woods and stones. Walking through the Adirondack forest, he'd see a bending spruce and translate it in his mind to a gracefully curved banister. Or he might notice a granite boulder and immediately picture a finely chiseled mantlepiece. Krissa had grown up with reverence and admiration for Covey's skills and talents; to her he represented all that was best in the dying breed of "Adirondacker"—independent, resourceful, self-sufficient. The values Covey had, Krissa felt, are lacking in most people today. On the first page of the notebook she used at the Mackie School of Log Building, Krissa wrote a tribute to Earl Covey. She later penned his epitaph, which is inscribed on a bronze plaque bolted to a boulder near the inn where Covey lived and worked. It reads:

In Memory Of Earl W. Covey
1876–1952

A master builder, who lived so much in
tune with the life of nature, that he
was able to duplicate and enhance its
beauty in the creation of beautiful
buildings from Adirondack trees and rocks.

As school progressed, Krissa's dream was to become the next Earl Covey, and her goal to keep alive the dying art of log building in the Adirondacks. She feels that because the woods were here before her and will exist long after she is gone, "I must tread softly, for my life is only temporary. I do not want to leave my mark upon the Manhattan shoreline as my grandfather did, but rather as one small log home on the far shore of Big Moose Lake. My goals are small and simple. I find joy and take pride in the little things."

The dangers associated with being a log builder are considerable, and Mackie taught his students to respect them. The kick of a chainsaw running at full power has roughly the force of firing a twelve-gauge shotgun, and a whirring saw can cut off a hand or a foot with ease and leave a mangled mess behind. Each student was required to have a chain-brake on his or her machine so that in case it kicked back or they fell off a building while sawing, the chain would stop instantly. Axes were kept honed razor sharp. Students were required to wear steel-toed boots to protect their feet. Eyes had to be protected by plastic shields or masks, ears by mufflers.

One afternoon Krissa slipped while doing a square notch and put a huge gash in her leg with a chisel. It was below zero, and she didn't even feel the wound until she came inside to warm up that evening. There was blood all over her long johns. She washed off the gash, slapped on two butterfly bandaids, had a couple of shots of whiskey, and went to bed.

Tools were all-important on the job, and they had to be kept clean and sharp. Krissa gradually assembled all the necessary tools of her trade—a pair of log scribers with level bubble (to mark notches), socket chisels, hammer, bong (large wooden mallet), axe file and broad axe, tape measure, peeling spud, lumber crayon and chalk line, log dogs (to hold two logs steady), draw knife, adze, auger, slick, peavey, timber carrier, whetstone, and broad hatchet. All were kept in a huge wooden toolbox.

As the lectures continued during October, November, and early December, Krissa and her fellow students gained a deeper respect for log building. Their days were long and hard. They began with a class, followed by work on a building, a coffee break, more work, lunch, and more work, until the afternoon grew dim. In British Columbia winter comes early. Snow fell. Winds blew. Ice formed. Students left. Krissa shivered in her log cabin when the fire went out during the night. When mid-December finally came, the class had dwindled from thirty-two to six students. They had grown efficient at running their saws, splitting roof shakes, selecting logs, and designing functional and aesthetic buildings. Now they were ready to graduate. Krissa had stuck it out and became the first woman to graduate from the B. Allan Mackie School of Log Building and, later, the first woman to go into log building as a contractor in the eastern United States.

She returned to Big Moose determined to use her training to start her own log building business. Her father encouraged her as he had all her life, "If you want something, go and take it." Krissa reasoned that she knew enough to make a go of it. She had already participated in building a blacksmith shop and a Russian-style log home at the Mackie school. She had grown up listening to construction terminology, seeing blueprints, going out on jobs with her dad. She'd helped repair and build onto the family's house at Big Moose and had earned money as a laborer on building crews while in college.

In founding her own enterprise, Adirondack Log Building, Krissa's rough-and-ready background on the north shore of Big Moose

Lake served her well. No roads ran to the family home. To get there she either canoed a mile over water or skied across the ice, and during freeze-up and break-up she had to walk around North Bay, roughly a two-mile trek. Behind their home lay a sixty-two-thousand-acre wilderness tract of Adirondack Park land. Living at Big Moose had taught Krissa respect for work, love for the woods, and values that today are often called old-fashioned.

"We had fun doing chores around the place. We learned that hard work was a pleasure, and sore muscles and blisters build character." Krissa and her three brothers were never sheltered. Their mother took the attitude that her "rug rats" could go any place as long as they could see the lake. Even when they were very little, she put lifejackets and cowbells on each child and threw them out the door. They all learned to swim and paddle canoes before they were seven. Krissa started camping when she was five and took her first trip in the woods alone at thirteen. Both parents were instrumental in bringing their children up to be self-reliant.

With this kind of upbringing, and the unconventional nature that an Aquarius is said to possess, it's not surprising that Krissa would decide to go out on her own. But she admits that "women are brought up to doubt, among other things, that we can use tools, run a chainsaw, and learn the skills we need to build our own homes. As women re-examining our roles in society, we have learned that we are responsible for our own welfare and survival. We must learn to love our own strengths and visions and capacities as a prerequisite to any other kind of loving."

Adirondack Log Building's first contract, in the summer of 1978, was to design and build a large log home, with a floor plan eighty-two feet by twenty-eight feet, in Harrisville, New York. The former structure had burned down, and the owners wanted it replaced. Krissa hired a friend and fellow student from the Mackie School to work with her on the house.

The two of them set to work in May. The house was finished five and a half months later with, Krissa admits, "much cussing and moaning. Men find it difficult to work with me. When I build something, I want it done my way. I am a perfectionist. Logs must fit right or become firewood. Actually I'd much prefer to have no one work for me at all."

Krissa explained that the Harrisville house was built by the scribed fit, also called "chinkless," method, which takes time and patience. Each log has to be carefully selected to be straight, knot-free, and with a mean diameter of ten to twelve inches. "We used red pine and, when we were done, there was not a chainsaw mark showing anywhere on those logs. But I did leave my own distinctive mark on one of the arches," Krissa says proudly. "Just like the old Russian builders.

"My work is a constant learning process. It is the transformation of design to an actual building that fascinates me. Building is very much like climbing a mountain. There are many ways to go about it. You can charge up or go slowly. I prefer to go slowly, as it's the process which makes the end product of high quality."

At the end of the contract, Krissa netted about $4,000. Her father was impressed. "If you can make that kind of profit in your first year, then Adirondack Log Building is a good venture."

Shortly after Krissa had finished this job, she came back to the Adirondacks and stepped into a local bar. She was wearing heavy boots, wool pants, and a flannel shirt. An old guide called Rockie was sitting on a stool. He took one look at Krissa and said, "Oh, God, I heard about you! You think you can build log cabins. You ain't gonna build shit, woman, up here!"

Horrified, Krissa stopped stock still, turned red, and wished she could disappear through the floor.

Then Rockie slapped his leg and guffawed, "Why, you're just a regular old woodchucker." It was his way of letting her know she was accepted locally, and since that incident Krissa's nickname has been Woodchucker.

Though she loves working with her tools and building from scratch, Krissa feels her greatest talent is in design. Her college courses in theater design and the structural knowledge absorbed from her father helped foster this gift. As a young man who does a lot of her drafting recently kidded her, "You are just a hack architect in logs!"

"A well-thought-out design will save a lot of time and money," she explains. "I recently finished designing a cross-country ski lodge out West, and now I'm working on a five-bedroom home and a log terminal building for a local airport."

Currently Krissa is busy building cabins, doing consulting work in which she designs buildings for other log contractors and promoting her Adirondack Log Building School, a nonprofit, two-week course for homeowners, based in Big Moose.

Krissa has two other strong interests in life. One is her relationships with women. Krissa is a very strong feminist, and she feels that the strongest influences in her life have always been women. She does not feel the need to have her identity linked up with a man. She believes that women are too often judged in relationship to men rather than on their own merits. Although she dates off and on, and may someday consider marriage, she has chosen independence for the time being. "But," she says, "that is not to say that I do not value intimacy."

Of equal importance in her life is being alone. "I need a lot of silence and wildness," she states simply. "Most people do not understand the value of spending periods of time with oneself outdoors. For me that time is spent in the woods. That isn't running away from things, it's running to find myself. In the wilderness I find it easy to keep an inventory on myself."

Taken together—her skill with tools and flair for design, her energy, independence, and love for the wilderness—perhaps Krissa's lifestyle and ambitions can be summed up most eloquently in a poem written by her Adirondack mentor Earl Covey:

A Woodsman's Prayer

Just let me live my life as I've begun,
And give me work that is open to the sky and sun,
Make me a partner of the winds that blow,
And I won't ask for life that's soft and low.

Chapter 9

Margaret Owings

An Artist in Activism

Wₕₑₙ MARGARET OWINGS was a child of six, her parents took her and her brother for a hike one Sunday in the tills above Berkeley, California. She remembers walking happily through eucalyptus groves, under giant oaks, and over grassy knolls. Golden light lay over the landscape. All was peaceful.

Her father carried a gun. The young girl had never seen one used before. She noticed a large owl take off from a tree where it had been sleeping and sail silently over the chaparral. Her father raised his gun and fired, and the owl fell to earth with a dull sound. Horrified, Margaret shrieked hysterically at her father, "*Why* did you do it? *Why* did you do it?"

Stunned by her behavior, her parent answered plaintively, "I don't know why I did it."

This incident made a dramatic impression on both Margaret's and her father's lives. It was the last time that her father ever carried a gun on their walks, and for her, the beginning of a moral ethic against killing wildlife. From that point on Margaret guarded the wildlife and wildlands around her home. She would attack boys who sniped at blue jays and scold children who picked wildflowers. No one encouraged her in this instinctive protection of nature; indeed, other children teased her. Yet, stubbornly, she persisted. Not until Margaret was fourteen did she read about or talk to

anyone who felt as strongly or acted as she did. Then a minister
gave her some of Albert Schweitzer's writings to read. At last, her
beliefs and actions were vindicated.

The same sense of outrage seized Margaret some forty years
later, as she and her architect husband, Nat, were enjoying a quiet
afternoon in their airy A-frame above the Pacific. It was June, and
the precipitous slopes of the Big Sur country baked in the late sun.
A fog bank hung far out over the ocean. From their porch the
Owings could look down onto a large herd of sea lions, some of
which frolicked in the waves while others slept on a rock-covered
beach. Atop a huge boulder towered an enormous white-colored
Stellar bull. The ruler of a large harem and its young, he had
returned here for years in breeding season.

Suddenly three shots from a high-powered rifle shook the air.
Nat and Margaret leapt to the railing as the sea lions moved into
chaotic retreat, and watched in horror as the great male toppled
off the rocks into the sea. A cloud of red blood spread out around
his body as his life poured out. In a few moments he had sunk
beneath the waves.

Above the Owings' house, on the narrow coastal highway, a lone
figure stalked away from the cliff edge and drove away in a truck.
There was nothing Nat and Margaret could do—no way they could
catch the culprit on that winding coastal road, no way they could
climb down steep slopes to the sea lion beach and calm the panicked
animals. Nothing except what Margaret did in the next hour: she
wrote an emotionally charged letter to the *Monterey Herald*, ending "I was strongly moved by this incidental, needless murder,
without reason, by a man who had extinguished a life quite obviously more noble than his own." Because of this letter (and the
dozens of others it engendered), Margaret earned the title of Sea
Lion Lady from her friends and supporters.

A short while later, in 1960, she and Nat learned that the State
Senate Resource Committee had approved a bill designed to kill
75 percent of the sea lions along the California coast. Less than
one month remained before the State Assembly committee would
meet to vote on it. Apparently salmon fishermen at the mouth of
the Klamath River in northern California were convinced that sea
lions were consuming their salmon catch. Although they already

*Margaret Owings silhouetted against the window of her home, Wild
Bird, with its dramatic view of the Big Sur coastline and the Pacific.*
Photo by Anne LaBastille.

had the right to shoot sea lions caught in their nets, they demanded
that the population of these sea mammals be reduced along the
entire coast.

The news made Margaret weep with rage and frustration. "I
knew nothing about bills or politics or Sacramento, the seat of
government in California," she explained, "and I couldn't conceive
of myself entering that realm." However, the next morning she
formed a plan of action. The first thing she did was to hire Kamini
Gupta, an attorney and professional legislative lobbyist, to stop the
bill in the Assembly. While he lobbied for the sea lions, Margaret
stayed quietly in the background and "steered." She sent out mail-
ings, alerted the Sierra Club, and helped arrange for expert research on sea lions' feeding habits.

The results of the research showed that the accused marine
mammals eat a number of items, including fish, but primarily

lamprey eels, which are a true curse to fishermen. Salmon are
relatively rare on their menu. Mr. Gupta presented to the Assembly a fact sheet based on data provided by the Scripps Institute
of Oceanography about the normal stomach contents of sea lions.
The information clearly refuted the fishermen's claims. Another
argument to protect the sea lions was the problem of just how 75
percent of the population could be eliminated. By bombs? Marks-
men with rifles? Poisons? In every case their bodies would wash
up on the beaches and cause a public uproar. The case presented
to the Assembly by Kamini Gupta, Margaret's competent spokesman, was convincing, and the sea lion bill was defeated.

Not long after this Margaret was alone in the Big Sur home on
a full-moon night. At about two in the morning a tremendous roar
echoed from the mountain behind the house, and the entire A-
frame shook. Dashing out onto the open sundeck, Margaret could
discern by the moon's light a group of dark figures throwing bombs
off the road onto the herd of sea lions sleeping below on the beach.
Again, there was no chance to catch the murderers. She spent a
sleepless night.

Even though the first bill had been killed, clearly the fishermen
were not about to give up, and it was not long before another
legislative attempt was made to destroy the animals. This time a
bill was drawn up to set aside the beach south of the Owings'
home, along with several other designated areas, as a Big Sur Sea
Lion Reserve. The rest of the coast was to be open for killing.
Again Margaret was appalled, and again she waged war. This time
Kamini Gupta's wife Ruth, also an attorney, defended the sea lion's
case—and won.

It seemed entirely fitting, when I visited the Owings in the
spring of 1979, to awake at dawn to the sound of some two hundred
sea lions barking and chuffing far below my bedroom window. It
was the perfect tribute to the woman who had fought to save them.
"I had to do it," she explains firmly but modestly. "We live with
sea lion voices along this shore; they would have been silenced if
we hadn't defended them."

Watching this tall, green-eyed, and gracious woman move about
her stunning home, I found it hard to believe she'd been called
a "tiger for conservation," and is one of California's leading envi-

ronmentalists. She seems more the elegant hostess, sensitive artist, world traveler. The interior of the lofty, spacious Big Sur house that she and Nat named Wild Bird is an expression of Margaret's artistic nature and training. She majored in art at Mills College and did graduate work in art history and museum operation at Radcliffe College. She has had a number of one-woman shows of her paintings from 1940 through 1969, and several exquisite arrangements of natural and hand-crafted objects adorn the rooms and garden of her home. Wherever one looks in the house, a bit of Margaret the artist beckons.

In a tiny basement room the impression changes. There hang her awards, pictures, and plaques: a conservation citation from the National Audubon Society; another from California Governor Edmund G. Brown "for saving the Big Sur country"; a photo of Margaret with then Secretary of the Interior Stewart Udall and another with former President Lyndon Johnson during her work with the National Park Service; the conservation service award from the Department of the Interior during Nathaniel Reed's brilliant tour of duty as assistant secretary; California's Golden Bear Award for conservation; and so on.

Just as the inside of the house is Margaret's spirit looking out, so the design of the outer structure captures Nat's. A leading architect and cofounder of the firm of Skidmore, Owings and Merrill, he has spent years making cities more livable, and dealing with such famous clients as Laurence and David Rockefeller, Weyerhaeuser, H. J. Heinz, and Zellerbach. But as he writes in his autobiography *The Spaces in Between,* "Wild Bird was something apart and special."

Growing out of rock and sea wind like Big Sur itself was our house. Two independent spirits met, crashed into a kind of numbing calm, then saved each other and the marriage by building a kind of shrine to a shared ideal—an ideal on which we have both been working since we moved into "Wild Bird" in 1957.

The A-frame is cantilevered out from a rocky nose of land six hundred feet long, six hundred feet high, and only thirty feet wide. Like a hawk-beak nose, the mountain slope arches out, then drops abruptly to the sea. Years ago Margaret brought Nat, her husband-to-be, here and showed the spot to him. They picnicked on fresh peaches and warm champagne and planned. Would it ever be possible to buy and build on that perfect promontory?

When at last they were able to realize their dream, old redwood bridge timbers, Big Sur boulders, huge log and cement rafters were melded together to create "Wild Bird." Pines and cypresses were planted all around the building to provide privacy yet still allow breathtaking views over the coast and east onto the Santa Lucia Range. Margaret was later to write in her introduction to the Sierra Club book *Not Man Apart:*

Those of us privileged to live on this coast, in the immensity of its scope and in its great proportion, enjoy a strong sense of belonging. Perched on the buttresses of the range, we might, with Sigurd Olson, call them, "the final bastions of the Spirit of Man."

From the 164,000-acre Ventana Wilderness in Los Padres National Forest behind "Wild Bird," many endangered forms of wildlife often venture down to the Owings' property. Ringtailed cats sniff for scraps on the patio. At least once Nat and Margaret have glimpsed a rare California condor soaring high above the ridge. Eagles nest up the canyon, and a peregrine falcon circles their promontory. Margaret has even found mountain lion tracks beside her mailbox in the morning.

Picking up the local newspaper from her box one morning in 1963, Margaret saw a picture of a dead puma—and for the third time was galvanized into action. The creature had been shot in the mountains directly behind the Owings house, and there was little doubt in Margaret's mind that it was *her* "mailbox mountain lion." The story reported that a boy had treed the animal with a dog and shot it to collect $115 in state and county bounties.

Margaret Owings vowed that the lion would not have died in vain. This time she flew immediately to Sacramento and took it upon herself to see a California senator directly. Her earlier qualms gone, Margaret argued fervently for the repeal of the bounty. Senator Fred Farr was convinced and agreed to present a bill.

"No one realized how green at politics I was; and I, in turn, had never known how blind the legislators were," recalls Margaret. "In fact, no one seemed interested in wildlife at all back in the mid-sixties. I formed a "lion committee" with distinguished, nationally known names in the wildlife field—but no one had ever heard of them in Sacramento. Finally I asked Rachel Carson [author of *Silent Spring*], to write a letter protesting the bounty. That helped convince a few people, particularly the head of the Senate Natural Resources Committee, who was also a woman, that we meant business. An astonished legislature soon found that, despite opposition from ranchers and sportsmen, a bill had passed which removed the bounty for a four-year moratorium."

For this accomplishment Margaret was honored in 1964 with a National Audubon citation, presented on the same day that Rachel Carson was awarded the prestigious Audubon Medal for her battle against the use of pesticides. It was an exciting experience for Margaret to meet at last the scientist she idolized, whose book *The Sea Around Us* she deeply admired, and whose poetic expression she cherished. To Margaret, Carson held the foremost place among women writing about the natural world.

At that time Rachel Carson was mortally ill with cancer. Speaking with Margaret after the awards, she referred sadly to *Silent Spring:* "I'm so worried about who will carry on my work when I'm gone." When she died a number of months later, Margaret took this plea to heart and resolved to see that something was done immediately. She wrote, designed, and illustrated a tribute to Rachel Carson for the purpose of raising a memorial fund to be administered through the National Audubon Society in New York. This fund, which is devoted to research on pesticides, poisons, and other environmental pollutants, still functions, and its work has been continued on a far larger scale by the Environmental Defense Fund.

Margaret remained concerned as to what would happen to California's mountain lion population when the bounty moratorium was over, and with good reason. Almost as soon as the time limit was up, the California Department of Fish and Game declared the mountain lion a big-game animal and sold 4,746 licenses to lion hunters. According to Margaret, their decision to open up the state to lion hunting was based on only hazy information about the lion population. The number had long been accepted as six hundred lions, but suddenly the Department of Fish and Game announced that two thousand existed.

Now Margaret came into her own as a political fighter and wild-life strategist. She made dozens of trips to Sacramento (six hours each way by car) and even chartered planes to pick up and deliver witnesses such as the noted wildlife biologist Dr. A. Starker Leopold to hearings. One day the fog and rain were so heavy that the pilot had to stay close to the ocean. "He could hardly decide whether to fly over or under the Golden Gate Bridge," she recalls. "Thank goodness we won that hearing!"

From Defenders of Wildlife and the National Audubon Society she obtained grants for a four-year study on the California mountain lion. Commencing in 1973 and conducted by Dr. Carl Koford, this study ran concurrently with a telemetric, radio-collared lion study on the coast ridge range in Monterey County. The results showed that the state was not exactly overrun with pumas. Koford felt that no more than one thousand lions existed in California. As a result, a second moratorium was declared and full protection extended for another four years. "I was driven," explains Margaret with the matter-of-factness typical of a Taurus, "and once I start something, I can't let go."

Alas, when I met her at Wild Bird in 1979, her peace had been shattered once again. A California senator had just proposed a bill to permit the hunting of mountain lions wherever depredations to livestock were reported and wherever a significant number of cats were reputed to live. Lion control areas, special big-game license fees, and hunts with dogs would be permitted under this new bill.* The sponsoring senator later boasted, "We can take three hundred lions a year."

That evening after dinner, while I relaxed by the fireplace, Margaret was busy phoning her allies and supporters. In between conversations she filled me in. "All this is based on a total of thirty-three confirmed depredations by lions during 1978!" she raged. "Already twenty-nine kill permits have been issued and twenty-one lions destroyed. We've got to alert the public and talk to a lot of people! This bill can lead once again to listing the puma as a big-game animal for the entire state. We can't allow that!"

*Fortunately the bill has been defeated, and the lions appear safe for the present.

She leaned back wearily in her desk chair. Her face, which would be extremely handsome at any stage of life, was illuminated by the fire flickering in the great hearth. Her long hair, piled on her head in Grecian elegance, glinted silver. "It's just as Rachel Carson wrote in *Silent Spring*," she sighed.

And so the effort must and shall go on. Though the task will never be ended we must engage in it with a patience that refuses to be turned aside, with determination to overcome obstacles, and with pride that it is our privilege to contribute.

The feisty environmentalist has not limited her concerns to wildlife. One major campaign that she joined was the effort to save California's redwoods. Perhaps it was inevitable that she would be drawn into the struggle to keep virgin redwood groves from being cut down for lumber and to make way for freeways. Her father, Frank Wentworth, was one of the early supporters of the Save-the-Redwoods League and had often taken his son and daughter into the magnificent two-thousand-year-old groves. Through the efforts of the League, citizens have donated over $25 million to acquire redwood preserves. The state of California has matched these funds and created an impressive number of magnificent redwood state parks.

At the time that Margaret took up the cudgels in 1964, she was a commissioner of the California State Park Commission. The matter which sparked her ire was the State Highway Commission's plan to route a major freeway through the alluvial flats of state parklands where the greatest redwoods grew. As a commissioner, she made an impassioned plea against this highway, bolding pointing out, "Three-quarters of our original redwood stands are gone. One quarter remains. Of this, seventy-five-thousand acres are in parkland. From the remaining privately owned land, about a billion board feet are harvested each year. This means that in a dozen years or so, no redwoods will be left except those in state parks."

She went on to explain to the Commission, "Redwood parks represent an investment of $250 million today, and in the decades to come they will be this area's greatest asset. Any further loss of trees would be a stark tragedy. Who would think of demolishing

Notre Dame to provide building materials for tract houses in sub-divisions? Well, when you cut a virgin redwood grove you destroy a natural temple. Yet lumbermen have stated that they too wanted to share the redwoods with the people—they wanted at least one redwood wall in every American home!"

She was to learn and explain the ecological consequences of lumbering—erosion, siltation in the watersheds, creation of wind tunnels through which the giant trees are toppled by storms, and increased vulnerability of the groves by changes in their moist, shadowy microclimate. She pointed out that, as it was, many of the smaller redwood parks were too small and isolated to survive very long.

During this three- to four-year battle Margaret learned two important lessons. One came from her husband, Nat. "He always goes right to the power source," she confided. "And he's indestructible, indomitable, intractable. I learned from Nat to fight steadfastly and stubbornly. He always supports and encourages me. He believes in me, pushes me, gives me strength. And that's a big thing.

"In my former marriage when I was young, living in the Chicago region, I felt like a displaced person, especially missing the High Sierra. I read John Muir like a religion in those days—read every word and lived every experience he related. I also longed to return to Desolation Valley above Lake Tahoe, where the granite was so magnificently clean and glorious. But my greatest wish was to do a book with my own ink drawings to accompany Muir's writings. This work-dream carried me through the war years. Then, too, age made a great difference in what I perceived I could or could not do. I got braver as I got older."

In addition to finding out the advantages of stick-to-it-tiveness and of going straight to the top, Margaret learned the power of women in politics and conservation. When the day came for the vote by the State Highway Commission, Margaret made a telling move. Sure that the vote would be unfavorable, as a last resort she wrote a letter to the wife of the governor, Pat Brown, begging her to influence the governor not to let any redwoods be cut in park-lands to make room for highways. She followed up with a phone call, and Mrs. Brown responded. The following morning, the governor spoke out publicly, surprising even the conservationists when he said: "I do not wish a single redwood in California to be cut for highway purposes!" (He forgot, at the moment, that the big battle was over the great groves within state parklands). The pronouncement hit hard, and those ready to vote for the highway route backed down. The long fight was over.

Margaret continued to attend hearings, along with many representatives from the Sierra Club, pushing for the establishment of a national park. Slowly opinions changed, and in 1968 the U.S. Congress created Redwoods National Park. "It's still too small and not really ecologically intact," sums up Margaret, "but it was a good political compromise, and it did save some priceless pristine groves."

Owls, blue jays, sea lions, mountain lions, redwoods—the list does not end here. Shortly after the redwoods issue, Margaret was catapulted into a new conservation campaign, this time to save the southern sea otter on the coast of California. Through binoculars the Owings could watch otters playing the kelp below their house; Margaret enjoyed them but did not anticipate becoming their advocate.

Sea otters had been a protected species since 1911, when they were close to extinction along the California coast. Once they had numbered in the hundreds of thousands, and ranged in an almost continuous arc along the Pacific coastline from Baja California up through Alaska, across the Aleutian Islands to Russia, and down to the Kurile Islands of Japan. Then for a full century the fur trade took its toll. Even after the slaughter was halted, it was not until 1938 that a few otters were noticed near Monterey. By 1970 there were 1,040 animals. They had been given further protection by the California legislature with the establishment in 1941 of a sea otter refuge, which was enlarged in 1967 to cover about 100 miles of coastline. Although the California otters have been slow to increase their population, they've been rapid in expanding their range. It wasn't long before a third of the population were living outside their designated refuge.

In 1968 Senator Fred Farr, who had handled the mountain lion bill for Margaret, invited her to attend a Senate Natural Resources Committee meeting in San Luis Obispo. Commercial abalone fishermen were blaming the otters for a decline in their harvest. True, the otters were eating abalone, but the other side to this coin was that the industry had been overharvesting this resource as the price of abalone rose and scuba diving equipment improved. To placate the industry, a legislative bill had been introduced which would make it permissible to "take" sea otters outside the California Sea Otter Refuge. This meant that one-third of the animals could be killed.

When Margaret returned from this hearing, she once again felt impelled to write a letter to the *Monterey Herald*. "The Otter Needs a Friend" was her title, and readers responded, urging the formation of "Friends of the Sea Otter." Margaret hesitated. "I could start it and run it just for a few months, as that would be the most difficult period," she explained to Nat, "and then I could pass it on to someone else to run." Eleven years later Nat chuckled. "To say that Margaret became *involved* is an understatement. She created an institution." A nonprofit trust was set up. The membership grew out of a single mailing of 250 personal letters and became an organization of some four thousand members from every state in the Union and eight foreign countries. Its advisory committee includes thirteen scientists, many underwater divers and photographers, a veterinarian, lawyers, and conservationists whose aim is "to aid in the protection and maintenance of a healthy population of the southern sea otter and its marine habitat." Dr. Betty Davis, a respected zoologist, joined the staff of the Friends as spokeswoman and scientific report writer. Friends of the Sea Otter gathered as many as seventy thousand names on petitions and published a newsletter called *The Otter Raft*, which is still ongoing, to inform the public. Their reports and public appeals were influential in placing the southern sea otter on the threatened species list. Today the animals are totally protected.

Margaret continues to spearhead the Friends. "Our campaign has taught me many things," she says. "Environmentally I discovered that sea otters are not the only issue. It's the whole ecology of the coast that needs protection—otters, kelp, urchins, abalone, clams, sharks, and human beings—the entire intricate web of life. Otters can be called a 'keystone species' of this special marine

habitat and are crucial to its wellbeing.* Yet kelp harvesting, abalone hunting, and clam digging, along with industrial pollution,
potential oil spills, increasing human population along the shores,
and human greed are intrusions into this web.

"Philosophically I think I learned something, too. I recall seeing
a pair of sea otters buffeted by a savage storm for an entire day
and night. The two moved together seeking anchor in scattered
broken sprays of kelp. All day they were rolled and spun and
inundated by the churning waters. The following night's action was
even more intense. At dawn I searched through binoculars, fearing
the pair had been smashed against the rocks. Nothing. By noon
the sea had subsided. Again I studied the waters—and there below
our house a relaxed little otter lay on his back, his hind feet out
flat and his tail stretched out like a blade of grass. Not a hundred
feet away another otter lay, rocking like a cradle. On her chest her
forepaws embraced the dandelion-light fluff of a newborn pup.

"What did I learn from this?" Margaret ponders. "That survival
is possible in the midst of an overwhelming force. Why can't we
survive impacts on our environment as the otters do—adapting
and adjusting as they do to the natural world through the ever-
changing phases of their lives?

"This idea had been germinating in my mind for a long time.
So much of what I see in nature strengthens it. When Nat and I
went to Africa on safari, those experiences opened more doors in
my mind."

The Owings camped for a month in East Africa, moving about
amidst wild animals, observing, not hunting, listening for the unexpected. From this trip Margaret produced a poignant essay entitled "Nerve Song of Africa." It seems to hint at the inner sensitivity and questing character of this talented woman, and at the
internal conflict which nourishes her energies.

The sky is turning copper now on the Uaso Nyiro River, sharpening
a silhouette of two vultures hunched on a bare limb. A covey of vulturine

*See Chapter 6, page 102, for further information on the sea otter's role in habitat
maintenance.

guinea fowl sift out of the undergrowth near the water's edge. Once again, an order predictable in its ritual takes place. The approach to the river for a few at a time to drink, and the watchful waiting for each to take a turn, holding their heads like embellished crooks inset with burning ruby eyes. A luminous blue, taffy-brown, and slate gray sweep up the bank and are propelled forward again for the intuitive procedure.

A hawk is wheeling overhead. Circling a tree, he reappears suddenly at an acute angle, dropping among the guinea fowl like an explosion. Out of the confusion, only the hawk remains; stretching his wings, he rises slowly up through the narrow corridor of the river.

On the earth lies a feather.

I slip off the tree trunk to claim it. Eight inches of exquisite under-statement—warm in charcoal-brown, pierced by a white quill with opposing elements of design on either side. Is it the symbol of life in Africa, these opposites paralleling one another?

Three steady, delicate lines march up the quill on the left; birth, life, death, while on the right, the staccato pulse of life, uneven, nervous, and varied, lies in four rows of dots.

So here is the rhythmic harmony, but, as this fallen feather indicates, without a guarantee. Give one the guarantee and vitality stagnates. The nerve song of Africa, found in this unexpected pattern, hidden beneath the vestments of the handsome vulturine guinea fowl, will be the tangible record of this journey I shall take home.

Turning it in my fingers, I, too, must accept the opposites in the rhythm as a part of the full harmony. I, too, must not ask for the guarantee. I look upon the feather with fresh insight.

Is it my life?

Margaret's African adventures also landed her on the board of the African Wildlife Leadership Foundation—its first woman member. Russell Train, then its president, appointed her because he appreciated her preservationist point of view as opposed to the big-game hunter mentality that characterized most of its members.

"I decided in Africa," says Margaret, "that women have more compassion for the single animal than men. It's almost impossible for them to think about wiping out animal populations because they focus on the individual death. There is a sensitivity in women that responds more to detail than to the vast panorama. Many like to probe in depth; I believe, and wait for the intuitive response."

Perhaps all of Margaret's dedication, worry, and hard work as an environmentalist have taken a toll. Three years ago, at ten thousand feet in her beloved Sierra, she had a minor heart attack and had to be flown out by helicopter. Now she can only go there in her mind. She has had to abandon as well her dream of illustrating Muir's writings from firsthand observations. Yet despite this physical restriction she still champions conservation causes. She justifies her actions simply. "If you believe in something, it will work—if you work hard enough for it. That's how I feel about wildlife and wilderness. Without wildlife and the songs of birds and insects, wilderness is a dead landscape. The mountain lion in our country— mostly unseen but leaving its print and scratch on the earth by the stream—is a symbol of wilderness. I've crowded a lot of things into my last twenty years, working to guard the wild things of our world. True, I've been caught up in the grinding wheels of government, of man's ways, of human problems and prejudices. But it's been worth it. For me wilderness is an escape and a freedom to discover and rediscover.

Chapter 10

Diana Cohen

A School Without Walls

THE GROUP OF backpackers scouted along the almost invisible trace through the Grand Canyon wilderness. In places it was barely a thread of dust among the sharp cacti and yuccas. Long-forgotten pioneers had worn a path and named it the Hance Trail. Now, over a hundred years later, the route was still practically unknown and unmaintained. For three days the students and their instructors, Diana and Mike Cohen, had trudged downward from the South Rim across the Tonto Plateau and into the mile-deep chasm, alert to distinguish animal trails from the long-unused human one. They passed cliffs and rocks of startling colors—buffs, purples, grays, tans, russets. They rested under gnarled old pinyons and junipers. They spooked wild burros, coyotes, rattlers, and coveys of quail. Their destination was the churning Colorado River, six miles below; their purpose, geological and ecological studies, liberally laced with adventure and exploration.

The third night out, disaster struck. A rare, low-altitude snowstorm blanketed the lower canyon, obliterating the trace. One student, Bill, fell, wrenching his knee, and was unable to walk. Tents were pitched on a narrow ledge, and everyone crawled into sleeping bags to wait out the storm. No evacuation was possible up the steep slopes in the swirling snow and wind. The hours dragged by ponderously. Group morale fell to a precarious low.

Diana Cohen on a winter campout in Maine. Photo by Mike Cohen.

As was their custom, the group talked over the crisis together. One girl began sobbing, "I want to get out of here. I want to get out of here. I want to go home."

Diana explained soothingly, "There's a real danger of hypothermia in this weather, or of getting lost. We have to stay put as a unit and then work our way out as soon as conditions break."

Some of the students began to worry aloud about their water supply, for there was no water on this high ledge and not enough

fuel to melt snow. Others begged to be allowed to pack out of the
canyon and search for help; two announced that they were ready
to carry their buddy out at once. Mike quietly described the possibility of all three slipping and falling into the lower canyon, where
rescue might be impossible. He was supported by other students
who opposed any precipitous action.

"The National Park rangers know our approximate location and
our route," said one girl sensibly. "Bill's not in a life-threatening
condition. If worse comes to worst, one of us can get out quickly,
and they'll use a helicopter to rescue him."

Diana offered further encouragement. "I'm sure we can all get
ourselves out of this jam if we take our time and use our heads.
This is a part of wilderness living, and it sometimes becomes a
matter of survival."

The next day, the snowstorm abated. Cautiously, the group hiked
back up the trail carrying their injured member. As they reached
the rim a couple of days later, shouts of jubilation echoed across
the Grand Canyon. Everyone was safe and enormously proud at
having extricated themselves from a threatening situation.

Such encounters have become par for the course for Environmental Education Expeditions and its leaders, Diana and Mike
Cohen. For the past ten years, this intense, dark-eyed, young
woman and her sturdy, sandy-haired husband have conducted wilderness expeditions. Their operation, at first a self-sponsored private school, has since become a training institute for the National
Audubon Society. Both Mike and Diana are expert naturalists and
committed educators who believe that not all classrooms and lab-
oratories lie within four walls. They feel strongly that through
constant contact with nature, young people can learn to sympathize
with and enjoy wilderness and wildlife, and gain an understanding
of fundamental ecological relationships. Acting upon this belief for
the last decade, Diana has hiked over five hundred miles annually,
slept outdoors eleven months of the year, and held her classes all
over wild America.

After they had reached the safety of the South Rim, the group
sat down to talk over their frightening experience. Such discussions
were extremely helpful to the students in understanding certain

ingrained attitudes and behaviors; gradually, they were able to talk about them honestly and openly. Practically all the students confessed that they had been scared and had wished they were back in their own homes instead of being trapped on a snowy ledge in the Grand Canyon. Diana and Mike suggested that as people get more and more civilized, they build more and more structures to insulate them from the discomforts and fears of the wilderness. The effort to construct an artificial environment has resulted in much destruction of the natural world. The goal is to conquer nature and to ignore, avoid, or reject primitive conditions, experiences, and feelings. Thus alienated from the wilderness environment, we forget that humans are part of and dependent on the natural world. Mike and Diana believe that relationships within the natural environment are based on cooperation. "And all human interaction," Diana argued to the group at the Grand Canyon, "should be based on the same concept."

Environmental Education Expeditions operates out of an old yellow school bus. Inside are shelves stacked with tents, sleeping bags, cooking gear, food, packs, and a rotating library. The bus carries classes of about twenty young men and women all over North America, starting on an island off the coast of Maine, ploughing across the Florida Everglades, dipping into the canyons of the Southwest, and ending up high in the Colorado Rockies. The curriculum features wilderness encounters with virgin forests, alpine meadows, and coral reefs; visits to strip mines, historical sites, and even officials at environmental protection offices; and encounters with a Mennonite community, Maine fishermen, and Hopi Indians. The students are exposed to a wide range of experiences in many different natural ecosystems and among people who interact with their environment more directly than do most twentieth-century Americans.

Diana is her school's best advertisement. She fairly burns with conviction and enthusiasm about the course. "The big difference between expedition education and many other kinds," she explains, "is that we don't fight against nature to become better people. We work at understanding nature, becoming part of it, and feeling good about this. Our most important function is helping students modify their culturally conditioned feelings, thoughts, and actions. Our school is based on the idea that when students choose to remove themselves from the overprotective home or school situation and expose themselves to the challenge of living in the wild, they ask important questions. Only in that way, Mike and I feel, can they grapple constructively with the seemingly unsolvable problems of life today.

"Our group sleeps and eats under the stars, under rain clouds, and in the middle of dust storms. We get to know each other and ourselves better than we have ever known anyone." She glances sideways at Mike, who nods proudly and thoughtfully at his wife.

"Our expeditions give students a chance to observe the web of life as it exists in many places throughout America, as well as within the social microcosm of the expedition," Diana continues. "They will want to discover the problems of various environments, while seeking workable solutions or alternatives. More than this, we both hope that any person who goes through a nine-month course with us will be equipped to help make the world a better place. A colleague of ours has called our expeditions 'perhaps the most valuable revolutionary educational program in the country.' "

How does a woman who grew up in a family which practically never left Brooklyn come off as an environmental guru? How did she take the giant step from riding her bike on New York City streets to driving thousands of miles from wilderness to wilderness across America? And from teaching in a city elementary school to conducting classes inside an old bus or under a tent?

"As far back as I can remember," Diana says soberly, "I didn't like cities, though I accepted them as the place I came from and would always live. I never thought of being anyplace else. My family didn't have funds to send me away to camp, so I stayed home and played baseball. I was jealous of all my friends who could leave. Our two-week vacation every year was to the countryside of New Jersey. I think that seeing my parents look forward to it so much and telling me how wonderful country was contributed to my later sense of being comfortable outdoors.

"My parents worried incessantly about my being a tomboy. My dad worked in a bank and my mother was a bookkeeper, and neither was actively involved in outdoors. I never wore a dress and I played outside constantly, so I got flak all the time. 'Diana, for heaven's sake, when are you going to grow up?' That's all I heard from parents, friends, and relatives.

"My first exposure to the real outdoors came when I was seventeen. Through the American Youth Hostels I got a job as a junior counselor with the director, who was Mike Cohen. I went to work for a summer at Mike's farmhouse, hostel, and wildlife sanctuary in Vermont. He was thirteen years older than I and had already begun taking groups out on traveling summer programs. I had an absolutely incredible time," recalls Diana, with a rare flashing smile. "And the second summer was even better. I was introduced to hiking, cave exploring, and tenting, and just loved it.

"Much as I loved being outside, though, I could think of no way to earn a living that way. So I did what I thought I should do— became a school teacher in Brooklyn and got married."

As it turned out, neither teaching job nor marriage was right for Diana, and within a few years both fell apart. She went back to work for Mike, helping in his office, assisting in summer programs, and running the farmhouse as a ski lodge in the winter. "Most of my appreciation and understanding for the wilderness has come out of my relationship with Mike," states Diana. "After a year or so two things became evident. Both Mike and I wanted to get married. And we decided to try our summer expeditions as a full two-semester school. We figured that after our summer successes eleven months would be smooth sailing."

It wasn't. They started basically as a thirteenth year of school, and their first year of operation was very hard. The kids were either too reserved or unwilling to work together. Perhaps the Cohens were somewhat too authoritarian. But they learned a lot. The second year they became more selective in choosing students—they realized they were not equipped to handle real "problem kids." And the school was conducted much more openly and democratically. "From then on, we operated as a private school. In 1978 the National Audubon Society became interested in us. We'd done some consulting for the organization, and they liked our ideas and work."

So their private school ended. The farmhouse-hostel-ski lodge was sold, and the National Audubon Society sponsorship began.

Now the school is recognized by over fifty colleges and universities. The Cohens run it full-time except for three months in the summer. Their vacation is spent in a cabin on the Maine coast near Lubec from which they can hear barking seals and watch soaring eagles. They live simply, without electricity, easy access, or running water—a fact that often astounds their students at first. They hope eventually to lead the expeditions during only one semester, letting their trainees handle the other. That way they would have time to write books, lecture, and search out new ecological encounters and wild classrooms.

A typical nine-month course with the school offers a scope of experiences that would require the combined talents of a travel agent, psychiatrist, university professor, and anthropologist to match. Come September, Diana and Mike meet the new group of students at the Audubon wildlife sanctuary in Sharon, Connecticut for an orientation week. After a brief explanation of the two-semester program, the young people go off to sit alone, out of sight of each other, for a half-hour "solo." Their reactions, which will form a basis for comparison at the end of the term, vary greatly. Some are bored. Some are worried. A few look half-heartedly at flowers or colored leaves. It's the rare person who just sits and enjoys the surroundings. At the end of their solos, the individuals tentatively discuss their feelings with the rest of the group.

The week passes pleasantly with Diana and Mike and other Audubon personnel in nature walks, demonstrations on camping, fire building, setting up tents, and going over the survival gear. Then the bus takes off for the White Mountains of New Hampshire. On the way up Lafayette Mountain, Diana points out the ecological changes from temperate hardwoods to boreal forest, and the tundra at the top.

Cutting across to Maine, their next stop is at a tiny Shaker village where nine elderly members of this religion still live in their traditional ways, which include celibacy and common ownership of property. The students attend a Sunday service, hear Shaker traditional music, and observe a tight-knit community living together. Also in Maine ten to twelve days are spent camping and studying marine biology between Acadia National Park and the Cohens' property near Lubec. The group camps on a Maine off-

shore island close to the Cohen property, getting glimpses of sealife
and aquatic mammals they never could have in a normal school-
room.

Because of Diana and Mike's intimate knowledge of the area and
their neighbors, the students get a real exposure to "down-East"
Maine folks. They visit sardine, cod, and herring factories, and talk
at length to lobstermen and fishermen. One year the whole group
became involved in the Eastport supertanker problem. They talked
to "Friends of Eastport" and heard the complaints of inhabitants
and conservationists whose livelihood and natural resources could
be snuffed out by a massive oil spill. Since the expedition's travel
plans are always flexible, Diana and Mike ended up driving the
yellow bus to Boston and escorting their students to the U.S.
Environmental Protection Agency offices there. A lot of direct
questions were asked about hard and soft energy and their effects
on natural resources.

"We didn't get very many straight answers back from the EPA,"
Diana recalls with a grimace. "However, it taught the kids how to
focus in on a broad problem and not feel helpless, and how to get
involved with big government. They ended up writing letters and
articles in protest of the superport, bugging the EPA, and finally
side-tracking the bus to Washington, D.C., to visit their congress-
men and senators."

Martha's Vineyard, off the Massachusetts coast, comes next as
the group starts heading south before winter descends. Here they
study colonial whaling days, listen to old sea songs, and observe
glacial geology. Later they visit the New England Aquarium.
Whenever historical places and events are considered, Mike and
Diana put the emphasis on the ways people formerly used natural
resources and how the present environment is the result of human
influence. The study becomes a look at how differing environments help to mold cultural identities.

The students get to observe another subculture of the United
States when they spend ten days on a Mennonite farm in Pennsylvania. The group work for the farmer in exchange for the privilege of asking questions and participating in this interesting culture, which favors plain dress and plain living, eschews television
and movies, and encourages hard work. For the first four years that

Diana and Mike visited the farm, the farmer's wife and daughters never introduced themselves or even talked to the group. Now they invite the students to meals and allow them to be taken to the meeting house.

In Washington, D.C. the yellow bus stops at the Smithsonian Institution, where a day is spent in the invertebrate paleontological collections in preparation for the fossils they'll find out West. Another day is passed with the folk archivist at the Library of Congress. The students learn how to tape the traditional music they'll hear throughout the year and will later deposit with the Library. Three more days are devoted to Colonial Williamsburg where, again, the group looks back at the way early settlers lived and what use and abuse they made of their surroundings. They study folk tales, natural foods and fibers, building materials, and wildlife.

Following Thanksgiving break a couple of weeks of winter tracking, camping, and cross-country ski lessons take place back in New England. Then comes Christmas vacation, and after that, the school is ready to head south and west for its second semester. On these long stretches of travel Diana helps drive the bus, does the paperwork necessary to keep the expedition going, changes library books to match the new countryside and peoples, and joins the nightly group meeting to plan the next day's activities and discuss any problems.

"This meeting serves as our 'escape valve,'" she observes. "Everyone becomes very open, honest, and self-evaluating. Everyone serves on a committee—to cook, to clean up, to shop, to repair equipment. There are no exams, but students do write papers. Everyone gets eight-and-a-half hours sleep per night, and no one uses drugs, cigarettes, or alcohol. Group safety is uppermost in people's minds. There's no distinction made between men and women; both do the same work."

The groups camp out whenever possible, even in winter, if conditions permit it. When they visit cities, they put up in hotels or private homes made available by generous friends of the school.

Diana goes on to explain seriously. "The wilderness may be the only place where barriers can be dropped between men and women, for in the wilderness each organism is mutually dependent upon all the other organisms within the system. That's how we work. The wilderness may be the only place where a woman can immediately be on an equal footing with men."

Okeefenokee, Georgia, means a four-day canoe trip into a southern swamp ecosystem. Then comes a four-week trek into the fascinating subtropical environments of the Florida Everglades. The group birdwatches at Audubon's Corkscrew Sanctuary and Rookery Bay Sanctuary; they snorkel in the Florida Keys, hike to tropical hammocks (islands of trees) in Everglades National Park, work for a day picking strawberries near Homestead, and visit the Miami Seaquarium.

"They soon learn," reports Mike, "that they can get along down here with about one gallon of water a day per person even in the hot weather, whereas the average American in Florida is gobbling up 150 gallons per day, mostly to water golf courses, fill swimming pools, wash cars, flush toilets, and take unnecessarily long baths and hairwashes."

"Another thing they learn," adds Diana, "is how their perception of nature has changed. When we hike out to that wild hammock in the Everglades, we all go on solo. It may be only half an hour, but now everyone is quiet, absorbed, delighted with the experience. They watch the vultures soaring or concentrate on ants with bits of food. No one wants to leave. No one talks. Quite a difference from their reaction at Sharon four months earlier."

Occasionally the group has real problems to face. Once, near Flamingo in Everglades National Park, they planned to follow an old road down to Florida Bay and find the site of an abandoned fishing village near Alligator Creek. It meant an eight- to nine-mile hike each way in hot, sticky, drizzly weather. Halfway there someone interested in botany pointed out what looked like manchineel trees. These can be highly poisonous if the sap touches human skin or if the small green fruits are eaten.

At once the group of backpackers sat down for a discussion. No one was positive if the trees were manchineel or not. However, it was raining, and everyone had touched branches and leaves already. The group decision was to play safe. They decided to forget the rest of the hike, go back the four miles to Flamingo, and take strong soapy showers. None of the participants got a rash.

Diana sums up the experience this way: "One hundred percent

of the people I meet are afraid of something like this in the outdoors—rashes, snake bites, spiders, skunks, and so on. Most of
these fears are handed down culturally over time. But once you
know about your environment, you stop feeling scared. You can
decide how to deal with a problem and not get hurt. You can go
outdoors comfortably from then on and enjoy everything."

From Florida the yellow bus heads to New Orleans for Cajun
Mardi Gras and more old-fashioned music. Then they go on to Big
Bend National Park in Texas. They spend a day hiking here and
a night at the nearby McDonald Observatory looking at stars. The
remainder of the second semester is divided up among the four-
corners states—Arizona, New Mexico, Utah, and Colorado.

The itinerary in this part of the country is heady—Carlsbad
Caverns, White Sands National Monument, and Coyote Gulch in
New Mexico; the Chiricahua Mountains and Grand Canyon National Park in Arizona; Mesa Verde National Park and Carbondale
in Colorado; Zion, Bryce Canyon, and Canyonlands National Parks
in Utah; and more. The students encounter a dizzying array of new
experiences—deserts, Hopi Indian dances, fossils, petroglyphs,
Mormons, an Arizona anthropologist. By May the summer heat is
mounting in the Southwest, and the bus heads home to Maine.
The school ends up with a hike and camping trip on the same
offshore island where it began.

By this time Diana and Mike have become role models to many
of the students, as have some of the interesting people met along
the way, especially old-timers. Most of the students have experienced great changes in their behavior and attitudes. If Mike and
Diana are right, the wilderness and wilderness values have done
it.

In the eleven years that the school has operated, both the Cohens
and their students have suffered remarkably few accidents and
mishaps. They claim that though exposure to risk is high outdoors,
they don't get hurt because everyone is careful and aware of potential dangers. They make it their business to know, for instance,
about hypothermia, poisonous snakes, and avalanches. Diana herself has been the victim of only two accidents over the years. One
took place on Assiniboine Mountain in the Canadian Rockies near
Banff. The group had set up camp, attaching their tarps to new

stand-up packs. That night—in July—it snowed. The weight on Diana's tarp pulled it in, and a fifty-pound pack fell over on her nose. She became dizzy and saw double. The group hiked four miles to a lodge which was a two-day horseback ride from civilization. Luckily a doctor was staying there. Worried about Diana's vision and continuing nausea, he had two kids hike out to the nearest ranger and get him to radio for a helicopter. Diana was airlifted out, conscious but with a bad concussion.

The second accident happened on Isle au Haut, ten miles off the Maine coast in Acadia National Park. The group had been five days on the island, exploring and camping. Wearing a new pair of boots, Diana jumped off a ledge and broke her leg. This time students fashioned a stretcher out of branches and jackets and carried her five miles to get a truck. She was driven slowly to a lobster boat and then transported to the mainland and a hospital.

These mishaps have not slowed down this intrepid woman of thirty-seven very much. While Diana admits to spending more time these days on her philosophical, rather than her physical, development, she's still camping out more nights and hiking more miles than any other wilderness woman in this book. She feels she may have calmed down a bit over the years, and she is less thrilled by the element of danger in the outdoors. Also she tries to find her enjoyment now in more "environmentally ethical" activities. "Nowadays," she smiles, "I'd rather swim with seals than go downhill skiing."

What reaction do most people have to a rolling stone like Diana Cohen, whose home is a bus or tent and who has few ties to the urban world?

"I've been accused of running away from society; of being unable to deal with its relationships; of not finding value in what the mainstream culture has to offer. I feel these reactions are coming from people who misunderstand not only what I am doing, but the realities of our culture today with regard to attitudes to the environment.

"I've often been asked, 'When are you going to settle down? When are you going to have children? Aren't you tired of living in a teenage society?' What's missing again is the fact that I'm living in a way that I believe can be a positive force in helping people to understand the natural world and how they relate to it. Going on these expeditions allows me to be the best kind of teacher, to still be a tomboy, to work as a team with Mike, and to take my dog Timber with me everywhere I go."

With her deep convictions and her loving, hardworking partnership with Mike to support her, it is unlikely that anything will swerve Diana from her goals. Her immediate plan to obtain a master's degree from Lesley College in Cambridge, Massachusetts should only further and deepen her life work. Diana's thesis will describe her experiences and observations in the environmental expeditions to show the importance of using the wilderness as an educator and the changes that occur within individuals in such a setting.

And what of changes within this Aquarian, living this exotic life? "Our travels have taught me three things," Diana states. "One is to believe in human potential—male or female—and to encourage the expression of feelings. Another is to respect and learn from old people. And finally, I have discovered what a different place the United States is than I once thought, back in Brooklyn.

"Best of all," she marvels, "is how I've come to see the world in a different way. I suddenly realized that while I was playing baseball on Saturday mornings in Brooklyn, the Hopi Indians were dancing in the same way they'd been doing for a thousand years. The people and environments of the United States are far more interesting and individual than I ever imagined. Once I thought our country was all the same. Plain. Now I know our country is made up of many, many pockets of people and ecosystems. Some fit together and support each other; some don't. It's my job to teach people how survival and mutual existence are possible in this world of ours."

Chapter 11

Eugenie Clark

Scientist in a Wetsuit

I WAITED A trifle nervously in the kitchen of a house in suburban Bethesda, Maryland, decorated with depictions of fish and whales. The internationally famous marine biologist, author of two books, five *National Geographic* articles, and over one hundred scientific papers, was due home any moment. What would she be like? Serious? Relaxed? Pompous? Cordial?

A car drove into the garage and the kitchen door opened. An attractive woman who looked about thirty-five, wearing jeans and jacket, walked in, her arms full of groceries and books. A graduate student, I thought, helping her with her things. I looked behind her, waiting for the renowned scientist to appear. No one else was there. Perplexed, I asked, "Is Dr. Clark coming?"

"I'm Eugenie Clark," was the amused reply, as she dumped paper bags on the countertop.

"But . . . you look so *young*," I blurted.

"Thanks, but I'm fifty-seven," was her candid reply. "I'm so sorry to keep you waiting, but there's always so much to do." Her voice trailed off, and she gestured helplessly toward the next room where a work table was loaded with papers, textbooks, yellow slide boxes, pencils, pens, and typewriter.

I took a closer look at this youthful woman who has spent thirty years diving in remote and wild seas and oceans. All that salt water must have agreed with her, for her tanned face was unlined, her skin smooth and supple, her posture erect and graceful. She has an ingenuous look and soft smile, yet her intense dark eyes and firm chin hinted at inner strength. To my surprise, Eugenie was tiny. (This may be due to her half-Japanese ancestry.) But it certainly hasn't kept her from throwing scuba diving tanks on her back and diving all around the world. Her long, thick hair casually gathered in a knot on her head gave the illusion of greater height, and the gray strands somewhat offset her youthful look and gave her a more academic air. Yet I still couldn't believe this diminutive woman was the bold "lady with a spear" of whom I had read so much.

Eugenie set about putting her groceries away and preparing supper. "I leave for the Red Sea in a couple of days," she said matter-of-factly, "so things are a bit disorganized. But I'll try to tell you about my career under the sea. I guess the most important parts are my Red Sea explorations and investigations, my work with sharks, and my early expedition to the South Seas to collect poisonous fishes for the U.S. Navy."

"What's the greatest underwater wilderness experience you ever had in those research trips?" I asked at once.

Without a moment's thought she answered, "Diving at Ras Muhammad in the northern Red Sea near the wild beaches of the Egyptian coast. It's so beautiful, so unspoiled, so rich in marine life. It's very hard now to find anyplace underwater where all the fauna and flora are undisturbed. To me an ocean wilderness has to be in a natural state, without people, and more important, without plastic bags floating around. I've been to some of the most distant islands in the world, like the Bonins in southern Japan, and even there I find debris lying on the bottom from ships which throw their garbage and refuse overboard far away."

She set out a plate of raw vegetables and crackers for me to munch on. "Oh, yes, one other wilderness experience stands out, not exactly underwater but definitely marine-oriented, when I slept overnight with sea lions in southern Australia. A graduate student and I borrowed blankets and heavy sweaters from the ship we were working on and humped our way on our hands and knees to the center of their little island so we'd look like female sea lions and the bulls wouldn't attack us. There we curled up among the rocks

Dr. Eugenie Clark in the Japanese-style garden she constructed at her home in Bethesda, Maryland. Photo by Anne LaBastille.

and listened to all the barking, bellowing, and confusion. Finally about midnight the animals fell asleep, and it became fairly quiet. It was a fantastic night being part of that marine mammal community."

Rice was steaming on the stove, and Eugenie was deftly slicing up fish and mushrooms. It looked as if a tasty Japanese dinner was in the works. "Tell me more about the Red Sea," I urged. "What have you done there, and why are you going back?" As Eugenie talked, I was given both a geography lesson about one of the world's least explored oceans and a voyage through a fairytale seascape.

The Red Sea, claims Dr. Clark, is unique among seas, geographically and ecologically a world apart. As the tail end of the great Indo-Pacific tropical waters, squeezed in between desert countries, it is at once the saltiest, the most minerally rich, and one of the warmest bodies of water in the world. The size of California, this sea is part of the Great Rift system. A mile-and-a-half-deep trench slices up its middle, and in certain places the sea floor drops thousands of feet within a hundred yards of the coral-fringed shore. The Red Sea opens only to the Indian Ocean by a narrow natural strait and to the Mediterranean by the Suez Canal. Hence it contains many unique endemic species of fish—maybe 15 percent of the entire population. Oddly enough, many other species have a remarkable similarity to Hawaiian fish, twelve thousand miles away! Eugenie speaks of the Red Sea as the most extraordinary body of water on Earth, with the greatest diversity of marine life she's found in her professional career as a diver and marine biologist. It is also beautiful, Eugenie told me. At times the cigar-shaped sea may lie untouched by wind or rain for months. The rising and setting sun turns the calm surface to crimson and tinges the desert mountains which rim the sea with glowing pink; hence, no doubt, the name *Red Sea*. Eugenie describes it best in "The Strangest Sea," her *National Geographic* article written in September 1975:

We swim through a curtain of marine gold fishes and catch the current that carries us toward the outer plateau. Propelled through a forest of sea fans, we glide like soaring birds, using our fins only to steer ourselves.

We sink deeper, where the current is gentler, and water darkens to midnight blue. At ninety feet—on the outer face of the Sinai's ultimate coral wall, the expelled air from our scuba tanks dribbles up the near-vertical slope like Alka Seltzer bubbles.

Surgeonfish in a giant school pass like a moving tapestry. A blizzard of silver jacks swims above a cluster of black-masked puffer fish that scurry past like bandits running from the scene of a larceny.

Sharks materialize from the blue and swim through orange-golden clouds of anthiases; then, fading away from the reef, they ride the current like giant condors.

It seems fitting that the first expedition to explore the Red Sea was sent forth by a woman, Queen Hatshetsup of Egypt, about thirty-five hundred years ago. Artists then carved representatives of its marine life on her temple. Today Eugenie Clark's explorations are carried out from Hebrew University's Heinz Steinitz Marine Biological lab at Elat, Israel, or from her original base, the Marine Biological Station at Ghardaqa, Egypt.

A native of New York, Eugenie earned her B.A. from Hunter College in 1942 and her M.S. and Ph.D. from New York University. During the late '40's she worked as a research assistant in animal behavior at the Scripps Institute of Oceanography in California and at the American Museum of Natural History. She first went to Egypt in 1951 as the proud recipient of a Fulbright scholarship to study fish life in the Red Sea. Part of her program involved collecting specimens for the U.S. National Museum, and part was capturing poisonous fishes for the U.S. Navy. During her year in Egypt she made probably the biggest collection of fish ever taken single-handed from the Red Sea—over three hundred species!

Also at this time Ilias Themistokles Papakonstantinou, a young Greek doctor with whom Eugenie had fallen in love in New York City, followed her to Cairo, and the two were married there in a Greek Orthodox church. They spent their honeymoon at the Red Sea, studying fish and hunting for sharks, using snorkeling gear. Ilias loved diving and became as enthusiastic as Eugenie about the sea world. After he got his first speargun, he became the most ardent spear fisherman Eugenie had ever met. All too soon, however, he had to leave for Buffalo, New York, where he had his residency in orthopedics; Eugenie joined him a few months later. In Buffalo she wrote her first book, *Lady with a Spear*, published in 1953. It is an adventurous account of her work as a young ichthyologist (fish biologist) and marine biologist; she also produced a major paper for the journal of Egypt's marine biological station.

Eugenie maintained her association with the Museum of Natural History through the early 1950's, and in 1954 she and her husband moved back to New York City, where Eugenie became an instructor at Hunter College. In 1955, she was appointed to the prestigious position of Executive Director of the Cape Haze Marine Biological Laboratory near Sarasota, Florida, and the young family settled there.

During her sixteen-year marriage with Dr. Papakonstantinou, they had four children, and both devoted much time to their specialties. Eugenie describes it as the best period of her life.

"This was definitely the most productive and happiest of my four marriages," she states in her candid manner. "You might say the other three were sort of 'legalized affairs.' I was such a prude in those days that I could never bring myself to live with a man without matrimony. With Ilias, however, I had everything I wanted most: the opportunity to study sharks and other fish, a laboratory and good collecting grounds in Florida, and my home and family."

Both Eugenie's scientific reputation and her work with sharks blossomed during the twelve years she was director of the Cape Haze lab. Located on the only unpolluted estuary on the Gulf of Mexico and Atlantic Coast south of Cape Cod, and supported by Anne and William Vanderbilt and Alfred Gwynne Vanderbilt, the lab began as a small wooden building with sinks and shelves, where people could learn more about the sea. It became one of the most respected marine study institutions in the world, as well as a famous center for shark research. There were shark pens to keep live specimens, a reference library, and a museum collection of marine life of the Gulf of Mexico and West Coast of Florida; a speedy Chris Craft for field trips; and plenty of scuba diving equipment. Over the years Eugenie Clark and her associates at Cape Haze handled several thousand sharks—18 of the 250 known shark species in the world. The lab supplied shark livers to one scientist for cancer research, skulls and teeth to others. Several hundred scientists from all over the world were aided and encouraged to do research there.

Some of Eugenie's most outstanding work on sharks came out of her studies of their food habits and learning behavior at Cape Haze. She mastered the skill of keeping sharks alive and healthy in captivity, finding, for example, that a nine-foot lemon shark needs only two pounds of raw food a day to keep active and well in such circumstances. She also discovered that most sharks in the wild eat over forty kinds of fish, eels, other sharks, octopus, sting rays, crabs, and shrimp. Rarely, they may gobble up a sea turtle, sea bird, or porpoise.

Eugenie's pioneering study of the learning behavior of sharks has confirmed her belief that they are feeling, thinking creatures, not merely "swimming noses" or "monsters of the deep." She proved that sharks could learn simple tasks, and more important, remember them over a span of several weeks. For example, she managed to 'teach' her captive sharks to recognize a special target, press against it with their noses, and then swim to the other end of the pen in order to get their rewards of food. One small,`two-foot nurse shark seemed the brightest of all—he learned the training pattern in only five days, whereas most individuals took much longer.

Eugenie was also the first to witness the courtship of sharks at sea. She has seen a male gray shark giving gentle "love nips" to a female's flank, and lemon sharks mating in the pens at her lab. The male's clasper undoubtedly was inserted into the female's vagina, and the back parts of their bodies were so close together that they looked like one shark with two heads. Their movements as they swam side by side in wide circles were perfectly synchronized.

Dr. Clark's shark research earned her the nickname of "shark lady" as well as the respect and acclaim of the scientific world. Her reputation became known to Crown Prince Akihito of Japan, who took a personal interest in the subject, and in 1964 he asked to meet her. (*Lady with a Spear* had been tremendously popular in Japan.) Eugenie decided to accept the royal invitation and took with her as a gift her trained nurse shark. This necessitated elaborate provisions for transporting the shark safely on an airplane from Florida to Tokyo. She and the shark made it successfully halfway around the world to Kyoto, where the Prince was waiting eagerly to see his present perform. Eugenie set up her target and bell in a specially built aquarium inside his palace. The little shark performed with as much aplomb as if it had been in its tank back in Florida and was rewarded with bits of lobster proffered by a servant with inlaid mother-of-pearl chopsticks!

Two years later Eugenie was able to repay the Crown Prince for his hospitality by teaching him to skin dive in Florida.

Eugenie's research with sharks continued long after she had been divorced from Dr. Papakonstantinou and left the Cape Haze laboratory to become a professor at the University of Maryland in 1968, where she still teaches. She was a consultant to the Shark Research Panel of the American Institute of Biological Sciences, and to the Office of Naval Research. In 1972, '73, and '74 she received grants from the National Geographic Society and The

Explorers Club, and additional support from the Mexican government, to investigate the behavior of a strange family of sharks
known as requiem, or "sleeping," sharks. For some unknown reason
these predatory fish swim into limestone sea caves off the Yucatan
Peninsula and remain there stationary, seemingly 'narcotized' and
unperturbed by divers. The immobility of these species contrasts
sharply with the ceaseless movement of most other sharks, which
must swim continually in order to 'breathe'—that is, to keep
enough oxygen-rich water moving across their gills. By contrast,
requiem sharks rest quietly for hours on end, pumping water over
their gills in as active a form of respiration as humans constantly
inflating and deflating their lungs.

On one of these expeditions, Eugenie, her daughter Aya, and
a graduate student, Anita George, came face to face with a requiem
shark. So close was the animal that they could see the ampullae
(pores) on its snout. These pores enable the sharks to detect minute
changes in the natural electrical currents in the sea. Such currents
are always generated by the water, other animals, and plants. Any
variation in them can signal the possible approach of dinner or
danger. Eugenie identified this species of requiem shark as Spring-
er's reef sharks.

The results of Eugenie's three research trips were somewhat
inconclusive. Her team of divers was successful in photographing
the sharks with their eyes wide open and in recording their respiration rate. She also discovered that fresh water was seeping into
the limestone caves from the mainland water table, and that the
salinity of the water there was low, the carbon dioxide content
high, and the oxygen content very high, as compared with the
open ocean. Because of fresh water seepage the electromagnetic
field also was different inside the caves than outside. In addition,
the sharks in the cave seemed to be getting a thorough picking-
over from small fishes called remoras, which carefully remove crablike
parasites from the sharks' gills, nostrils, mouths, and skin. Eugenie
speculated in her 1975 National Geographic article on the study
that the less salty water might cause these parasites to loosen their
hold and make them more available as fish food.

After ninety-nine dives and encounters with seven sleeping
sharks in three different caves, Eugenie is still considering several
explanations for the behavior of the sleeping sharks. They may be

"But as soon as I had my teeth in something and could show my earnestness, the scientific community came around. People have always been truly helpful and good to me, from the very first time I visited the New York Aquarium at nine years of age, right through school, all during my research work at Scripps, the Museum of Natural History, Woods Hole Oceanographic Institute, Cape Haze, and right up to today. I find that once women have proven themselves, they usually get more credit than a man gets on the same job."

Eugenie went on to recount some of her early experiences when she was virtually the only female marine biologist in the field. In 1949 she went to Micronesia to investigate poisonous fishes for the Office of Naval Research and the Pacific Science Board. During this four-month reconnaissance trip she collected specimens and information at Kwajalein, Guam, Siapan, the Palaus, and several of the most remote islands of the Carolines, all part of the U.S. trust territory or possessions of the United States. Here she had her first encounter with a big shark. It swam up to her, and she stopped swimming at once. The shark came closer. She began to admire its shape, grace, and speed, rather than feeling frightened. Eugenie could have almost touched the animal before it turned and swam away. (All her other meetings with sharks have been harmless except for one incident. On that occasion the dried and mounted jaw of a tiger shark fell onto her arm as she slammed on the brakes at a red traffic light. Just this once her arm dripped blood after a shark's teeth sank into it.)

I interrupted Eugenie's reminiscences to inquire about the emphasis on conservation in her work.

"It's a major concern," she replied. "I've participated in three international congresses on behalf of marine conservation, and represented the U.S. National Parks and Conservation Association at the first international conference on marine parks and reserves in Tokyo in 1975. There are so many problems threatening the sea. Even my favorite ocean wilderness, Ras Muhammad, is being endangered by development and the dangers of modern technology. Ras Muhammad is the closest tropical coral reef to Europe, so it's a perfect target for tourism and hotel building. The nearby ports of Aqaba and Elat are obvious potential sites for oil pollution, and one major spill could cause a disaster to the coral reefs. The many ships which unload their bilge water in the sea are already causing oil slicks. Then I've seen increasing numbers of poachers and spear-fishermen taking lobsters and shells and shooting everything that swims. One aquarium company has even secured permission from Egypt to capture tropical fish here and sell them in Europe. And there are plans to build an electrical power station, a refueling tower for boats on the reef, and a commercial harbor. I just pray that permanent peace and wisdom will come to this area so that, although more and more visitors are arriving, the coast of Sinai will still be unpolluted. Fortunately, both Jordan and Israel are taking measures to preserve wilderness areas along their Red Sea coast-lines. But there is still much to do."

We were both silent. The fire was crackling. A full moon was rising outside the window, bathing Eugenie's miniature Japanese garden in bluish light. She was probably thinking of her beloved sea life half a world away, while I was wondering what new dis-coveries this remarkable woman would come up with next. Coming from New York City, the only child of a hard-working, widowed Japanese mother, she has had accomplishments nothing short of incredible.

"Has your career been an obstacle to your marriages?" I asked.

"Not in general," she replied. "I've always had to have a career to support myself, and at certain times to support my husbands and my children. I would never throw away my profession to tag after a man. Unfortunately, husbands come and go, whereas one's career grows and endures. The paradox is that men are attracted to me because my work makes me an interesting person, but after they 'possess' me, they want to make me a house pet and become jealous of my career. That happened with the last two. I think they were envious of my involvement with the Red Sea."

Between 1964 and 1975 Eugenie made a series of summer trips to the Red Sea with her four children, students, and underwater photographers. Grants from the National Science Foundation, the National Geographic Society, The Explorers Club, and the Smith-sonian Institution supported these investigations, which have re-sulted in at least three remarkable reports on garden eels, flashlight fish, and the Moses sole, a shark-repelling fish.

Eugenie found that garden eels anchor themselves by their tail tips to the sea floor where they live. When danger approaches, the eels will disappear tail first into the sand, tunneling faster than a diver can dig. The males have harems of several females and control a small territory around them. Eugenie describes them in her *National Geographic* article of November 1972, "The Red Sea's Garden of Eels."

Before five a.m. we reached Colony Number 2. An oval nearly 300 feet long, the area supports more than 1,000 eels. When we arrived, they are already swaying and writhing in their habitual ballet. . . .

The silvery gray eels stood like plant stalks, projecting a yard above the bottom. Bodies arched, eyes alert for food, they curtsied and dipped, bowed, and swayed. To the orchestration of invisible currents, they perform their tireless serpentine dance, like cobras spellbound by a snake-charmer's flute.

The three-inch, black flashlight fish, *Photoblepharon*, a fascinating companion of their night dives, was the subject of a study published in *National Geographic* in 1978. These fish come out in the dark of the moon to feed, and their light organs give off one of the brightest glows of any creature in the entire bioluminescent realm. Eugenie found that she could actually read her watch under water at night by the light of one fish. *Photoblepharon* might be called the fireflies of the sea because they blink from the pouches under their eyes and give off light for hours. Their blinking may be to attract food, to communicate between fishes, or to confuse predators.

Even more intriguing is the Moses sole *(Pardachirus marmoratus)*, the Red Sea's "sharkproof" fish. Normally it lies quietly on the sandy sea floor, well camouflaged by its beige color and dark spots. If frightened, however, it secretes a lethal milky fluid from glands along its dorsal and anal fins. Eugenie was to discover that even the most dilute mixture—1:5,000 parts—will kill small captive fishes in minutes. Mice injected with the toxin will convulse and die in two minutes. Apparently sharks can detect minute amounts of the repellent, and hungry sharks will shun the sole and its environs for up to twenty-eight hours after the toxin is secreted. The toxin of the Moses sole is the first known chemical substance that can actually prevent a shark from biting. In addition to this powerful hemotoxic chemical, the Moses sole has a built-in inhibitor which neutralizes its own poison and which, when extracted and tested by researchers, has also been found to counteract the venom of bees, scorpions, coral and mamba snakes, and cobras. Eugenie was quick to see that both toxin and inhibitor had promising medical possibilities. "Maybe someday," she says, "we will spray our wetsuits with synthesized Moses sole poison, then dive and swim at ease with sharks."

Determined words! Perhaps this will be the "shark lady's" greatest contribution to science.

Meanwhile, Eugenie may soon be able to take much of the credit for ensuring that her favorite place in the world, Ras Muhammad, is protected from further development. In the course of her work there, she struck up a friendship with an avid young diver who happened to be the son of Egypt's president, Anwar Sadat. On a visit to Egypt at the end of 1979, this connection resulted in an unexpected opportunity to meet Sadat himself, who was much impressed with Eugenie and her work. (Mrs. Sadat, incidentally, has long been a strong supporter and patroness of Egypt's fledgling conservation movement.)

During their talk, President Sadat indicated to Eugenie that he would be favorably disposed to making the area around Ras Muhammad a national park, and that a proclamation to that effect might be forthcoming at the January 1980 ceremony in which control of Ras Muhammad was officially transferred from Israel back to Egypt. Israel's vigorous guardianship of the area in the past is the main reason, according to Eugenie, why its marine life is so abundant and accessible to observation. Unfortunately, there ensued a chill in the delicate political relations between the two countries just at the time of the transfer ceremony, and Sadat cancelled his plans to attend—so the possible announcement was postponed. However, in reporting these events to me some time after our interview, Eugenie expressed confidence in Sadat's sincere commitment to the preservation of Ras Muhammad; and the prospects look hopeful for a park in the not-too-distant future.

Eugenie Clark's last words before I left her home in Maryland were very much in character. She must have been reading my mind, for she pluckily predicted, "I plan to keep on diving and researching and conserving until I'm at least ninety years old."

Judging by past performance, she will.

Chapter 12

Peggy Eckel Duke

Monitoring the Olympics

A MOBILE RADIO set crackled ominously from inside the knapsack on Peggy Duke's back. "Blasting on tower 8, lift number 6 at 10:10 A.M." said a crisp voice.

Peggy glanced at her watch, then motioned me abruptly uphill. "That's in less than seven minutes, and we're headed right into the blast area," she explained tersely. "Let's work our way up to that island of trees between the two trails and hide on the west side. The trees will absorb any flying rocks."

We scrambled back up the steep ski run and crouched down behind tall spruces and a fallen log. "This should be a big one," muttered Peggy, casting a look at her watch again. "Ten seconds. Now stay *down!*"

I tugged my hardhat on more firmly and nestled closer to the ground. Peggy's frosty blue eyes scanned the slopes as she adjusted her own hardhat. Then the explosion came: thousands of fragments were thrown into the air and a few stones hurtled into the woods behind us, dropping harmlessly to the ground. A puff of smoke wafted across the trail.

"All clear!" crackled the radio. Peggy eased her lean body out from behind the log, brushed off her blue denim shirt, and grinned at me. "Let's go," she said energetically. "I want to check the tree cutting and trail widths on the men's downhill course. Under state law a ski center trail can't exceed eighty feet on Adirondack Forest Preserve land."

She plunged downhill on legs strong as steel springs from weeks of climbing up and down Whiteface Mountain. Somewhat less nimbly I followed. As New York State's only female environmental monitor, Peggy was in charge of inspecting the 1980 Winter Olympic Games construction at Lake Placid, New York and its impact on the state lands within the six-million-acre Adirondack Park. In order to protect this uniquely beautiful area, the Economic Development Administration, the federal agency funding the thirteenth Winter Olympic Games, hired three environmental monitors. Their job was to review and inspect engineering and construction activity before and after the Games. Peggy's chief concern now was the work being done on Whiteface Mountain for the downhill and giant slalom ski races. She also was responsible for work at Mt. Van Hoevenberg, including the Nordic (cross-country and biathlon), luge, and bobsled facilities. In both places she was working on New York State land classified as Intensive Use bordering state-designated wilderness areas. After the Olympics she would make sure that all of the projects were cleaned up, the temporary facilities such as safety nets and judging stands removed, and the natural condition of the land restored. These guidelines were all set out in a final environmental impact statement (FEIS) prepared for the Games. Peggy reported her field inspections to an engineer who handled the administrative end through New York State's Department of Environmental Conservation (DEC). In a way, the monitors played "Big Brother" (or in Peggy's case "Big Sister"), overseeing $170 million worth of construction with a 2,300-page FEIS as their bible.

To see her in action, I joined Peggy in the field during the summer and again in winter, 1979. She keeps a rigorous schedule. At Whiteface we met at the bottom of the ski slopes and drove a truck around and up the 4,867-foot peak. (It's the only mountain in the Adirondack Park with a road to the top.) Then we took a chilly, damp elevator through a rock shaft to the summit. When we stepped out, a clinging gray mist smothered us. Every sound was muffled. Visibility was zero, the roads and village of Lake Placid lying far below in summer sun had disappeared. The magnificent

Peggy Duke and a colleague confer about the grading of a downhill ski run on Whiteface Mountain for the 1980 Winter Olympic Games. Photo by Anne LaBastille.

views of Adirondack high peaks to the south and west; Lake Champlain to the east; and distant rivers, ranges, and lakes were totally blotted out. The temperature stood at a chilly 42° that July morning, as Peggy switched on her radio and shrugged into a rain suit. Nonchalantly, she told me that we'd be dodging dynamite blasts all morning from 4,400 feet down to the base. But right now we needed all our agility and caution just to find our way safely over the slippery rocks and off the fog-shrouded summit.

Keeping in sight of one another, we picked our way along, sliding, jumping, and slipping down a narrow trail. In the distance I
heard a jackhammer blatting. How could that be, way up in this
mountain wilderness? Minutes later we broke through a dwarfed
forest of balsam firs and spruces onto a cleared track. "This is the
start of the men's downhill run," Peggy pointed out. "They race
from 4,306 feet to 1,578 feet, sometimes attaining speeds of eighty
miles per hour on the steep stretches! It'll take *us* about four hours
to hike down; in February 1980 the skiers will make it in just under
two minutes!"

Shadowy figures moved ahead of us. The jackhammer stuttered
again, closer now. I began seeing portable generators, long lengths
of pipe for snowmaking, thick cables, and jumbles of tools.

"The men are cutting and making this trail strictly by hand,"
said Peggy. "Everything is brought up and dropped by helicopter
in order to minimize environmental impact. After seeing construction done this way, I can say it's really a matter of 'men over
mountain.' " She looked closely at some ruts in the ground and
frowned at a pile of blasted rock in the trail. "The soil mantle is
so thin and fragile at this elevation," she explained, "that we must
be extremely careful about erosion and landslides, for which the
steeper peaks in the Adirondacks are notorious. In fact, Whiteface
is so called because slides have resulted in white slashes of anor-
thosite rock showing on both sides of the mountain."

As we dropped down below the 3,500-foot mark, the fog began
to thin and the sun appeared. Behind us the workmen and jackhammer were swallowed up in the mist. We headed for a wide
open section where three trails converged.

"See those trees lying over there?" asked Peggy, pointing. "Well,
one day I found the men beginning to cut those islands between
the trails. I knew that was not an activity covered in the environmental impact statement, yet I couldn't confront the construction
workers and say, "Stop cutting!" It's a very delicate thing. I got to
the bottom of the mountain and spoke with the mountain manager
and other DEC officials about the activity. The result was that the
cutting was stopped until a supplemental EIS was prepared. After
that the work continued because it was needed as a safety consideration on this Olympic trail, but the environmental impact had

been addressed. I had a similar experience at Mt. Van Hoevenberg. But that's my job. It's a unique experience to be involved in the implementation of an EIS which is really being strictly adhered to."

We passed a group of laborers in muddy boots and hardhats who were connecting some of the snowmaking equipment. Peggy nodded to them and greeted the foreman. The men paid little attention to her, instead riveting their eyes on me. One whistled softly. I felt a blush creep up my face. When we were out of earshot, Peggy grinned and said, "You got those guys curious. New girl on the mountain."

I grimaced and remarked, "Why do workmen always act so silly? Did you see them leering? How come they didn't bother *you?*"

She laughed and said, "In the beginning, they did somewhat, but word got around fast that I was some sort of 'inspector.' Besides, I'm always very businesslike on the job. I've had people tell me I seem so friendly in town but out on the job site I'm just cordial and polite. The guys are great, but it's very important to remain professional. They've accepted me at that level now." Moving downslope, Peggy continued. "I have to work with over two hundred men on this mountain and relate to several different groups—the Lake Placid Olympic Organizing Committee, the DEC, the Economic Development Administration, independent contractors, the Adirondack Park Agency, environmentalists, and construction engineers. The environmental monitors have enough clout to recommend withholding funds in an unresolved dispute over environmental damages, but we almost always solve problems long before that."

Now she had her tape measure out and was laying it over the ground. "It's a bit confusing," she continued, "because state and private lands in the Adirondack Park are normally managed and protected by the DEC and the Adirondack Park Agency. They have *their* land use plans and *their* rules and regulations all established (Adirondack Park Agency, 1972 and 1973). But here come the world-famous 1980 Winter Olympics, which are costing close to $200 million and will bring in thousands of visitors, taking place right at the heart of the park. There are all kinds of environmental hazards associated with preparing for the Games. Yet a lot of people wouldn't mind bending, even breaking, the conservation rules for the sake of the Olympics."

"What kind of hazards?" I asked, hopping from rock to rock over a little stream.

"Well, take this creek, for instance," she replied. "Too much bulldozing too close to a stream will cause erosion and siltation. That kills trout and other fish downstream and certainly makes the water unfit for drinking or swimming below.

"My second month on this job the guys really tested me. I spotted muddy water running directly into a protected brook and saw a bulldozer working right above it. I knew I had to lay out a drainage ditch that would divert the runoff away from the stream, but that takes some calculations. The foreman kept needling me, 'Where do you want it? Where do you want it?' I barely had time to check out the contours or anything. I just pointed to the logical place and said, 'Put it there.' The bulldozer chugged right over and dug the ditch. Luckily it worked out fine, and the brook cleared up. After that they didn't give me a hard time anymore."

Suddenly the sound of a helicopter reached to us from the foot of the mountain. A beelike object began buzzing up the slope.

"Finally!" exclaimed Peggy. "Here comes the hay for mulching. I've been after them for days to protect these raw slopes before a heavy rain falls."

The helicopter roared closer. Now I could see the cargo of hay bales slung underneath it by a cable.

"Watch out," called Peggy heading for the trees again. "There's nearly two tons of hay up there and when the pilot releases them he might be off his mark a little."

Holding my ears against the terrific clatter, I squinted up at the belly of the giant Sykorsky and watched the bales tumble out of the sky. Some burst open on impact. Hay flew everywhere.

"He'll make dozens of trips today," Peggy explained, "to cover up the mountainside. It's an expensive way to do it, at $60 a load, but there is no other way. Machinery is not allowed at this altitude, according to the FEIS, because the slopes are too steep and fragile."

"I'll bet a lot of people misunderstand these mitigative measures you've told me about," I ventured when we sat down in a sunny patch of grass for lunch. "And resent you, a *female* environmental monitor, for enforcing them."

Peggy smiles ruefully at me. "A few. I was in a bar once when a contractor barged right up to me and said, 'I hate your guts! You've cost me so much money on Whiteface! What the hell's a pretty woman like you doing in this business anyway? Saving the environment? Saving the wilderness? Telling contractors what to do! Bullshit!' That's what I have to deal with sometimes."

She pulled off the blue hardhat and shook out her honey-colored, shoulder-length hair. With the grace of a dinner hostess, Peggy poured my Sierra cup full of white wine and offered me a liverwurst-on-rye sandwich, dates, and cheese.

"Well, things aren't *too* rough out here on the mountain," I joked, sipping the unexpected treat.

"Oh, no," she agreed. "In fact, I think I'm making an impact. One day not long ago one of the workmen came up to me to talk. He asked how I had learned what I'm doing now and told me his daughter was interested in environmental work. He said he hoped someday she could do what I was doing. It had taken him a very long time to decide to ask me, and I was flattered."

I nodded enthusiastically and asked for more wine. "Tell me what you did before this, Peggy. Were you always in this profession?"

"No, actually I wanted to be a veterinarian. I went to Colorado State University in Fort Collins and took two years of prevet medicine. But it was evident I wouldn't get into vet school. This was back in 1969 when I was eighteen. The school was still touchy about having female vet students—even if they had perfect grades. Ninety students were admitted, and they expected ninety to graduate four years later—no marriages, no babies, nothing. They virtually thought you should be sterilized. It was the old way of thinking. So I changed my major to the environmental field. I did work as a veterinary nurse for a while and later ski-bummed all over the Colorado resorts. I took 'survival jobs'—waitress, maid, clerk—just to be able to ski and save up money for my next quarter of college."

The relaxing lunch gave us time to admire the scenery. From time to time a distant blast rocked the air, or the helicopter buzzed by and dropped more hay. The fog cap on Whiteface had disappeared entirely.

Peggy continued telling me about her life. "My first full-time job was as environmental planner for the Lake Champlain–Lake George Regional Environmental Management Council and associated with the Regional Planning Board. What a job! There I was—my degree in hand but no experience. I didn't really know anything. I didn't even know how to run a copy machine! The very first day I was asked to prepare a directory of all the agencies dealing with environmental problems in that region. Pretty soon I was giving presentations on environmental topics, reviewing reports, going out in the field, and coordinating with many agencies. Eventually I was made chairwoman of a regional water management planning group. After two years I decided to obtain my master's degree. I was lucky enough to be awarded a fellowship in water resources from the EPA (U.S. Environmental Protection Agency) while studying at Rensselaer Polytechnic Institute." She stretched out supine in the sun. "After getting my masters I took a job as a senior water resources planner for the Hudson River study with the Department of Environmental Conservation in Albany. I was active in water conservation programs and writing a comprehensive plan for the river basin. One day in 1977 I received a call asking if I was interested in working on the Olympics. I was interviewed and offered this job. And I love it!"

"Do you spend a lot of time outdoors like this?" I asked.

"Not enough," sighed Peggy. "I'd be out every day if I could, but there are always reports and paperwork to do in the office. But I go camping, hiking, fishing, and skiing around here, and I used to live in a log cabin in the woods near Saranac Lake. As you know, the Adirondacks are the wildest area left east of the Mississippi. On state lands we have over 1 million acres of pure wilderness—no roads, buildings, or motorized vehicles. And then there's another good million acres classified as primitive, canoe, and wild forest areas. And that doesn't even take into account 3.7 million acres of private lands which have plenty of foot paths, camp grounds, and cross-country and snowmobile trails open to the public. I often hike by myself, and the men I meet along the way are incredulous that I am alone in such wild woods."

The next time I saw Peggy was on a frigid day in December 1979. She was going out to Mt. Van Hoevenberg to inspect a new stretch of biathlon trail and a footbridge that had been built over it. She wore heavy snowmobile boots, powder blue jeans, and a bright blue ski parka. As we drove, Peggy told me about her childhood. She had grown up in the country in Massachusetts with a large forest and swamp right at her back door where she spent hours exploring. She also had horses and much preferred going for all-day trail rides in the quiet woods by herself to being in a riding ring.

"I never stayed in the house," she reminisced. "I spent my time cleaning the stables, not my room; currying my horses, not dressing dolls. I liked horse work, not house work. My parents never objected. They supported my interests and bought me books on science and natural history, took me and my sister and brother to national parks. They never told me that as a woman I couldn't do certain things. In fact, it was just the opposite. They never mentioned that some day I might have to consider a home, marriage, and family in addition to a career. They just said, 'If you want to do something, then do it.'

"I always thought I'd have a career. My father was an electrical engineer, and my mom was a registered nurse. Dad took me along on jobs and spoke engineer's lingo, so I learned to think like an engineer even though I never thought I'd be one. Funny thing, a guy I now work with closely once said, 'Hey, you're okay, Peg. You think like an engineer!' It was a nice compliment. Anyway, I guess I decided early on that it was more interesting and more fun to work with men, and to be involved in fields that were traditionally theirs. Maybe it's my competitive nature.

"As for the outdoors, my feeling is that attitudes toward wilderness are a matter of individual differences among men and women. Though women are not equal to men in brute strength, they can find ways to compensate, and generally they are able to endure just as well. Many women I have come in contact with (roommates, friends, acquaintances) have come to believe they are helpless in the out-of-doors and that wilderness is a man's world. They are a product of society's traditional attitudes. Thankfully, though, I see this changing now."

We reached the end of the road, parked, and strapped on snowshoes. The snow lay three feet deep on the level, and the forest was draped in white. As we trudged back toward the rustic bridge, a flash of red, white, and blue passed by us. It was an Olympic contestant out practicing—a year in advance. His cross-country skis moved in parallel precision and made a soft swishing sound. "Wow! He must have been going twenty miles an hour," I marveled.

The bridge lay ahead. Peggy began darting about like a blue jay checking the underpinnings, the slope of its sides, the angles of approach, and the trail width. The forest lay absolutely quiet except when a tree trunk cracked in the −10°F. temperature. I hopped up and down on my snowshoes, trying to keep my feet warm.

The afternoon was dimming, and the blue winter twilight was deepening. "I'll have to come back tomorrow and ride out on the new snow-grooming equipment to check their widths on these cross-country ski trails," Peggy said. "I really would like to see how they operate. Some of the new equipment makes a pretty wide swath. Just one machine can rack, chop, pack, and smooth the snow all at one pass. One of them costs $22,000 or more! But, once again, such specialized equipment has the potential of damaging the environment. If the snow is too thin and if young seedlings are in the way or the soils are exposed, they can really mess things up. They must be handled carefully and only under the right conditions."

On the way back to town we stopped at the home of a friend of Peggy's for a hot cup of tea. Peggy settled back in a comfortable stuffed chair and crossed her legs. Our discussion focused on her work briefly and then switched to another popular topic, sports. Both women play on the local women's basketball team and ski together.

"How's Louie?" interrupted Mary.

A warm glow spread over Peggy's face, and she flashed a smile. "Fine, fine." Then, as an explanation to me, she said, "He's the man I'm married to. He does a variety of things—tennis pro, antique and art appraiser, theater, and now business investments. He is also involved with sports timing for the Olympic Committee." She warmed to her subject. "I was so lucky to find him up here. It's wonderful to live with a man in a totally different profession; it gives us so much to talk about. And Louie's extremely understanding and trusting." She gazed out the window toward the high peaks, backlit now by a faint greenish afterglow.

"I feel I'm truly fortunate in my profession, too. I work with men a lot and get along well with them. I find I can tease and joke easily with men. Of course, I feel I could work with women, too, except there are so few in this type of work. I've found that professional women have good attitudes. If they have a conflict, they address it and say so. They seem to know themselves better than those women with no business experience and limited education. The ones who have delayed marriage or lived alone handle themselves best of all, I think. They take pride in being independent. After all, a woman can't afford to be helpless if she's on her own— if there's no man around to help change a tire, wax her skis, or hang a curtain rod."

Her friend's voice brought her back to the present. "What will you do, Peg, when the Olympics are over and your contract ends?"

"Well, I'm not really sure at this time, though I've been thinking lots about it. I love field work and enjoy the people I've been involved with here. Certainly I'll continue in environmental work, hopefully in or near the wilderness, probably as a consultant.

"Whatever, Louie and I will stay together no matter where we are," Peggy continued in her husky voice. "Actually, I'd like to move back to Colorado. I love those mountains, and the hard winters, and the super snow out West. You know that poster on my wall, Mary." And then, with the typical optimism of an Aries, she added, "It doesn't matter. Things are so great now. I know they'll be fine in the future, too."

We thanked Mary for the tea and said goodbye. Something nibbled at my mind. Just as Peg was closing her car door, I remembered.

"Hey," I called, rolling down my window. "What *does* the poster on your wall say?"

"Oh, that." She cocked her head, remembering. "It says:

> *I live not by myself,*
> *But become a part of that around me.*
> *And to me,*
> *High mountains are a feeling,*
> *And the hum of human cities torture.*

"That's my philosophy."

"Not bad at all," I nodded appreciatively, "for an environmental monitor."

Chapter 13

Sheila Link

A Modern Diana

THE NEW JERSEY Pine Barrens were frigid and silent in the grip of winter. The stunted pitch pines and scrub oaks stood twisted and tangled; tawny grasses and burgundy brambles covered the rock-hard ground. Patches of black ice in the swales glinted somberly. A winding sand track ran through dark clumps of laurel, past frozen fields of corn stubble, and around an abandoned farm house shot full of holes. Nothing moved save for a jet high overhead whining its approach to Newark Airport far to the north. The state's largest remaining wilderness area seemed absolutely devoid of life on this January day.

Suddenly a white setter ran into view, followed by two figures dressed in bright orange and khaki, and carrying twenty-gauge shotguns over their shoulders. The dog stopped stock still and went into a point, its tail quivering excitedly. Deep in a little copse of oaks and hickories a covey of quail crept through the dead leaves. The two hunters swung smoothly into action, shotguns braced and ready to fire. A tense moment passed. The smaller of the two hunters edged toward the covey. All at once a dozen birds sprang into the air flying every which way. Both guns spat, and two birds tumbled to the ground, a flurry of feathers falling like snowflakes. The dog leaped forward to retrieve the dropped quail while the two hunters grinned broadly at each other.

Sheila Link on a quail hunt in the New Jersey Pine Barrens. Photo by Anne LaBastille.

"That makes a total of twelve!" exclaimed Sheila Link. "Good shooting, Pete!" Her face, framed in dark brown curls, was radiant. She intercepted the setter and took the birds from its mouth. After stuffing them into the back of her hunting coat, Sheila opened her gun and put new shells in the chamber.

Pete glanced up at the sky which was thickening with clouds and prophesied, "We'll have snow before long, Sheila."

"It doesn't matter," she said blithely. "You know me, Pete. I hunt as long as we can, no matter what the weather or terrain."

The occasion was the New Jersey Outdoor Writers' annual invitational quail hunt, hosted by the New Jersey Division of Fish and Game. Pete McLain, assistant chief of the department, was one of its genial hosts. And Sheila Link, outdoor writer, sportswoman, and firearms expert, was the sole woman invited. Little wonder, since she is a crack markswoman, a consultant to the National Rifle Association, and a deputy conservation officer and hunter safety instructor with New Jersey's Division of Fish and Game.

The pair continued hunting through the wintry countryside, stopping occasionally to listen to the booms from the guns of their companions in the distance. By the time they had their limit, it was noon and the first flakes were drifting down.

"How about some lunch with the guys at the Log Cabin?" suggested Pete.

"Sounds good to me," nodded Sheila, swinging her shotgun onto her shoulder. They called in the dog and headed back to the car. It had been a good morning. But the snow was worsening, and eventually it would cancel out the afternoon hunt. After lunch Sheila spoke a few goodbyes to her buddies, waved crisply to Pete, and headed for home. She planned to spend the rest of the day in her study working on a new article for *Sports Afield* magazine.

To step into Sheila's study is like going into a miniature sportswoman's "Hall of Fame." Dominating the room is an antelope head that comes within four points of the Boone and Crockett record book of trophy animals. Photographs show her hunting stone sheep, elk, and other big game mammals. Plaques commemorating her outdoor photography and radio shows hang on the wall. A backpack stands against her filing cabinet. Papers and books clutter the desk. It is the study of a hard-working, determined, outdoor woman.

The rest of Sheila's house, two blocks away from where the Atlantic laps calmly on Bradley Beach, is comfortable, clean, and attractive. Pictures of her four children stand on the piano. Except for a canoe rack out back there is very little about this setting or about the house to suggest that a woman like Sheila lives here. But, as she says, "If I was limited only to New Jersey, I'd be so frustrated that I'd probably forget all about my outdoor life. Fortunately, the whole United States is my backyard."

Actually Sheila did spend many years in this house and town as an ordinary "devoted mother and housewife." She did not enjoy going camping, hunting, or backpacking with her babies when it meant having to change diapers in the woods, so she stayed home until her kids were at least partly grown. Her husband of twenty-five years, Fred, is a high school English teacher and a professional musician—drums and piano—and Sheila regularly joined him as a bass fiddler during their early years together. The vivacious woman with the piercing grey eyes and her mild-mannered, quiet husband were much sought after for weekend bands. Sheila cared for her children, cooked, and did housework all week, and then turned into a musician on weekends.

During this period of her life a tennis-playing acquaintance one day asked Sheila to go bird shooting. When she was growing up, she had often shot .22's, gone hiking, and tracked wildlife, and she kept skillful at target practice, so she accepted. Her friend was impressed by how well she handled firearms and by her knowledge of the outdoors. Eventually he suggested that Sheila write an outdoor column for the local paper.

Intrigued by the idea, Sheila decided to try. It wasn't easy. It took her a month to produce three stories, but finally she was ready. The editor read them over and asked, "Could you start writing for the paper right away if you're not committed to anyone else?"

Sheila laughed and said, "I'm not even a writer, much less writing for any other paper or magazine."

Events were to belie her words. She wrote for the small local paper for two years, then in 1970 graduated to one with a circulation of 127,000 as an "outdoor editor." As difficult as she found writing at first, she was determined to do the best she could. She wrote primarily about camping, fishing, hunting, outdoor equipment, and canoeing. Sheila got much of her first-hand information by taking her children on trips. Her son Greg grew to love these excursions so much that they became "partners in crime," devising all sorts of excuses to get outdoors. In "A Gun for Greg" Sheila described how she taught her boy to hunt. *Field and Stream* (1968) magazine bought the article at once. Shortly after this coup she became the regional field editor for *Metropolitan Camper* magazine and saltwater fishing columnist for the *Bucks County Courier-Times,* a Pennsylvania newspaper.

Sheila's quick success was misleading in a way. "How easy it is," she thought, not yet aware of the stiff competition in the world literary market. Throughout these early endeavors she was aided by Fred, who patiently coached her in style and format, grammar, and vocabulary. "He was wonderful," claims Sheila. "I never could have done it without Fred."

Subsequently her freelancing landed articles in *Redbook, Sports Afield, American Rifleman, Better Camping, American Hunter,* and other magazines. She joined the Outdoor Writers Association of America, a fifteen-hundred-member organization of journalists who write about the outdoors. This group gave her the encouragement and support a beginning writer needs. Later Sheila became the first woman to be elected to its board of directors; she is slated to become its first female president in 1981.

Success in radio also happened at this time, with seemingly equal ease. Sheila had been a guest on several local radio shows when it suddenly occurred to her to start her own program. The forceful Leo-born woman went right out and found a sponsor and a station, and devised a five-minute show called "Outdoors Unlimited." The program ran for three years on one station and two years on another, and in 1974 won the Outdoor Writers Association of America's Deep Woods award—for achievement in the outdoor-oriented media—in the radio category. This efficient, no-nonsense woman also directed her energies to photography, becoming so adept at illustrating her own articles that she won another Outdoor Writers Association first prize, this one for outdoor photography.

During this period of development and growth Sheila gave up her music and turned more and more to writing and outdoor skills. Fred had told her, "You've paid your dues. You've helped me get through college, brought up our children, and kept house. I want you to do whatever makes *you* happy. Just include me out." A pacific man, he dislikes firearms and hunting, so Sheila goes on most of her excursions, particularly hunting and fishing ones, without him. Twice she has driven across the United States to take her children on camping trips. She also bought a kayak to increase her outdoor sports coverage.

In 1975 Sheila began teaching an outdoor skills course at New Jersey's Brookdale College, taking her class on such field trips as backpacking on the Appalachian Trail and canoeing through the Pine Barrens. She went elk hunting with a woman friend in Colorado and bagged a bull elk and an eleven-point mule deer. She's fished for trout in Idaho and northern pike in Minnesota, and hunted wild turkeys, black bear, upland game, and waterfowl all across the country. She began attending the big sporting goods shows, inspecting and evaluating outdoor goods for her columns and classes. Eventually various companies started sending her products to test. Now in her mid-forties Sheila is on the go constantly. "I have lots of energy and get cabin fever if I'm inside too much. The outdoors and outdoor skills are the overriding force in my life now."

One of her pet peeves is women's outdoor clothing—or the lack of it. "It presents problems for being comfortable in the bush," she explains. "In the first place, it's hard to find women's things. Companies just don't make enough money out of it because up to now the market hasn't been large enough. So women tend to buy men's clothing. Men's pants? Well, it feels like straddling a clothesline, and they make you look like you're standing in a Dixie cup. Not flattering at all. Men's jackets? The sleeves are invariably too long, and the shoulders hang off our frames. Boots? Usually only the boys' sizes will fit a woman, and they are generally 'bottom of the line' in terms of materials, ruggedness, and design. Women have been badly neglected in this whole outdoor field. It's only recently that modern camping gear and accessories have lured women into the outdoors. There's still a lot to be done."

Sheila has also become interested in survival training. Perhaps her longest and most frightening survival experience took place in New Mexico, and it surely paid off—in self-knowledge and wilderness expertise, in a 1976 *Field and Stream* article, and in a book for young people called *The Hardy Boys Handbook: Seven Stories of Survival*, published in 1980.

In 1976 the National Rifle Association and Council for Survival Education in Denver contacted several people, among them Sheila, with an idea for a five-day survival leadership field exercise on the 38,000-acre property the NRA owns in the New Mexico mountains. The purpose of the five days of travel on foot through the wilderness at zero (and lower) temperatures was to establish proven guidelines for survival in the winter mountain wilderness—information that might someday save the lives of lost or injured hunters, campers, and car breakdown or aircraft crash victims. It was also to provide advanced leadership training for survival instructors, and to field-test equipment. Four teams were sent out with no food (other than five candy bars), sleeping bags, tents, or regular matches. Sheila was put with five other women, the only female team. A prearranged system of daily flyovers and distress signals would, it was hoped, ensure that everyone would survive this grueling experience safely.

The time was mid-January, and the elevation was six thousand to eight thousand feet. The teams had to cover thirty miles through the mountains using topographical maps and compasses. They were to rendezvous briefly on the third day and then be picked up on the afternoon of the fifth day at a prearranged point on a jeep road. Hunger pangs were most intense during the first two days, Sheila recalls, but nobody wasted energy trying to hunt or snare game. They just went hungry and kept moving. Feet became wet and chilled. Nights were cruel and sleepless. The teammates huddled close to the fire, which they started with a metal match, and dozed in their parkas.

On the third night Sheila began acting strangely. She started shivering violently and uncontrollably, unbuttoned her jacket, and talked with slurred speech. Her companions noted this and suddenly realized she was in the early stages of hypothermia. This chilling of the body's core can be fatal in as little as two hours if nothing is done to warm the victim. Immediately one woman built up the fire. Someone else started melting snow in a metal canteen and forced Sheila to drink the hot water. Two other women sat down next to her and enveloped her inside their arms and parkas. (Without sleeping bags they could not practice the bare-skin-to-bare-skin warming technique which is considered the most effective way of combating hypothermia.) The battle to keep Sheila alive lasted till midnight. By then she had recovered her normal body temperature and fallen safely asleep. Come morning, she could not remember her brush with death.

The overall experience made a lasting impression. "I wasn't afraid of *anything* anymore," declared Sheila later. "I felt equal to any wilderness situation. In fact, my wilderness training has taught me complete self-confidence. Now I know that I'll always go down fighting."

Sheila had a chance to prove that attitude recently when she went rafting down the Chatooga River in South Carolina. This is the same river system where the movie "Deliverance" was shot and which she'd run in a kayak two years earlier. The raft she shared with five others capsized in a series of rapids near a bluff, and the hydraulic current dragged her deep beneath the craft.

"I was fighting to come up, needing air, and exhausted," she recalls. "The raft was still racing downstream, pulling me along directly under it through the rapids. All I could think of was, 'Fred will be madder than hell if I die. He's always telling me I do crazy things.' Then I thought to myself, '*I* have something to say about dying or not dying. There must be something I can do."

She began fighting harder and pushing her face up against the raft floor, where she know there would be an inch or two of air trapped against the boat's rubber bottom. This air kept her alive until two of her companions, who were clinging to the side of the raft, felt her body thrashing underneath, locked arms together, and dragged her out.

Sheila has taught wilderness survival methods in courses given in New Mexico by the NRA. The courses are offered four times a year, for six days each time. The first two days are spent in a classroom learning basic techniques. The third day the students are given demonstrations of outdoor skills in the field, and that night they camp out in small teams. The next three days are for "solos," during which each participant will stay alone in an isolated part of a canyon, without books, companions, or food. Each will build a shelter and campfire. Before the solos some students invariably mention concern about loneliness. Sheila says implacably, "If you're afraid of your own company for three days, think of your friends." As the students go out alone, each one up a side canyon, Sheila leaves them with this sage advice: "You know what to do and how to do it. Keep your head; don't panic."

The first day and night they are frightened. The second, bored. The third, they have it all licked. "When the students come back," describes Sheila, "it's a beautiful thing to see. Their grins literally split their faces. They all say, 'It was the greatest experience of my life. It gave me a chance to know myself.' "

The seeds were planted for Sheila's rough-and-ready lifestyle when she was a child, though they lay dormant for many years while she was a housewife. She grew up a "rolling stone" and very independent as a result of a choice made by her parents when she was very young—and made in a most unusual way. Her father, an oil company administrator, and her mother, an executive secretary, had made their home in northern New Jersey. Both sets of grandparents lived nearby, and there was constant haggling about who would invite the three children over and when. One night when Sheila was about seven, the young parents decided it was time to pull up stakes and seek a more quiet and private life. They spread out a map of the United States on the dining room table. "We'll close our eyes and point to a place and then move there," they determined. Holding hands, with the three children watching agog, they put their index fingers on San Diego. Soon everything, including a large Airedale, was packed in the car, and they were on their way.

In southern California Sheila ran barefoot on the beach and shot jackrabbits in the canyons with her own gun. She was tan, tough, and wild. Yet she and her brother and sister still made several trips to visit their grandparents in New Jersey. In those days one didn't just jet across the continent for the weekend; one stayed for a good long visit. So Sheila had another life—that of the spoiled, beloved, fancy little grandchild who was taken to concerts, art galleries, or skating in Central Park, and who always dressed up for dinner.

During those formative years spent bouncing back and forth between California and the East Coast, she attended thirty-two grammar schools, two junior highs, five senior highs; and she spent two years at a junior college in San Mateo. As a result, she can say matter-of-factly, "If I had to pack up tomorrow and leave home, it wouldn't bother me at all. As a young woman I never wanted a career, or a home, or a family, even after I fell in love with Fred. But I did dream of having a horse ranch in Montana." She goes on, "You see I learned to be an outdoor woman purely by chance, the hard way—no formal education and all by myself with lots of self-determination. Also I have a marvelous, supportive husband who always encourages me to do what I want, plus four wonderful kids who love to go camping with me, and who are among my best friends. I'm the luckiest woman I know."

Late that evening after the hunt, Sheila is in her kitchen cleaning the quail she shot. Fred is in the living room playing the piano. Strains of "Full Moon and Empty Arms" flow through the house. Large wet flakes of snow are piling up in the yard and hissing into the cold Atlantic Ocean. "What a great hunt!" exclaims Sheila, stretching out her legs in cowboy boots and tight jeans. "It would have been good with or without killing any game, though. Hunting is a complicated and touchy issue today, and while I respect the personal viewpoints of people who choose not to hunt, I think that many who disapprove of the sport miss this basic point: that for most hunters the heart of the experience is the combination of developing and using outdoor skills and pitting these against the superior physical capabilities and instincts of wild creatures and their intimate knowledge of their own terrain. It's not necessary to win all the time.

"I also believe that human beings have a place, like all other forms of life, in the ecological chain. Like lions, wolves, striped bass, or hawks, we are predators; and even though we have learned to breed and raise certain animals for food, many people—including me—prefer stalking wild game in a fair chase to buying meat other people have raised, slaughtered, and butchered for us. Except for prairie dogs, which are systematically poisoned to keep their incredible reproduction rate in check, I kill nothing we don't eat. And, of course, I stress sound conservation practices in hunting, in my personal life, and in my roles as hunter education instructor and commissioned deputy conservation officer for the state.

"Hunting with good companions is sharing a primitive gut experience. It touches you deep inside. And I really like to be with men—in fact, I have ever since grade school. When we moved around so much, I found that boys were always open and nice to me when I began in a new school, but the girls were not. Later I found that men can be the most close and confidential friends.

Also I like sports traditionally considered men's much better than domestic pastimes. I hate sewing, cooking, and cleaning. I'm female by nature, but unfeminine in my interests."

Quail feathers are floating around the kitchen. Twelve plump little carcasses are lined up on the sink edge. Sheila begins to wrap them for freezing. "I'm not competitive in my outdoor sports," she explains. "There's no room for that. So I'm not a threat to most men. They know I'm not outdoors with them to snare a mate, or to make brownie points with my boyfriend, or just tagging along with my husband. I really want to hunt, long and hard, and to enjoy a wilderness experience."

Closing the freezer door, she walks back into her studio, stopping to straighten a small plaque on her wall. It reads:

Press On. Nothing in the world can take the place of persistence. Persistence and determination alone are omnipotent.

A few minutes later the rattle of Sheila's typewriter mixes with the soft chords of Fred's piano as she continues with her latest article.

Chapter 14

Carol Ruckdeschel

Island Naturalist

A TOWERING, BLACK-BOWELED thunderhead loomed over the Atlantic, flashing intermittently and rumbling ominously above the flat gray sea. Internal streaks of lightning turned it mauve and pink and pearl and ivory. A few feet from the retreating tide a line of gulls slept, each on one foot. A moody twilight glowed briefly on the waves and wet sand; then night fell over the deserted beach.

From the island's interior came a chugging sound, the glimmer of lights. An open jeep emerged from under the wind-bent maritime forest, crawled up one side of a steep dune and down the other onto hard-packed sand. At the wheel sat a wiry, pigtailed, pug-nosed woman with a shotgun across her lap. She steered toward the ocean, tugged her safari hat down more firmly onto her forehead, and switched off the headlights. Any light now could frighten away egg-filled female loggerhead turtles who were homing onto the Georgia coast to unburden themselves and to perpetuate their species. Carol Ruckdeschel turned hard left in front of the foredunes and parked her jeep parallel to the sea. The gulls jumped into the air with screeches of annoyance and flapped sleepily away. She waited for her eyes to adjust to the dark. It was very quiet except for distant thunder and the soft lap of waves.

Anticipation ran through the young naturalist. Every sense was alive, alert, ready. Would the turtles come in to lay tonight? How many, and where along the five-mile strip would they arrive? Would she be able to tag and measure more than last night? The past week had been poor. Very few females had come ashore, dragging their two-hundred- to four-hundred-pound bodies across the wet sand, leaving broad marks like tracks of bulldozers. One just never knew with these turtles when they would come or when they wouldn't.

Only a few precious miles of Georgia's Barrier Islands, and even fewer of the Florida and Carolina coasts, are still undeveloped, dark, and wild, and so acceptable and safe for the huge reptiles. Loggerheads are the only sea turtles which regularly breed on the southeastern U.S. coastline, although green and Ridley turtles (both endangered species) and, more rarely, leatherbacks and hawksbills, have been seen off the shore. Several sea islands used for nesting sites have been under study for varying amounts of time in an effort to save these species from extinction. Much of the sea turtles' life history is still a mystery. Because they range far and wide at sea, they are difficult, if not impossible, to track or observe. Part of the program, therefore, has included tagging turtles when they come up to lay eggs. If the tags are seen and retrieved, biologists can learn where the adult turtles go each year and how they die. The other part of the turtle program involves patrolling the nesting beaches and protecting the eggs of females from any form of predation.

A few hungry mosquitoes began whining around Carol's ears. A fantastic bolt of lightning lit up the beach for an instant. The humid night seemed haunting, exciting, mysterious. Starting the jeep, she began her patrol—five miles down the beach, five miles back. Far ahead, she saw a dark spot on the sand. The spot grew to be a three-hundred-pound female loggerhead, lumbering straight toward the high broken line of foredunes. Carol braked to a stop, cut the engine, and waited. The turtle slowly dug a hole several inches deep with her rear flippers. When her cloaca (rear external uro-genital opening) was directly above the pit, the miracle of birth began. Slowly, without sound, her eggs dropped out— white, leathery, the size and shape of ping pong balls. It would be an hour before the eggs—up to 150 of them—were extruded and the turtle had covered up her nest hole.

Carol Ruckdeschel and friend outside her island home. Photo by Anne LaBastille.

Carol decided to continue her patrol and come back after the laying was over and the female resting quietly. Then she could easily tag her without upsetting the animal. Further up the deserted beach Carol met a turtle already heading back to sea. To tag the beast meant immobilizing her. Carol squatted beside the left rear side of the monster, grabbed the edge of the carapace (shell) with her hands, and strained upward with her strong legs. As the turtle began to lift, the sturdy woman gave a hefty shove, flipped the turtle onto its back, and then somersaulted over it onto the soft sand. The feat was deftly done.

Once, Carol recalls, a female biologist came down to help and could not budge a single turtle an inch. "She had smooth hands and long nails," Carol said mockingly. "She seemed surprised that loggerheads were so heavy. Turtles do have a very low center of gravity. It's kind of like grabbing the bumper of a Cadillac and trying to lift it in order to change a tire."

After applying a bright tag to the female's front flipper and mea-
suring her overall length and width, Carol straightened up. She
rubbed her aching lower back a moment, then sighed and flipped
the turtle back onto its feet. Relieved of eggs, the animal now
would follow an ancient instinct to head toward a bright, open, flat
horizon—the sea—rather than the black, high, broken silhouette
of dunes and vegetation which edged the nesting beach. This
amazing set of signals, evolved over the ages, keys the turtles into
dark, uneven horizons before laying; light, flat horizons after laying.

Carol rested awhile on a dune and watched the loggerhead begin
its elephantlike walk back to the sea. Then she jumped in the jeep
and began another run. So she spent the night—searching for
turtles, flipping and tagging seven more, keeping a close eye on
the storm which hovered out to sea. At one point a spatter of rain
began, so she took shelter with her notes and knapsack under a
giant wooden cable spool which had washed ashore. It was the
perfect hiding place because she could shift 360° around the spool
while still staying dry under its wide lip.

When 4:00 A.M. came and the first faint streaks of gray showed
in the east, Carol drove her jeep behind the dunes, found a sandy
dip with hummocks of beach grass all around, and fell asleep immediately. It had been a good night. Eight turtles were tagged and
two "beach pigs" shot. Part of Carol's duty as a consulting naturalist
to a governmental agency was making sure the eggs were protected
from human poachers and feral (wild) animals. Domestic animals
had been introduced on many of the barrier islands of the southeastern coast during Colonial days. After slavery was abolished and
plantations went out of style, the animals were often turned loose
to fend for themselves. Adapting to the wild, the pigs, cows, don-
keys, horses, cats, or dogs often managed to survive and eventually
to wreak havoc on the natural vegetation, soils, and wildlife. Some
feral pigs actually "learned" to venture boldly out onto the broad
beaches, root up the tasty, nourishing turtle eggs, and eat them.

Once as she was driving Carol thought she saw a jeep without
lights heading down the beach. Who could be on that desolate
stretch, she wondered? The "jeep" turned out to be a huge hog,
which was destroying every nest it could find. The gun stood her
in good stead then, as well as other times. On one occasion some

drunk picnickers began trespassing and had to be asked "polite-
ly"—but at gunpoint—to leave her private land. Carol's reputation
as a "pistol-packing mamma" began with her protecting turtles on
the island and eventually spread to the mainland.

As soon as the sun was up and getting hot, Carol awoke and
headed home. She never gets more than two to four hours sleep
a night during the summer, living on a perpetual "high." To her
the beach is "always just perfect" at night, whether it is raining,
blowing, or clear. Sometimes the sky is shot through with meteors,
other times hung low with dancing stars. Once she saw a dim
rainbow at night. Another time she had the feeling of driving 'under
the horizon' when clouds formed a strange luminescent ceiling. No
matter what she sees, it is never the same. She lives for the nights.

Yet her daytime work is equally important and exciting for it
concerns her own survival. She spends all day working on her
home and organizing her possessions and zoological specimens.
Four years ago Carol completed lengthy legal negotiations to buy
a black farm hand's shanty built in 1895. When the family had
finally moved off the island after three generations, the title was
fuzzy and nine heirs had to be contacted to straighten it out. Some
joints were rotten, and the rafters sagging, when Carol became the
new owner. Yet it was her long-time dream to live on the island,
and this was the only feasible way she could manage. Today she
beams and says, "An old shack never made anyone so happy. I
wouldn't sell it for any price! Money spent on peace and happiness
is not wasted."

And peace indeed lies inside and outside her home—peace as
glowing as the golden Georgia sunlight. There is peace in the
delicate skeins of Spanish moss hanging from the giant live oak
trees backlit with a pearly pink dawn sky. There is peace in the
contented clucking of chickens as they peck around the yard, and
the pair of pileated woodpeckers shrilly courting each other in a
big long-leaf pine nearby. There is peace in the distant roar of surf;
in the fresh green smell of spiky palmettos and resurrection ferns
after rain; in the flash of red cardinals at the window feeder and
the lazy armadillo sleeping under the porch stoop. Carol fits into
her own little ecosystem as easily as an otter flips through the
water.

Inside, wide, weathered cypress board lines the walls of her peaceful studio, and a hundred-year-old K&E drafting table stands by a window. Old red bricks form the hearth of the fireplaces. The sink countertop in Carol's roomy kitchen is made from sturdy three-by-ten-inch boards, still bearing traces of barnacles, which once were part of a dock. Rustic bookshelves hold a wealth of natural history and zoology volumes. A Siamese cat dozes in a graceful rocker beside an antique leather chest. Varnished turtle shells decorate the walls, while an intricately balanced mobile of ribs and vertebrae hangs in white splendor from the living room ceiling. No modern sculpture could rival it. Almost every item in the "shanty" was found washed up on a wide beach and artistically crafted into Carol's home.

The nicest touches are two black and white portraits of the original owners and a rubbing from the tombstone of an early island resident on the walls. As Carol explains, "The original inhabitants of this house and this island built the same way I am doing. They scrounged for boards and furniture on the beach. It makes me feel real close to them."

Such homeyness and artistry were not come by easily. Carol had to renovate the entire structure. Alone, or with help from a close neighbor, she replaced joists, pointed up the chimney, and strengthened rafters and roof. Then she turned every board on the outside backward, so the original pink paint would not show and the natural pine could weather gracefully. She covered the entire three rooms on the inside with plywood before paneling it so that her home would be cockroach-proof. Some of the cypress paneling she used was transferred five times before winding up on her walls—from the mainland on truck, to a boat, to a truck, to a storage pile, and finally to the house.

After two years of labor Carol was finally able to invite her parents to spend Christmas with her in 1979. "I could offer them two beds with a sound roof over their heads, a flush toilet, a shower with hot and cold running water, and a kitchen to cook in. Mind you," she continues smiling, "I still sleep outdoors in my 'conch shell' (a kind of chicken coop) and have only flushed that john myself once, just to see if it was working."

Carol is a "nature girl" in still more ways. She virtually lives off the land. Potatoes, collards, onions, parsley, corn, Jerusalem artichokes, and sugar cane flourish in her garden. A line of fresh green garlic sprouts by the back stoop. There are clumps of catnip for her cats and other herbs scattered about. A gnarled old grape vine and arbor covers half her backyard. She fertilizes strictly with natural compost, fishheads, and any dead animals she finds on the beach. "See that cabbage?" she points. "The reason it's so big is that I buried part of a stranded shark there."

For meat Carol goes down to the creek which meanders through a saltwater marsh at the end of the island. "You can always find something to eat here," she reports. "Fish, clams, shrimps, oysters. Just throw in a cast net, and the sea will provide. The saltwater marsh, like the southern swamp, is one of the most productive ecosystems on Earth. All you really need is a pan with butter to make a fine meal from the gifts of a salt marsh."

She often receives "wild gifts" for herself and her cats from Jesse, a sixty-year-old black resident of the island who loves Carol dearly. "I trim his hair, and he brings me meat," she laughs. "Like squirrels, marsh hens, mullet, armadillo, even venison. I always cook up mullet for my cats. I don't believe in *them* eating store-bought food any more than *I* do."

Only when the freezer is really empty will Carol and Jesse resort to killing a feral hog—and then only one which has been routing around damaging turtle nests or vegetation—or a rattlesnake, whose meat tastes like chicken. Carol supplements her meats and greens with grapefruits from the sites of old abandoned plantations, holly leaves for tea, honey from wild beehives, and occasional wild fruits. In preparing all these foods she never uses a cookbook or recipe, but improvises to make truly delicious dishes. When I asked Carol what she did need to buy from stores, she shrugged and said, "Well, I guess just liquor, butter, and milk." She reflected a moment. "I'm lucky. Usually friends will bring those luxuries when they visit their camps on weekends. It's always like Christmas because they may bring cookies and other neat stuff. Oh, yes, and my mail, too. Otherwise I'd have to make a five-hour trip on foot and by boat to the mainland just to get to a post office or a phone."

"What about soap?" I asked. "How do you do your laundry?"

"In a pail or tub with a bar of laundry soap, like everyone else did before washing machines," she replied. "To me, you can tell clean clothes by their smell, not their color. Whiteness and brightness don't necessarily mean cleanliness. All my clothes tend toward gray, and gray is my favorite color. It blends with greens and browns, and those muted shades help camouflage me in the woods."

When Carol finishes her house and studio, her next big venture will be to complete her museum and laboratory-workshop. Carol has a keen interest in zoology; she has run her own trap line for small mammals for two years and regularly picks up DOB's (dead on beach animals) which may include stranded whales and sharks, sick loons, sea birds coated with oil, turtles, and other animals. She has both state and federal authorization to handle any of the endangered marine mammals. "What I want most in the world is to make my work with dead animals available to the scientific community. I collect specimens, sketch them, dissect them, really study them thoroughly, and then store them away. There are so many projects that might need my help, and so little is known about the Georgia barrier islands."

Already Carol has provided one scientist at the Smithsonian Institution with teeth from dwarfed and pigmy sperm whales which had been washed up on the beach. He is doing a careful dissection of the teeth to determine the ages of these rare cetaceans. She has provided the state with a first record of a beaked whale and prepared the skull for a museum. On rare occasions she's picked up shells of Ridley turtles, one of the most endangered sea turtles.

Another interesting and worthwhile job she has engaged in on the island is taking sand samples for a study of the drift and movement of dunes along the beach. Without these all-protecting barriers of sand, the entire island would be vulnerable to the sea and its fury. She's also kept records of vegetation plots to analyze the effect of feral animals on the local plants.

"The more I do, the more I learn," she asserts. "Eventually I want to work on a series of field guides for all the fauna and flora of the coastal islands. Nothing like that exists. I'm in a perfect position to do it and also to produce, over time, a serious and consecutive recording of life on my island." From the shelf she pulled a couple of black notebooks filled with her fastidious and accurate notes, sketches, and references. Page after page is done in indelible ink in a beautiful, flowing hand. "I've lived here six years now, three as a caretaker and three on my own land. I feel I'm almost ready to write something worthwhile."

Carol is her own self-appointed conservation watchdog. Nothing escapes her notice—planes flying too low over the beaches, the rank sulfurous stink from air-polluting paper mills nearby, the threat of nuclear submarine bases and giant tanker terminals on the coast, rumors of poachers, or backpackers molesting the fauna. She keeps up a steady flow of letters to conservation and scientific organizations, such as the National Park Service, the Georgia Nature Conservancy, the Wilderness Society, the Smithsonian Institution, and the National Audubon Society.

"For the first time in my life I'm content," she says with satisfaction. "All my life I've known what I wanted to do. Lucky for me I didn't have to wait until I was sixty-five to do it. I'm not willing to forfeit all the freedom I have for the security most people want in their jobs and lives."

The logical question seems to be, "But aren't you lonely out here in the wilderness all by yourself?"

"Never!" she says staunchly. "I have my three cats—Killer Frog, Coon Cat, and Spider Wharton—fifteen chickens, and two roosters. From time to time I'll take in a feral piglet which has been injured. They tame up really nicely. I wish I could have a dog, but the ticks are just too bad over here." As she has been talking, Carol has been cuddling one of the Siamese cats in her lap. She continues, "The wild creatures are my brothers and sisters, too." Carol has kept as pets seagulls, black widow spiders, a rattlesnake called Zebra, a red-winged hawk known as Big Man, spotted salamanders, and a tree frog that lived in a huge brandy snifter for several months.

"Besides,'" she adds, "this island isn't really a wilderness to me. Wilderness is what you call that stuff out there where people don't go—land that has never felt the hand of man. This island has been used for centuries, and there's still people coming over here to get away from it all." Now another cat has jumped on her lap, and she accommodates the two. "I like to be alone and really delve into projects. It's hard to always have someone else around. I guess maybe I'm a kind of a misfit by now, but this lifestyle suits me."

The description does not match the picture of this vivacious, youthful woman of thirty-seven who wears tiny gold studs in her ears and flashes a smile as radiant as any American toothpaste ad. I asked Carol to explain.

Carol grew up in Rochester, New York in a typical suburban setting. Her father worked there for the Kodak Company before he was transferred to their plant in Atlanta. Carol remembers that she always felt different.

"My parents were so conforming to society, so conservative. I was an only child, and they wanted me to be a perfect little lady. No animals were allowed in the house, and my mother always told me it wasn't ladylike to play with frogs or to get muddy in swamps. So, of course, I went outdoors more and more to find animals for comfort and companionship. Some of the best times I had were floating in an old inner tube down the Chattahoochee River with my German shepherd swimming beside me. I had a dog and a bedroll—what else did I need?" She went on, "I was the only human being there. It was like my own personal river. I don't go near it anymore. It hurts my heart to see it the way it is, full of garbage and pieces of broken styrofoam coolers. We all want some things to remain static, the way they were. Anyway, I guess the whole time I was growing up I was almost a disgrace to my folks.

"Then when I got to college in the early 1960's, I began to find other people who felt the same way I did. It took me a long time to build up my self-confidence and follow my natural bent for animals and zoology. Up to then no one had encouraged me at all. Then a really nice woman—a fellow student who had married at fourteen, had four kids, and had finally come back to school for her master's degree—urged me to stay in college and be a misfit, if that's what it amounted to. Right about then I quit trying to make everyone else happy. All that did was cause everyone to become unhappy."

Carol didn't quite get her degree because she married a zoology professor at her university instead. Yet her education continued as she helped him run field trips, set up labs, do library research, and write up papers. The marriage lasted two years and then "evaporated," to quote Carol. She found herself alone in Atlanta with a small house full of animals, a pickup truck, and a German shepherd named Catfish. At this point she took a job with the Georgia Natural Areas Council which would have far-reaching effects on her life. She teamed up with Sam Candler, a philanthropist and amateur naturalist to explore, survey, catalog, and register outstanding wild places in the state. Since Georgia is one of the largest states east of the Mississippi, and is less developed than most, it still has considerable wildlife and wildlands. As part of Carol and Sam's survey, they plotted the ranges of river frogs and picked up "DOR's" (dead on road animals). The skulls, pelts, and skeletons, later turned over to the University of Georgia museum, provided invaluable information about Georgia's wildlife.

In the process of combing the state, Sam and Carol developed a strong hatred of the U.S. Army engineers and their channelization and dam projects. They found that the Soil Conservation Service and Corps of Engineers had tampered with at least 166 watersheds in the state in an ill-advised effort to practice flood control on small streams and rivers. Their method was to cut the timber back one hundred feet from any stream, then widen, deepen, and straighten it with a drag line. The effects on the southern rivers and swamps were tragic. There could be little recovery of plants or wildlife or of the natural drainage pattern after such massive surgery.

Carol, Sam, Carol's ex-husband, and many others protested, pointing out that these southern rivers had been flooding the land since time immemorial and leaving an annual gift of rich silt to fertilize the land. They explained how swamps are the natural storage areas of flood waters and serve to recharge the aquifers which supply water to the coastal plains of Georgia. Swamps can clean pollutants from the water—human wastes, toxic pesticides, petroleum spills—and turn them into organic material useful to the entire biotic community. For example, they showed that six miles of a typical Georgia coastal stream has the same cleansing action as a city sewer plant serving fifty thousand people. They also described southern river swamps as the last truly wild places left in the Southeast, the last refuges of many rare animals, and the last sanctuary for city-sick people. Channelization, they predicted, would cause up to 50 percent mortality among the wildlife and fisheries by impoverishing the ecosystem. After the drag lines got done working, the minnows, turtles, otters, coons, hackberries, catfish, tree frogs, deer, and trees, which are interrelating and producing energy in the food chain, would be destroyed. And ultimately human beings, who are the benefactors of all this wealth, would be hurt.

It was at this time that Carol and Sam attracted notice through a 1973 article by John McPhee in the *New Yorker* magazine describing their natural area survey work and their conservation fight against channelization. Subsequently, these two dedicated naturalists had the honor of escorting Jimmy Carter, then governor of Georgia, down the Chattahoochee River. For Carol, coming back many years after she had floated there with her German shepherd, it was quite a change. In the four hundred miles that it travels through the state, the Chattahoochee is nearly wild—that is, until it enters Atlanta. There it is subjected to millions of gallons of raw and partially treated sewage; hot effluent from power plants; and leaching and seeping of salt and petroleum products from highways, parking lots, and storm sewers. The purpose in canoeing Carter down the Chattahoochee was to show him the flagrant abuse of this river and to convince him of the need for conservation and land-use planning.*

While Carol was traveling for the Natural Areas Council, she came out to survey many of the barrier islands—the so-called Golden Isles of Georgia. She loved them at once. This feeling, coupled with her desperate desire to move out of the city, led her to take a closer look at the islands. She decided to take a job as caretaker on an island estate, and this led to her eventually settling there. Now she leaves only once or twice a year, usually for an annual booksale in Atlanta or perhaps an important public hearing relating to the conservation of the islands, or to buy Christmas presents.

Carol has never been seriously ill or hurt on the island, but she usually gets sick when she leaves it (all those germs and people on the mainland, she explains). There are diamondback rattlers and cottonmouths all over the island, so she takes proper precautions when hiking through the palmettos or dense swamp grass and never walks out at night without boots and a flashlight. Carol has

---

*Subsequently it has been legislated to be a national river park.

always had a feline grace and agility. Her five-foot, six-inch, 120-pound frame is that of a tumbler; she can stand on one hand and drink a glass of wine with the other, and until recently she could climb any tree and jump and catch any animal. Now she stops to think before doing it. "Maybe that's getting older, or growing up, or taking safety precautions. I don't know. But it *is* a long way to the hospital from here. Otherwise, I'm far safer alone in this tangled bit of back-country Georgia than in any city."

Carol's volatile Sagittarian nature keeps her moving. When she's not hammering on her house, or cataloging her specimens, or feeding and playing with her animals, she is cruising the beach in a friend's borrowed jeep. A day spent with Carol is an active one. Driving down the beach, she never stops scanning the sand, the dunes, the circling vultures, the sea. Her broad Aussie hat, in which are stuck various feathers and a pencil, protects her tan face and long braids from the sun and wind. She brakes the jeep to a halt. A four-foot fish, picked clean save for head and tail, lies at the high water mark. Carol jumps out and investigates the skeleton, then measures its length, jots in her notebook. Back in the jeep, she cruises on. Next it's an immature common loon partially buried in the sand. Again Carol measures, pokes, unbends wings, postulates the cause of death. The young bird is very gaunt. Did it starve? Why? She throws it up on the closest dunes. "Food for the buzzards," she explains. The next stop is at a string of shells left by the waves. Sea pens, cockles, moon shells, and whelks lie in pretty disarray. Carol picks out two huge paired cockles. "I use them to bake in," she tells me. "My old ones are cracking. I'll make some stuffing and roast a nice chicken for supper tonight."

Another loon, this one sticky with black tar, lies ahead. And then a pelican. Carol marvels at its huge inflatable pouch with the delicate tracery of blood vessels. And so it goes. The sea gulls and terns wheel and cry. The sun plays hide-and-seek with an approaching cold front. A group of shrimp boats put out to sea. Carol stops, gets out, and stands with her arms akimbo on her slender hips, gazing at them.

"Those shrimpers are one of the chief *un*natural forces threatening the turtles," she states emphatically. "There are almost fourteen hundred vessels licensed in Georgia for commercial shrimping, including the 'weekend warriors.' Those are just folks who go out and catch bait on Saturdays and Sundays. But the big commercial boats—they are the *real* threat. One conservative study in 1975 estimated a capture of 9,417 turtles by commercial shrimpers during a six-and-a-half-month season. That's 30.7 turtles per boat per year!" she says agonizingly, unconsciously grasping the sharp hunting knife which is always strapped to her wide belt. "About half the boats throw them back, the other half don't care. They view turtles as a nuisance to haul up and a danger to their nets.

"Now if you plug in all the other unnatural factors . . ." she stopped abruptly and shook her head despairingly. "Lights on the highways and in houses upset the nesting females and the hatchlings, causing them to respond negatively to their internal signals. Why, I've seen young turtles just out of the nest turn from their way back to the sea and follow a vehicle onto the beach. Then they become sitting ducks to all kinds of death traps—predatory birds, ghost crabs, being run over under wheels, and so on.

"And then there's their habitat being destroyed. Every shoreline from Virginia to Texas is getting chopped up, built up, and developed with homes, hotels, and condominiums. All those lights! Those turtles which nest on lighted beaches are doomed—both adult females and youngsters. At least here," she spread her arms wide, "there are no lights on the beach at night. It's the way it was in 1500, 500, 1 A.D."

We continued driving down the beach, Carol shouting above the wind about the turtles. "If you add in all the normal *natural* limiting factors facing the turtles—coons, ghost crabs, gulls—you get a survival of eggs and young of maybe 25 percent on the beaches. And an overall survival to adulthood of probably less than 1 percent. That's why I think those shrimpers are so critical to the species' survival." She suddenly decelerated the jeep and turned squarely to face me.

"Did you ever see a drowned turtle?" she demanded, brown eyes turning liquid with tears. "You open the lungs and see salt water pouring out of this superb, healthy sea turtle. You know it got caught in a shrimp net and was towed along helplessly by the force of the drag under water until it drowned. Or if it does get hauled aboard alive, the shrimpers may shoot it in the head and dump the body overboard. In my opinion, the shrimping industry is inducing serious mortality among turtles.

"Actually, there now is a special double shrimp net with big mesh outside and a smaller mesh inside. It serves to shunt out the turtles and still catch shrimp. It also excludes jellyfish, which are a big annoyance to shrimpers. The safety net device cuts down the overall catch of shrimp by only 10 percent, so it's not such a big price to pay for saving such beautiful creatures."

The jeep picked up speed again as Carol turned her attention to the beach and its flotsam and jetsam.

"But it can never be the way it was," I yelled at her, gesturing around at the island and the sea.

"No," she shouted back, "but we can do something about educating shrimpers, protecting wild beaches, and shooting hogs. When I first came out here and began patrolling, not one single nest survived the poachers and predators. Now it's different. We *do* have the power to change those circumstances."

That night a tangerine full moon rose slowly above the salt marsh behind Carol's house. A floodtide was creeping in among the spartina cordgrass and covering the salt marsh with silver plate. We stood silently, looking out from a sand bluff under the live oaks. "At times like this I imagine that's a quiet lake in Michigan or New York State," she said wistfully.

"Would you like to go back?"

"No, no, this is my home. I don't want to go anywhere else. There's so much to do. Someone has to take care of things here. I could never go back and live on the mainland or enter the mainstream of civilization again."

I was reminded of the acknowledgment in a National Marine Fishery Service report written in 1977 about sea turtle captures in Georgia. It reads, "We are compelled to singularly acknowledge the valuable contribution of Carol Ruckdeschel; sea turtles have no greater ambassador."

I glanced at the lithe woman beside me. Her face was in shadow beneath the broad-brimmed hat, two long braids hanging down jauntily, the hunting knife glinting in the moonlight. I gazed out over the silvery inundated marsh where a clapper rail squawked briefly. I'm glad Carol is here.

Chapter 15

Margaret Stewart

The Frog Professor

THE MEADOW LAY green and vibrant, and the air hummed with the singing of frogs. A cool evening breeze rustled the tawny grasses. On the distant horizon the high hills of the Nyika Plateau stood barely visible against the hazy blue African sky. It was October, spring in Central Africa, and the air was smokey from thousands of bush fires. No rain had fallen since last March, but the wet season would soon begin.

A tall, black-haired women in high rubber·boots moved slowly through the little swale. In one hand she carried a collecting net; in the other, a canvas sack. From time to time she swished the net vigorously through the grass, then gently emptied its contents into the sack. Already she had deposited a dozen frogs, two toads, and a small lizard inside. Occasionally she straightened up from her work to listen to a distant bellowing sound. Thinking it was oxen, which were used locally as beasts of burden, she bent again to her task. As shadows lengthened, Meg Stewart turned and slogged out of the meadow up toward the small forestry station near a pine plantation.

On the porch Meg saw her husband intently scanning the rolling grasslands with a pair of powerful binoculars. The minute he saw her, he started beckoning furiously. "My God, Margaret, where have you been?" he greeted her anxiously. "Didn't you hear the lions roaring? Come on up here!"

Dr. Meg Stewart botanizing with a hand lens around a stone wall in northern New York State. Photo by Anne LaBastille.

"Lions?" she said uncertainly. "I thought it was the oxen."

"No, no," he grimaced. "It was the lions that live back in the pines. They broke into the corral and killed an ox this afternoon. It's really causing a hullabaloo among the Africans. I'm glad you're back safely."

Sinking down on a rocking chair, Meg drew off her boots, wiped clean her peaches-and-cream face, and removed her broad-brimmed hat. She sighed with relief. "Well, I'm glad to be back, too, Paul, even though we both know that lions almost never harm humans except under rare circumstances."

With that calm academic comment both biologists fell silent, gazing out over the six-thousand-foot plateau where zebras and antelope roamed. As darkness fell, they went indoors, lit a fire in the hearth, and ate supper. Outside the lions continued to roar.

It was 1963, and the couple had recently come to Malawi, then called Nyasaland, on their respective year-long sabbaticals from the State Univeristy of New York (SUNY) at Albany. It wasn't an ordinary vacation. Dr. Margaret M. Stewart, a herpetologist and associate professor of biology, was planning to study frogs, lizards, and snakes. Her husband Paul, an ecologist, would make an evaluation of the Nyika game reserve in hopes that it might become the country's first national park.

Malawi is often called the Switzerland or Scotland of Africa because of its rugged mountains which rise sharply from the plains. It surpasses much of the rest of the continent in natural beauty and variety of landscapes—magnificent blue Lake Nyasa (now Lake Malawi), massive rock outcrops, rolling green hills, and mountains rising to nine thousand feet or more. Meg found working on the high Nyika Plateau safe and pleasant. The cool temperatures, lack of poisonous snakes, and absence of *bilharzia* (snail fever, which is endemic to much of lowland Africa) made it especially easy to do field work there.

Down in the village of Rumpi, where the biologists had rented a cottage, complete with servants and an English garden, the situation was different. Leopards sometimes walked through their backyard. Meg once found a tiger snake curled up in her toilet, and a night adder in the garage. Spitting cobras were fairly common, being attracted by the rats and mice around the natives' huts within the fenced compound. Meg had had a narrow escape right in the front yard of this cottage, in fact. She had wandered out one evening to observe a puddle of water which formed in the grassy driveway after every rainstorm; amphibians of all kinds could be seen there. She heard something large rustling in the grass, something too big to be a frog. Instantly she jumped back. A spitting cobra "stood up," about two-and-a-half feet tall, and gave a threat display. These snakes are notorious for their ability to squirt venom into the eyes of intended victims as far as eight feet away. Meg had always wanted to see one and was so fascinated that she forgot to be afraid. Besides, the snake was not aiming straight at her in an attack posture, but rather behaved as though out hunting. Soon it dropped down and slithered away. Meg discovered a huge toad by the puddle, looking like a sack of jelly. Apparently the cobra had bitten it, preparatory to eating, before she came by. Already the venom had digested the toad's insides by hemolytic (blood-destroying) action. She left the toad by the puddle, hoping that the cobra would return to eat it so that she might get another look at the snake. But it didn't come back, she reported sadly.

"You soon get accustomed to all the snakes and other 'creepy crawlies' in Africa," she explains. "It becomes a way of life. One is always careful. The natives are sometimes bitten because they walk around barefoot at night without flashlights. Since they cannot afford shoes or batteries, they're vulnerable and deathly afraid of snakes. Otherwise, people are seldom harmed. Even the tiger snake in my john wasn't so bad. They aren't aggressive or very poisonous, and they feed heavily on geckos, small nocturnal lizards which often live inside houses. The geckos are good to have around to control the many insects. I had a great grey tree frog on my window sills for months. He just sat there looking like a Big Mac hamburger—same size, too. He liked to stay dry, being especially adapted to arid conditions. When the rains came, he left. I really missed him."

Cool words—and why not? Margaret has spent almost fifty years outdoors, first as a child, then training as a herpetologist in school, and later doing field work in out-of-the-way places. She always liked the idea of doing something extraordinary. She feels she was conditioned to being different at an early age and had no desire to live the humdrum lives of so many people she knew. From the time she was little Margaret found all reptiles and amphibians fascinating, not only for their beauty, but because so little is known about their biology.

Her main purpose in coming to Malawi was to study as many of the native species of frogs and toads as possible and to produce an illustrated field guide to these amphibians. No such work existed, other than in obscure scientific papers, and she wanted a book from which anyone could learn about the beautiful amphibians of Africa.

Meg enlisted the help of many friendly Africans in her collecting work. At first, it was difficult. Since reptiles often feed on frogs

and toads, they usually occur in the same places, and the natives'
dread of snakes hindered them. Some Africans considered Meg as
something akin to a witch because she would handle snakes and
other reptiles at all. Slowly and patiently she had to explain her
purpose to the villagers. After the first few days the men would
relax and provide superb assistance. Without exception, her African helpers and colleagues treated her with respect, dignity,
courtesy, and servility, which she ascribes to the colonial tradition
left by the British.

Meg found somewhat different attitudes among the African wom-
en. She recalls the day she drove into a tiny hamlet in a Land
Rover. She was soon surrounded by curious women and children,
surprised to see a white female there. "How many children have
you got? Where are your children?" they asked. When Meg explained she had none, they turned hostile and started murmuring
among themselves. Meg quickly explained that she taught other
people's children. That seemed to appease the women, but Meg
was glad to drive away from the crowd, which apparently believed
that a woman's chief function in life was to bear young. In general,
Meg recalls with amusement, most natives she has worked with
think all white people are a little crazy but calmly accept the weird
projects they work on.

Sometimes the natives were not quite as helpful as she could
have wished. For example, little boys would catch frogs for her but
drag them back on a string to avoid touching them. By the time
Meg examined the specimens, they were almost unrecognizable.
One time an African brought her a huge live python. All told, Meg
collected and studied forty species of amphibians in Malawi, out
of the total of sixty-four varieties now known in that country.

Many amphibians in the tropics are extremely colorful. "You
cannot help being attracted by their brilliant patterns," says Meg.
"That's one factor compelling me to work on this group of animals.
Some are so magnificent that it's a more aesthetic experience than
seeing a work of art. I found one species of frog on the Nyika
Plateau that had ten polymorphs (color patterns). At first I thought
I was seeing ten different species, but they were really only color
variations of the same species."

Meg loves to teach that toads and frogs have played an important
role in human history. "The Bible mentions 'plagues of frogs' in

Egypt, so they evidently made a large impact on people along the Nile. Many native tribes have revered amphibians and named gods after them. Pre-Columbian Indians in Panama worshipped a toad as earth mother; their gold work is rich with figures of frogs and toads. Other tribes have stuffed them as decorations and used them as lucky charms. The Indians who live high in the Darien jungle of the Central American isthmus squeeze the secretions from the skin glands of the 'poison arrow' frogs and tip their deadly blowdarts and arrows with it. Many forest people listen for the cessation of frog and toad calls as an indication of danger.

"Even in our own times," she goes on, "certain species of frogs have been vital for pregnancy tests, as laboratory animals, and for beginning biology students. One never knows when results will have direct significance for humanity. Indirectly, any knowledge we have about populations and ecology of other animals may help our understanding of the ecological relationships in which human beings and other life forms live. Besides, we can get answers much faster when we study amphibians than when we study similar processes in *Homo sapiens!*

"In South Africa there is an appreciation for frogs matched in this country only by our fondness for birdwatching and horseracing. The people hold 'frog Olympics,' which draw thousands of spectators. In Puerto Rico the everpresent *coqui* is very much a part of the culture of the island, and everyone knows this little frog. Then, too, amphibians are very unusual. The Goliath frog of West Africa, for example, is the size of a small dog, while the tiny tree frog of Cuba is less than half an inch long. Then there's the giant salamander of Japan, a five-foot fellow. And the snoring frog, which lives in Jamaica but is endangered by forest destruction, makes a sound exactly like a human snore."

Meg thinks that the ecology and behavior of amphibians are by far their most intriguing aspects. She explains that amphibians form an important link in the food chain by transferring insect biomass to bird-reptile-mammal biomass; that is, 'amphibs' eat bugs and then are eaten in turn by the higher vertebrates. Amphibians, like birds, are ecologically safe insecticides!

While in Malawi, Meg had a nasty experience with another of her loves—snakes. A native brought in a Zanzibar burrowing viper about twelve inches long. It looked very much like a harmless, glossy burrowing snake. It happened that her husband was there and took the reptile, grabbing it behind the head as any good biologist does. To his surprise the snake's jaws began moving from side to side and two long fangs emerged sideways! Such movement by a snake is extremely unusual; this species is capable of independently erecting its flexible fangs and protruding them from the side of the mouth as an adaptation to catching rodents, its principle food, in burrows. For this reason, the burrowing viper has probably bitten more experienced herpetologists than any other African species. Paul released the adder immediately, but not before he'd been bitten alongside the nail of his left forefinger.

Meg immediately began searching through the only field guide available. She was shaking so much she could hardly hold the book. She read that the bite was "usually not fatal." Small comfort! Paul was already experiencing intense pain in his fingers and back of the hand. She killed the snake to make a positive identification and administered one ampoule of polyvalent tropical antisnakebite serum, hoping that it might counteract the venom and not set up an allergic reaction. Her husband spent a sleepless night, wracked by pain, swelling, fever, headache, and later a large oozing blister. On the next day he was transported to a hospital fifty miles away and treated for secondary infection. Weeks later part of the finger began to heal; however, it gradually shrank to two-thirds its normal size due to tissue loss. A year later Paul still had trouble bending it.

In spite of the shock of this incident, both biologists continued with their field work and writing. Meg did all the illustrations and photographs for her book—more than eighty, all told. She traveled to the University of Natal and the University of Rhodesia to examine museum collections and identify her specimens. Coming back to the states via London, she followed up at the British Museum, the American Museum of Natural History, the Harvard Museum of Comparative Zoology, and the Field Museum in Chicago. These final checks enabled her to construct a key for identification of the various species and complete her illustrations. Meg's book, *Amphibia of Malawi,* published by the SUNY Press, was the first such guide for African amphibians.

Meg's dream to return to Africa with Paul for five more years of study was shattered by their divorce. So, too, her romantic, and long-sought goal of being married to a biologist with whom she could work compatibly in the field hadn't worked. So she devoted herself to teaching and soon became a full professor at SUNY, where she still teaches. As she explains sadly, her divorce had nothing to do with professional conflicts; it was strictly personal differences. She and her second husband, George, who is also a professor and a mathematician, have been married ten years. They get along beautifully in the field and have coauthored a scientific paper. "It's a plus when both partners are professionals and busy with their own interests," Meg smiles.

Meg's sunny, warm nature, scientific expertise, and contagious enthusiasms for her subject have won the regard and affection of many students. "I love to see *them* get excited about the things that excite *me*," she exclaims. "That's one reason I chose teaching as a career. It's the best way I can transmit my concerns, attitudes, and excitement to others. Luckily, my classes are field courses, and I take my graduate students on field trips and expeditions. I interact best with people in the field, in the natural world. That's when I can really attract their attention and pass something on. We're on a one-to-one basis; it's not straight lecturing to large groups. We have a great time in the wilderness, and the students love it. Many of my students are from New York City or Long Island and have never been exposed to the outdoors. Some of them come back to visit years later and tell me that a particular field trip with me was the most exciting event in their lives. That's nice to hear!

"The other reason I went into teaching is because the academic life offers such a wide range of work. I can interact with people part of the year, plus have my summers and vacations free for field work and writing, plus do my own research. It's got to be the most fascinating *and* frustrating profession I know." Dr. Stewart's dedication to her students won her the SUNY Distinguished Teaching Professor award in 1977.

Meg attributes her love of the outdoors and of travel to wild places to a number of factors. She spent her first seventeen years on a hundred-acre farm in rural North Carolina. Most of her family's time was occupied with pure survival: farming crops, raising stock, and growing flowers for sale. Meg's life demanded that she spend a lot of time outdoors, and in her free time she and her older sister and brother explored the surrounding woods, streams, and fields. Her mother often took the children on picnics and walks, teaching them the local flora and fauna. "My mother had a great love and curiosity about the natural world, and she instilled those qualities in us," Meg reminisces. "My sister loved nature, too, and steered my interests toward learning bird songs, nests, butterflies, and so on. My brother made a telescope and showed me the rings around Saturn, Jupiter's moons, and other astronomical delights."

Then she read a lot. Osa and Martin Johnson, the famous pioneering filmers of exotic cultures and wildlife, made a deep impression on Meg. Osa was her idol. And the *National Geographic* was her escape to the wide, wide world. Furthermore, a few cousins were foreign missionaries, and Meg's mother often sent money to help support their work abroad, so it was common in Meg's household to speak of far-away lands.

When she went to college (largely supported by the "flower money" her mother saved for this purpose), Meg found ornithology, zoology, and marine biology courses and field trips the most rewarding. How did she decide to specialize in amphibians? Again, her early life made a lasting impression. "We got our drinking water from a spring at the foot of the hill, and when I went for water, I amused myself by watching salamanders crawling around on the spring floor. Catching frogs was a frequent pleasure as well. But actually," she admits, "I chose that group because so little was known about them, and finding good research topics was no problem. I reasoned that an area relatively free from human competition should be most appropriate for a specialty."

Meg did both her master's and doctoral theses on the ecology, physiology, and morphology of salamanders. Part of her time was spent at the Highlands Biological Station in western North Carolina, the "salamander capital of the world." This was the young biologist's first contact with the wilderness. She began climbing and hiking in the Great Smoky Mountains.

"I found it a glorious and exhilarating experience, and I never got enough of wandering through the then-primeval forests. Munching sandwiches on top of Whitesides Mountain, with views over the vast ranges of the Blue Ridge, surely 'set' my love of mountains and climbing them." When she moved to New York State, the glens of central New York and the Adirondack trails were her favorites for getting away. It's the peace, serenity, and fascination of exploring which appeals to Margaret most about the wilderness. "I can deal with it at my own choosing," she comments. "Besides, going into the wilderness is the only way I know to escape that 'madding crowd.' "

Meg Stewart first went to the Caribbean in 1966 as a visiting lecturer to the Caribbean Biological Center in Jamaica. She was so amazed by the frogs she found that she resolved to go back. This idea was strengthened after she remarried. Her husband George had no interest in long treks to Africa, but he did like the Caribbean, where they could go more easily, more cheaply, and more often. So Meg transferred her herpetological interests there. She could study many unknown aspects of amphibian behavior much closer to home. Her first Caribbean research trip was to Jamaica in 1973. By combining their sabbatical leaves, she and George were able to make two long field expeditions there.

Meg's research goal this time was to study the little-understood Jamaican species of one of the largest genera of frogs in the world, *Eleutherodactylus*. Specifically, she wished to compare the ecological and physiological requirements of four different species of the frogs, two that are native to Jamaica and two introduced by human beings. The newcomers appeared to be doing well and displacing the native species. Why? It seems a simple question, but the answers are hard to find.

First, the intrepid woman spent a lot of time digging up piles of old coconut husks which dot the coastal coconut palm groves of Jamaica. These husk-heaps are a favored habitat for frogs—Meg found up to 150 frogs per husk pile. It was hot, heavy work, made more tricky by spiders, scorpions, and eight-inch-long centipedes with poisonous pincers.

Meg discovered that the native frogs were far more sensitive to heat and drought than the exotics. Therefore, the invaders are in a good position to move in, adapt, and occupy niches undesirable for the native frogs. Such behavior is similar to the way English sparrows, pigeons, and cattle egrets, to name a few non-native species, have taken over habitats in America that became inhospitable for natives due to human disturbance.

As part of her investigation Meg carried frogs back to her university in plastic bags within insulated containers. In the laboratory she houses them in terraria and feeds them fruit flies, beetle larvae, crickets, and mealworms. Besides the physiological testing being done on these tropical creatures, Meg is attempting to breed them in captivity in order to study their life history and growth rates. This may be the first time these species have reproduced in captivity. So far, she's been quite successful.

As interesting as her field work has been, the political and racial upheavals in Jamaica have made it too difficult for Meg to continue research there at present. She has turned to nearby Puerto Rico, where she can study the same group of frogs and feel safer working alone or with one or two graduate students in the bush.

Dr. Stewart's scientific involvement includes other animals and wildlands besides amphibians in the Caribbean. Her research papers reflect work done on small mammals in New York State; timber rattlers in the Allegany Indian Reservation of southwestern New York; the marbled and two-lined salamanders of the eastern United States; and minkfrogs, bullfrogs, and green frogs in the Adirondacks. She also belongs to an impressive number of professional societies, including Sigma Xi, American Women in Science, and the East African Wildlife Society. She's been listed in *Who's Who*, *Who's Who of American Women*, the *World Who's Who of Women*, *2000 Women of Achievement*, and *American Men and Women of Science*. In 1979 she was President of the Society for the Study of Amphibians and Reptiles, the largest herpetological organization in the world.

Meg has definite opinions about the roles of women and men in professional and academic field work. "My gut feeling is that many men try to prevent females from working out-of-doors. They think women are incapable, or they fear the competition. I first encountered this resistance as a graduate student at Cornell University, a male-dominated place. Then when I started looking for my first job, one university wrote back that they had never hired a female professor and would not do so, but I could go ahead and apply if I wanted to. That attitude has continued right up to today. It was reflected in the tone of the rejection of my first National Science Foundation proposal (1972). 'A woman can't go to the wilds of Jamaica and study frogs!' sort of reaction. Even today certain of my male colleagues feel insecure and jealous because I'm a full professor. One even told me that I'd cut off his balls! Both men and women seem afraid of an educated woman. The women are envious because they'd like to be doing some of the things I'm doing, and the men resent me because I have been successful in getting grants and interesting projects. Of course, not all people are like this. Some compliment and encourage me. But still, it's often a lonely existence.

"Curiously," she goes on, "the wilderness is the only place I've not felt discrimination or been afraid of being molested by men, where I'm not afraid of being alone. This fear is a major factor in the life of any woman. I've walked for miles across the high Misuku Hills in Malawi, and to the top of Blue Mountain in Jamaica. At Cranberry Lake Biological Station in the Adirondack Mountains, I roamed freely, working alone in bogs and swamps. None of these wild places made me uneasy."

Concerning her feelings and approach to female graduate students, Meg says she tries not to discriminate in any way. "I respond to good, bright students who do their work well, and I attempt to give them the confidence I lacked when I was younger. I've been accused once or twice of being too hard on women students, but I think it was said by students who got poor grades. I always encourage girls to do the things I was so fearful of as a student. There are so many more opportunities open to women today and, of course, the whole job market is far more accessible than when I searched for my first job.

"Some professors think that males tend to be more aggressive and curious as students, but I find plenty of women with those qualities. These are individual characteristics. I'm seeing many more talented and self-confident women students than ever before. And I like to see girls stand on their abilities, not on their sex appeal."

Meg's biggest commitment right now besides her ongoing research in Puerto Rico, is trying to save the Pine Bush, a wildland-

relic of the Ice Age which lies between the cities of Albany and
Schenectady, New York. It's an odd, miniaturized world of twisted
pitch pines, scrub oaks, clear creeks, emerald-green swales, and
sand dunes. Beneath the Pine Bush lies a giant aquifer (water table)
of pure water capable of supplying thousands of people. Biologically
speaking, the Pine Bush is a treasure trove of rare species and a
unique biotic community. The sandy oasis has over thirteen
hundred species of plants, seventy-three of which are protected
in New York State, plus several kinds of amphibians and reptiles
rarely found elsewhere north of Long Island and the New Jersey
Pine Barrens. Prominent scientists from all over the world have
studied the life of these barrens over the years. One such was the
renowned author Vladimir Nabokov, who came to see the rare
Karner blue butterfly, which is threatened by development of the
Pine Bush. Meg Stewart often penetrates the Bush with her biology
classes and conducts field trips for conservationists and naturalists,
both independently and under the auspices of SUNY and conservation groups.

The Pine Bush used to cover well over twenty-five thousand
acres, but today it encompasses barely four thousand. Four-fifths
of it is gone, disturbed, or developed. Urban sprawl—condominiums, office buildings, apartment complexes, highways, industrial
parks, and sand-mining operations—have carved away chunks. The
reasons Meg is fighting to preserve the Bush from such unneeded
building are many.

"Ecologically, this is one of the most unusual areas in the whole
state. It's neither wilderness nor virgin countryside. Yet once
you're in the Bush, it 'feels' wild even though you may hear the distant
hum of traffic on the Northway. This is the only green pocket
within easy reach of the entire metropolitan area. It could become
the Central Park of Albany. This will be extremely important as
gasoline shortages prevent people from traveling to more distant
recreational areas.

"People can cross-country ski, hike, picnic, fish, horseback ride,
camp, and study nature here. There are endangered animals that
deserve protection. My biology classes love their trips here, and
at least ten other colleges, and I don't know how many high schools,
make use of the area. Damage to this fragile ecosystem is irrevers-

ible. Once you start bulldozing those sand dunes that took ten thousand years to evolve, the creation can be undone in two days. Worse, sewage, oil and chemical spills, and pollution in general, easily leach through the porous sand and glacial gravels right down to the aquifer, which lies about ten feet or less below the surface. If we lose this, we lose our best source of drinking water anywhere around. Who wants to drink the Hudson River? It has already been ruined!"

On a broader scale Margaret worries about endangered species everywhere. She's deeply concerned with the balance and imbalance of nature. In her lectures she impresses on students that time is running out. Wrinkling her brow behind horn-rimmed glasses, she predicts, "Unless we slow down the present rate of destruction, most species of large wild mammals could be extinct in thirty years—and *Homo sapiens* may well head the endangered species list!

"Human actions have been responsible for 75 percent of all animal extinctions over the past few hundred years. In recent times we have not been close enough to the natural world to feel a responsibility for it. We have been users, victims of a 'frontier philosophy'—move into a pioneer land, take as much as you can, and don't worry about the future. Things are bad, and the time to reverse the trend is long overdue."

Then, abruptly, she flashes the smile which lights up her face and which has endeared her to so many young people. "Human awareness is improving," she says. "Animals such as the trumpeter swan, beaver, bison, and wood duck have made real comebacks from near extinction. If we combine informed citizenry, protective legislation, world cooperation, and money, then we may be able to save the plants and animals—and man."

She laughs. "And, of course, I mean woman, too!"

Chapter 16

Rebecca Lawton

Crusader for Whitewater

Becca lawton braked to a halt at the edge of the lookout, hopped out of her car, and leaned against the high wire fence. I followed slowly behind. Looming in front of us was a giant mass of grey rocks and soil—New Melones, the largest earth-filled dam in the world. In the canyon bottom at the base of the huge bulwark, two round culverts gushed water. That was the Stanislaus River, or what was left of it. The river had been trapped, harnessed, and beaten, and was about to be buried. The next day, April 1, 1979, heavy gates would close the culverts, and the water would start to rise.

Becca stood quietly, staring at the dam, her knuckles white where she gripped the fence. "That's the river where I learned to raft and kayak, and where a lot of my friends did, too," she said grimly. "It was one of John Muir's favorites. Can you believe what they're doing to it?" She shook her head in angry disbelief.

We peered over the edge of the lookout. Far below us spindly looking transmission towers with spidery lines marched away from the turbines and generating plant, up the steep canyon walls, and over the greening California hills. "What a price people in this country are willing to pay for promises of power and irrigation!" Becca exclaimed. "Why, the 'Stan' is probably the most well-traveled river in the United States, the most popular short whitewater

The Stanislaus River sparkles in the California sun as Becca Lawton rests during her farewell kayak run. Photo by Anne LaBastille.

run. Over sixty thousand rafters and kayakers ran it and the South Fork of the American River in 1975. You should see its rapids all sparkling in the sun, its limestone canyons, its . . ." The professional river runner stopped abruptly and ground a tear from her eye with a tight fist. Turning quickly, she said, "Come on. I'll show you. You'll see for yourself why Bill McGinnis, one of the most famous river runners in the West, said, 'The Stanislaus can supply more food for men's souls than it can ever supply for their bellies.' "

With the skill of a racing driver, Becca maneuvered her old Volkswagen, crowned with a beat-up but still-beautiful kayak, down hairpin mountain roads to a bridge seven miles upriver near the town of Sonora. "Parrott's Ferry," she indicated as we parked. "This is our battle line. The Army Corps of Engineers versus Friends of the River. The Friends are the recognized conservation group to protect rivers from damming, and shoreline development, and erosion damage caused by clearcutting," she explained. "I help them with the North Coast River chapter, which I've come to the Stanislaus to represent."

We untied the kayak and shouldered it, the paddle, and a canvas bag full of wet suits, sandwiches, beer, and cameras. Together we lugged everything along a trail bordering the river. The grass was emerald green, dotted with small blue flowers. Overhead the poplars were unfurling fresh leaflets. Warblers, magpies, woodpeckers, and kingfishers sang, croaked, tapped, and rattled. The water was running clear, green, and fast between steep, pine-clad slopes. The air smelled fantastic. Becca quickened her pace, her somber look changing to one of childlike expectation as we neared the river.

"See this flat spot right here?" She motioned with her chin. "I spent a whole summer living under these trees, learning the river, running the rapids every day. We made a sauna of willows and plastic tarps and then jumped into the river afterward. Warm, innocent, summer river nights!" She then motioned toward the river. "Just up ahead are the best rapids."

She dumped her kayak and gear onto a silvery sliver of sand and strode to the water's edge. "It'll be smoking real soon with the spring sun and warm temps melting those snow drifts high up in the Sierra." She rubbed her hands together gleefully, and her eyes scanned the river. Then, suddenly, she remembered—April 1, 1979. Her face saddened, and she turned to me, scuffing at the sand with a worn sneaker toe.

"The Corps plans to inundate the Stanislaus River Canyon from New Melones to here between April and July," she explained morosely. "A few months later they'll begin again to try to fill up the remaining twenty-one miles of canyon behind the dam. Within a year or so the canyon could be buried under as much as 625 feet of water. That means goodbye forever to this wilderness recreation area with its wildlife, old mining towns, pioneer sites, and all the close personal ties people have had with the Stan.

"We're protesting in every peaceful way possible. We've proposed a compromise: to fill the canyon to Parrott's Ferry and no further. That will save at least the upper part of the Stanislaus, which has some of the prettiest rapids, still-water stretches, and canyon walls. If that doesn't work," she prophesied grimly, "we may resort to civil protest. I know people who are considering offering their lives for this river. They won't stand to see it sucked dry."

"You mean they'd die to save the river?" I asked incredulously.

"Perhaps," she sighed. "But before anyone does that, we'll take part in the Stanislaus River Canyon Witness and Encampment, a continuous camp by the riverbanks which will move upstream as the reservoir rises. It's our final opportunity to show the world a dramatic example of the destruction of a living piece of our planet. We can make the burial of the canyon's lower stretch one of the best publicized funerals in history. That *may* save the Stan above Parrott's Ferry. In any case, it'll sure inform the public about the Corps and all its plans to dam more of our country's last wild rivers. You and I will join the Witness tonight," she said, "and camp beside the Stan."

Rebecca began stripping off her clothes and wriggling her long, lanky body into a bathing suit, full wetsuit, wool socks, and rubber booties. I walked to the river's edge and put my hand in. Almost at once my fingers turned numb. "It can't be more than forty-five degrees, Becca," I cautioned her. "Are you sure you want to go out?"

She nodded determinedly. "It may be my last chance. It's my way of saying goodbye to the ol' Stan. I wish I could show you some of the great rapids—Cop Rock, where seven drunk policemen wrapped their boat; Chinese Dog Leg rapids by an old gold mine; Bailey Falls; Death Rock; the Devil's Staircase; and Chicken Falls. There's a path around those last rapids if you're too scared to run 'em."

Becca stood up, tucked her riot of brown hair under a helmet, and grabbed the paddle. She was transformed. The black rubber suit molded her frame to elegant leanness, and the helmet emphasized her wide-set brown eyes, enormous in her thin, delicate face. She slipped into the kayak and pushed off from shore, then turned and smiled back at me sadly. "Here goes my last run."

I watched her dart diagonally across the rapids as lightly as a water beetle. For the next hour she performed what seemed to be a ballet upon water. She zipped into the frothing whitewater, raced downstream, swerved behind giant rocks to rest in their backwater eddies, shot out again, worked her way upstream, glided into still pools, executed a couple of Eskimo rolls (tipping over the kayak and coming back up the other side in a complete 360-degree revolution), and finally paddled back to the beach, dripping and sputtering with laughter. She eased out of her slim craft, drew it onto the sand, and flopped unceremoniously beside me.

As we lunched on cheese sandwiches and beer, the tragedy of the whole situation became apparent to me. This smooth sand beach, the poplar groves, the singing birds, the fragrant pines, those cascading rapids might all disappear in the next few months. I lay on my back and visualized the huge mass of dark water pushing down from above, blotting out the cobalt California sky. It was very depressing. To lighten the mood, I asked Becca how she had become a professional river runner.

"Tim, my older brother, was working as a boatman for ARTA (the American River Touring Association) in 1972 and invited me to go on a trip with him down the Stanislaus. I'd never experienced anything like it before in all my seventeen years," she grinned. "I remember I didn't even take a hairbrush on the trip, I was so excited about going. The other members of the group were from a 'swinging singles' club. I was totally out of place and didn't even know it. Our days were hot and full of waterfights. The rapids were such a new, foreign thing, and the mode of transportation was the cleanest I'd seen before or since. The boatmen exuded unparalleled energy. It was beautiful and refreshing.

"I had plans to go to Alaska and work on the Pipeline, but one of the boatmen talked me into the idea of being a boatwoman and river guide. The more he talked, the better it sounded. And I remembered seeing the Walt Disney film 'Ten Who Dared,' about John Wesley Powell's journey as the first white man to go down the Colorado River. So that winter I interviewed with a small rafting company, Mother Lode Raft Trips, in California. They were looking to balance their crew by hiring women. I got the job and began training that spring in paddle boats on the American River. After rafting down it three times, I 'got my oars.'

"I spent a lot of time on the Stan that summer. It was really our stomping ground. That same fall I rowed the Tuolumne River, which is quite close to the Stanislaus, with an ARTA group. It's a very technically tough trip, with over sixty rapids and canyons. Some river runners call it 'the supreme whitewater adventure.' "

"What's involved in learning to run a river?" I interrupted, opening another bottle of beer.

"You learn to read water," she replied, "and you learn to handle different types of rubber inflatable boats. I've rowed everything in that line from little Avon 'Redcrests' to twenty-two-foot snoutboats. You learn to be fast and well-coordinated. You come to know where the big holes, the 'rooster tails,' and the 'keeper waves' are. Rooster tails are waves that kick up from behind a submerged rock. A keeper can suck your raft back in and hold it in its reverse wave. You need as much momentum as possible to punch through one of those mothers. You can't fight it. Once it's got you, you stay until it spits you out. And you also find out about falling in and swimming safely out. One thing that can happen is that you get pulled down into a whirlpool or deep hole with your life jacket on. The current at the bottom of a hole will eventually push you out of there, but the life jacket hinders this natural safety exit by floating you to the surface—so you have two forces fighting against each other."

"What other dangers are there?" I asked, spellbound.

"Oh, not many," Becca answered calmly. "Mostly it's peaceful and beautiful and nice weather. Of course, in early spring, like now, you need wetsuits and wool clothing, or you could get hypothermia. You also can suffer heatstroke or sunstroke on blistering hot days. And starting out the season everyone earns some blisters from not being in shape. I guess the biggest danger is on land— breaking a leg on rocks, stuff like that."

"What if you flip over in the raft?" I persisted. "Isn't that awfully dangerous? Supposing you got caught on a line or trapped underneath the raft, or your food and camping gear got lost in the water?"

"Those are real dangers, but they can usually be minimized by not making mistakes," she answered firmly. "If you don't concentrate, you pay. The only way to be really safe is to run the river correctly. The only standard of success is to be upright and in one piece at the end of the rapid."

Rebecca stripped off her wetsuit and lay flat to sunbathe. Drowsily she continued her personal account.

"In 1974 ARTA wanted a woman who knew something about natural history to go down the Yampa and Green rivers through Dinosaur National Monument in Utah. So I went and worked a season there. I was overwhelmed by the beauty," she exclaimed. "I was the only boatwoman rowing in Utah then. But I blew the run—made a few mistakes, lost my oars and filled my raft with water once, although I never flipped. That's when I found out a woman can't afford to make mistakes. Even when I make a perfect run and do better than all the boatmen, I might still get a bad letter from a client who felt insecure with me. It used to bother me terribly; it doesn't much anymore, though, since I've become more skilled and boatwomen more accepted. That same summer I had a chance to try the Colorado River through Westwater and Cataract canyons for the first time. What a terrific river!"

The next year Becca returned to Utah and worked under her brother Tim, who was then area manager and head boatman for the Dinosaur and Canyonlands trips.

"It was my best year yet," she smiled. "I moved with the water conditions, north or south. Tim gave me lots of good feedback, and that's real important. Also I began selling the desert to my passengers. Most didn't care much about it at first; they were just along for the thrills. But by the end of the trip they loved it just like I do and wanted to preserve it from the heavy exploitation the Colorado and other river systems are subjected to today.

"In the fall of 1975 I went up to Idaho to train on the Main Salmon River and the Middle Fork of the Salmon. I learned more about rowing up there than anywhere else. And I met Harvey. He's the boatman I live with now.

"The next summer we had to split up temporarily. Harvey went to work in Idaho again, and I was made ARTA's area manager in Utah. I missed being near him, but the management experience was really worthwhile. I lived in a tepee by the Green River near a dinosaur quarry. It was a cozy and easy way to live. I was able to get enough data to write a short paper on the taphonomy of the quarry in Dinosaur National Monument, which was later published in *Contributions to Geology* by the University of Wyoming."

Seeing my puzzled look, she laughed and added, "Taphonomy is what happens to animal remains between death and burial. In the case of those dinosaurs over a thousand bones were transported by ancient Jurassic rivers at flood stage for several miles and then dumped in this quarry area. I found all kinds jumbled up there; it was really an interesting paleoecological study."

"Tell me, Becca," I went on, "what did you do during all those winters?"

"That's what everyone asks," she chuckled. "I finished school at the University of California at Santa Cruz, with a bachelor of science degree in earth sciences. Then I did a few months of volunteer work as a geologist for the National Park Service and later as a physical science technician for the U.S. Geological Survey. Also I worked as a maid and a weaver's apprentice. I learned how to use a large loom. It was during this period that I decided never to buy a big house and fill it with knickknacks that collect dust. Instead I've traveled nomad-style across Canada and the states, visiting friends. And I've even written a couple of historical pieces and a children's book, though it's not yet published. To stay in shape, I swim whenever possible and ride my bike. I do any odd job that'll see me through till spring when the rivers come alive. Usually Harvey and I manage to get in some really wild trips then. For instance, we've made a one-day run through Cross Mountain Canyon on the Yampa, which for a long time was thought to be an 'unrunnable' stretch. My friends figured it was a first for a woman. I also made the first inflatable kayak trip through that canyon—and I hope my last. I'd never do it again; it was just too dangerous. I was also the first woman to row commercially on the Selway in Idaho, which is considered by some to be the most technically difficult whitewater in the United States.

"One of our best private trips was two weeks on the Dolores River in Colorado. We started in mid-April, got snowed on several times, and were visited by cowboys. We watched the San Juan Range of Colorado fade from sight as we approached the LaSal Mountains near Moab, Utah. In the last canyon on the Dolores, Mesa Canyon, spring finally hit us: sego lilies, claret cups, dock, apricot mallow, bee plant, yucca in bloom. On that river trip we realized what it must have felt like to make the early runs on the

Green River and the Middle Fork of the Salmon. We saw few people; we doubted the maps; we got cold; we portaged; we ran rocky rapids that others before and after portaged around; we re-supplied in small towns on the river. I kayaked the two hundred miles; the others rowed rafts. We all had plenty of quiet to watch the river change and enjoy it."

"Which river do you like the best?" I asked.

"Utah rivers are my favorites because I love the desert and some of the still waters in the canyons. But Grand Canyon tops every-thing. I was given my own boat to handle and started running there in September 1977 and half of 1978. Once you've done that, nothing else compares. I like the Grand because of its greater physical challenge."

"Will you go there next summer?" I asked her.

"I hope so, but first Harvey and I are going to work together in Idaho for a while. I've been with ARTA for seven years now, so I have some choice and mobility with them."

The sun was sinking lower, and our beach would soon be in shadow. A late afternoon chill crept into the air. Time to go. Becca stood up and stretched, then suddenly struggled into her wetsuit again. "One last run. Do you mind?" she begged. "Pick me up down at the bridge, O.K.?"

"Sure," was all I could say, thinking again of the river's future.

At sunset we crossed a low bridge and drove down to the ruined town of Old Melones, where the vigil would take place. The first campers were getting settled, and a brooding silence filled the air. Already the giant willows closest to the river bank stood in about three feet of water. Off to our left lay the abandoned mines and tumbled-down walls of this early gold town. Walking around in search of a campsite, we joined other people who were protesting the flooding of the canyon.

"The water's going to rise a foot or more a day starting now," warned one camper. "Don't tent too close to the banks. God, there's gonna be a lot of water in here. That bridge'll be hundreds of feet under."

"Did you know that 85 percent of all the water in the state goes to agriculture?" remarked another. "And we still need more! California's been the leading agricultural state for twenty-five years, with more irrigated land and a greater variety of commercial crops than any other state. California supplies two-thirds of the country's vegetables and fruits. That's one reason the Corps will keep on damming our rivers. The other reason is power. The way our population is skyrocketing we're due to have seven million more people here by 2000 A.D. So naturally our rivers are being dammed."

"But the state's going to grab water anywhere and any way it can," murmured the shadowy figure of Becca. "Each year people in California *waste* many times more water and power than the New Melones Dam and reservoir can produce. Our wild and scenic rivers are really threatened unless people consciously start cutting back on use and unless new sources and techniques are found to produce power and save water."

The group fell silent. It was almost dark. Becca and I moved off to make a campfire and set out our sleeping bags. Over supper I asked her more about her work. "What are boatmen really like?" I wondered, "and more especially, boat*women*?"

"Self-sufficient," was the reply. "Most are well educated and friendly, and they love their work. We're a tight little microculture, and we're transients—we go where the water is. We have to know how to navigate, cook, do first aid, repair motors, patch up rafts, set up camp, read a compass and map, guide our clients in geology and natural history, pack and stow gear so it stays dry and safe. I always carry my own waterproof metal case stuffed with wilderness gear—maps, field guides, sun clothes, extra boots, salt pills, gloves, books for bored clients, and first aid stuff. Oh, and my guitar goes, too.

"Since I've been running rivers, my competence and strength have grown. I've always liked the feeling of being strong in proportion to my size," said the Leo-born Becca. "I don't want to brag, but I've spent these last six years, summer and winter, learning the skills to be an excellent guide. I feel I can work as hard and interpret a river as well as many male guides I work with. It was easy for me to learn to maneuver a raft with a minimum of muscle because that's what I was working with. When stronger people are learning, they rely on their power more, so they often learn technique more slowly. Of course, over the years rowing has helped build my strength and endurance, so I can use them in addition to finesse. I do have problems with cold because I'm thin, but I've learned to handle it, and even to like it, by being very well prepared."

"How did boatmen treat you at first?"

"Most of them were great. In the first place, my brother, who I already told you about, gave me lots of confidence and support. Then all my buddies did, too. Boatmen showed me everything I know, encouraged me, even pushed me into getting jobs. I really owe them a lot. But it's tough to get romantically involved with a boatman and still maintain a professional relationship."

"How's that?" I stoked up the fire.

"Sometimes when a woman gets good at her job, her man's encouragement drops away. There are still a lot of threatened egos around. Harvey and I have had competition problems, but we managed to talk them out. Now we both support each other as much as possible."

"What about passengers?" I asked. "Do they ever give you a hard time?"

"For sure," she exclaimed. "There have been small discouragements like men not boarding my raft the first day or making snide comments; women not trusting me. I notice guys hurrying to relieve me of any burden I might be carrying (which is a part of my job, and I like it). I guess they're not used to seeing skinny little things throw their weight around. Those are the not-so-wonderful moments. Over the years, though, I've grown more adept at handling these problems and allaying people's fears. Still, stereotypes do remain, and I find myself attracting certain types of passengers and putting off others. However, I'm satisfied that I do well and try hard. The problems others have with me being a boatwoman are often their own image problems."

The flames were dimming and the night growing cold. I snuggled into my down sleeping bag and turned companionably toward Becca, still seated cross-legged by the fire.

"Are there many boatwomen besides yourself?" I asked drowsily.

"Sure. Lots of competent women are rowing boats all around the country now. I was just fortunate to start early and to pioneer on a couple of rivers and get a full range of experience in many places. Yet I know that some boatwomen have problems with their own self-images. Some have been married once or twice before, going the route of the haircurler and electric range, or have had high-pressure jobs in big cities. They've taken to their new jobs with a vengeance—some even in bitterness. In any event, our daughters will see more and more of us thumb our noses at Madison Avenue stereotyping. If they choose to be china dolls and not boatwomen, it certainly won't be because they don't know any alternatives."

I chuckled and rolled onto my stomach. Becca stood up, listened carefully, then slid into her bag. "I almost thought I could hear the river rising a little," she whispered.

"Don't fall asleep yet," I begged. "Tell me what you were like as a child and how you got interested in the outdoors."

"I feel I was weaned on the outdoors as a way of life," she answered, yawning. "My parents used to take us everywhere— camping in the Mohave Desert, by the seashore, hiking in the redwoods, or just skiing where we lived near the Columbia River in Washington State. It gets in your blood. And in your house, too," she said happily. "My parents' basement is jammed with sleeping bags, pads, and tents; our bedrooms are packed with outdoor books and equipment. Even when economics forced my parents to the California suburbs—my Dad sells large industrial printing equipment and my Mom teaches at Audubon nature training classes—the outdoor values were always there. They gave me an eye to ecology and wilderness and quiet. I guess that not fitting in with the urban high school scene is what inspired me to take that first job as a river runner. Tim and my older sister Jennifer also run rivers. We're so lucky to be able to educate other people to the right ways of enjoying wild places. We feel like we're turning people on to something really important, something to protect."

"Will you keep on for several more years?"

"I don't know. I guess so, unless I get burned out. I'd like to learn to be a cowgirl as well as a boatwoman. Also, I intend to put down roots so that in winters to come I can grow some greenery and raise some hogs. But I'll stick to my way of life for now, because it's the only one that makes sense to me.

"For me the river is the ultimate teacher for all life's lessons. Rivers have helped teach me to deal with psychic as well as physical hardships more easily—though I'm still learning. A lot of people want to fight the river, and that's stupid. It will exhaust you in a single day. You have to flow with the river."

White midnight frost was settling on my head and pillow, so I scrunched all the way into my bag and fell asleep. Dawn came at 5 A.M.—cold, still, golden-green. Quietly, so as not to wake Becca, I dressed and packed up my car. I would leave her here to stand her sad vigil at the funeral of the Stanislaus. As I drove up and out of its deep canyon, the question lingered hauntingly in my mind: What will the Beccas and the boatmen of this country—and the millions who enjoy wild rivers—do when all our rivers have been buried?

Chapter 17

Margaret Murie

A Long Life in the Wilderness

Bettles, alaska in 1924 was nothing more than a row of little log cabins on the banks of the Koyukuk River. It was from here that Margaret Murie set out in late October with her new husband, Olaus, by dogsled. Their goal was the distant Endicott Mountains in the Brooks Range; their mission, to gather facts about the biology and the migrations of the vast Arctic caribou herd. Now the cabin was bare. All their possessions were packed and the log room was already growing cold without a fire. Mardy took one last look around, swallowed a lump in her throat, and pulled on her mittens. It wasn't easy for the young bride to leave Bettles, where she had spent her brief honeymoon and made her first home.

As she writes so beautifully in *Two in the Far North*, her book about life with Olaus on the Alaskan frontier, "It had been perfect here, but was I going to measure up as a staunch and capable enough partner in the next chapter? Confusing, being a woman, eagerness for new adventure fighting within one with love of cozy home-keeping. Did men ever feel pulled this way?"*

*Most of the quotations dealing with the Muries' Alaska experiences are from *Two in the Far North* (1962); those covering the period after the Muries moved to Wyoming in 1927 are from *Wapiti Wilderness*, co-authored by Margaret and Olaus (1966), and *Island Between* (1977).

She closed the door and went outside, where the yipping dog team waited. As soon as Olaus gave the command to them, she had to be ready to run along behind the sled. A few old-timers waved goodbye from their cabins, and suddenly they were off like a shot. The dog team disappeared through a break in the forest, racing down to the river, across the ice, and up to the portage trail.

Within an hour after they left the cabin, they drew up a long hill and looked down on the Koyukuk River curling between banks of bare gray cottonwoods. The broad valley below lifted into blue hills and, still farther off, into the white mountains which were their destination two weeks hence. At times during the first day's nineteen-mile trek, Margaret rode the sled to conserve her strength. It felt like riding a bronco, as the long, loaded sled thumped along over tussocks and stumps and hollows. Olaus ran in front, trying to keep the dogs in line and prevent fights among them. But as they moved on after this brief pause, Mardy jumped off the sled and jogged along behind, bareheaded and barehanded. She tried to put the cabin at Bettles out of her mind and look ahead.

As she wrote in *Two in the Far North*, "Days on the trail taught us that there is always and forever something to rejoice about. It was a fairyland, this highland, skyland, on a glorious blue-and-gold day. Our seven dogs, the two of us, alone up there, sliding along the top of the world."

But it was not all beauty and enjoyment. At times the sled would tip over on the trail, and it would require the combined efforts of both Olaus and Mardy to pry it back up. There were riffles to go around on the river, and worst of all, overflows—hazardous layers of ice and water that form at the edges of shallow streams when intense cold forces water out from the stream. This can be the most sinister of arctic dangers, as the process weakens the ice covering the stream. Sometimes teams and drivers broke through and drowned; or if they did manage to scramble out, their hands, feet, or bodies might freeze when wet at 40° below zero. Then, too, it was easy to be thrown off the rear runners even when grasping the handlebars firmly. Twice on that trip Mardy was catapulted into snowbanks beside the trail. Once she wrenched her shoulder

Margaret Murie at home in Wyoming. Photo by Anne LaBastille.

against a hidden stump and burst out crying. The second time Olaus dug her out sputtering with laughter.

"As a result," smiles Mardy, "Olaus decided early on that he'd never understand women."

At night the couple would usually camp by the river in a "siwash camp"—a rope tied between two trees with a tent thrown over it as a back wall. In front Olaus placed a thick bed of freshly cut spruce boughs, their two sleeping bags, and a small Yukon stove.

"Here was home," Mardy wrote: "fire and the smell of meat sizzling, the sound of the man's ax blows in the woods near by, the figure of the woman kneeling busily before her hearth fire, and the honest dog faces in a wide circle beyond the fire. This was total peace and contentment."

As the pile of firewood grew, Mardy would prepare a skilletful of ptarmigan and rabbit, fry potatoes, heat up beans, and dish out applesauce. She claims that food never tasted so indescribably good, nor is there such a thing as overeating on the trail. They just ate until they thought the meal would keep them nourished till morning and then stop.

Sometimes at night she awoke to a moon shining through the spruce trees, the sky white with stars, the river a dazzling white ribbon beyond the campsite. A dog might stir, an owl hoot, the fire crackle. "I could not analyze my feeling as I lay there watching and listening, but I felt somehow privileged, humble yet triumphant," she recalls, "waking so in the night hours, as though I had found omnipotence at work undisturbed."

The next day they would be off again, jogging along behind the team for miles and breathing the keen air, always gazing in excited anticipation toward the rugged white peaks ahead. Margaret recalls that it was "a joy to feel blood pounding in your cheeks, every ounce alive and going, feeling the ecstatic warmth of vigorous exercise."

When they arrived in the Endicott Mountains, the Muries set up camp thirty miles above the settlement of Wiseman. This was the area in which Olaus would collect caribou specimens, study their winter food habits, observe their migration down out of the Brooks Range, note racial differences, and try to fill in the gaps in his study. Here Mardy got her first lesson in making a winter camp. She learned how to tramp down a ten-foot-square space for the tent, put up the tent, and cut poles and pegs and firewood; feed the dogs; mix up trail food; help Olaus with his specimen tags, dress out caribou carcasses, and care for the meat. She also learned some of the more bizarre aspects of marriage to a field biologist:

Now, supper over, our 8' × 10' tent holds a rather interesting scene. While I sit on the sleeping bags writing notes, Olaus, across the tent, is cleaning the caribou skulls. I was quite horror-stricken when a cow caribou skull with its stubby antlers was shoved through the tent flap and the operation began, but the process has a fascination after all, and where but in the tent could it be done at twenty below zero?

At this same tent site the young Mrs. Murie had her first experience camping alone. For six weeks the newlywed couple had
been apart for only a few hours at the most. Then, abruptly, things
changed. One day Olaus had to hunt for more caribou atop the
mountain across the Koyukuk, so Margaret stayed by the campsite
to keep the fire alight in order to dry the hides. She shared the
tent with three caribou skins, various camp equipment, and no
reading material. Only the dogs were there to keep her company.

"I sat for what seemed endless hours, listening to the dark
sounds—owls, trees cracking in the cold; sat and gazed at the red
eye of the stove draft and wondered—*if*—should I go look for him
myself or hitch up the dogs and go to Wiseman for help, and how
quickly could I make it?"

When Olaus was not back by seven in the evening, long past
dark, Mardy crawled into her sleeping bag and burst into tears.
"I wasn't afraid for myself," she declares. "I've never been fearful
or minded being alone in the wilderness; it has always seemed a
friendly place. It was imagining that something had happened to
Olaus and then not knowing if I could manage the dogs to go
downriver or up for help."

Olaus came in about 8:00 P.M., heavily loaded and slowed down
by a huge caribou head, hide, and meat. He was scared that something had happened to her when he found her crying. "Mardy, my
darlin'," he explained calmly and simply, "things take longer than
you think."

It was then she realized what it really meant to be a naturalist's
wife and that she had better accept it. "It was that or grow into
a nervous, nagging, unhappy woman," she states. "The work came
first, and Olaus had to keep his scientific integrity. I had to learn
not to worry, because as far as I knew, our life would be one long
field trip.

"I had never faced the fact that sometimes I would have to stay
behind in camp, and wait after darkness, and wonder. I must learn
to trust, to wait serenely. That hour on the snowy mountainside was
good for me," she writes. "I came to terms with being a scientist's
wife."

Mardy Murie's childhood actually had prepared her quite well
for a life in the wilds. When she was nine, her family moved from

Seattle to Fairbanks, Alaska, which in 1911 was a town of about
ten streets—a mere pinprick in a "wilderness so vast that it could
not be visualized—defying the cold and loneliness and all the powers of the unbeatable North." Fairbanks lay eight days by horse
and sleigh to the nearest town in winter, ten days by river steamer
in summer. The only "lifeline" was the Valdez Trail, now part of
the Alaska Highway.

Mardy's home was the last log house on the last street of Fairbanks. It was a happy-go-lucky town, she recalls, full of characters
with plenty of room for humor but very little for morals. Life was
exciting, and each day was a story in itself. Nothing was worth
worrying about in that gold rush town that Mardy adored. Her
parents called her a gypsy because she was always roaming out
into the forests or swamps. But whereas the child was comfortable
and at home in the wilderness, her mother was not. Mardy feels
now that her mother must have felt an unspeakable isolation,
though she never said anything. "She was a sweet, respectable,
Victorian lady and a skilled secretary who went about creating a
home and family on that far frontier with the man she loved."

"Respectable" women apparently coped with their trying situation by setting up "a regular routine, a definite project for each
day, a regular program with other people," explains Mardy. "It
was all part of the bulwark these women built, consciously or
unconsciously, against the isolation, the wilderness, the cold, the
difficulties of housekeeping. *They* set the pattern for the kind of
town Fairbanks was supposed to be—the town you could talk
about—not the seamy side of it."

Monday was washday, so extra water had to be brought in by
bucket, the stove stoked up, and the wash boiler heated. Clothes
were scrubbed on a washboard with Fels-Naptha, then hung
around the kitchen. Outside they would have frozen immediately.
Tuesday was for ironing (they did have electricity) and baking. On
Wednesday various ladies' auxiliary groups met. Thursday the ladies made formal calls on one another with fancy engraved calling
cards. Friday was sewing day with perhaps an informal visit to a
friend for tea and cookies. Then came Saturday with cleaning and
more baking; and, finally, Sunday, church and rest. Through it all,
people gossiped, lived and let live, and helped one another out in
emergencies.

Mardy believes her mother had little or no influence on her love of the outdoors. From her natural father, however, a cannery owner and fisherman in southeastern Alaska from whom her mother was divorced, she inherited her adventurous and curious spirit. "Anyone who is a fisherman has to be a gambler and adventurer," she states. "Besides, my father was a dynamic, magnetic man who came from New Brunswick and had spent years facing the sea." From her stepfather, the assistant U.S. attorney in Fairbanks, she learned to read and write and love words. "I was devouring *King Lear* at age ten," says Mardy, "and always enjoyed writing, though I never took a course in it."

Mardy began her wilderness travels as a teen-ager, when she twice left Fairbanks to go to school in Chitina, a nine-day trip by horse sleigh. The first time Mardy made the journey was one of the last voyages of the stage line on the Valdez Trail before the government railroad was built, and the last trip of the year before ice break-up made the rivers impassable. Since days grew warm and the snow mushy, most travel was done at night, when everything was frozen hard again. The fifteen-year-old Mardy calmly and cheerfully put up with detours, fordings, snowstorms, primitive accommodations in roadhouses, narrow bridges, and long hours. At the end of the trip the driver turned and looked at her steadily and said, "I guess you'll do."

Just before she left Fairbanks Mardy had asked her mother if there were any more things she should know. Her mother merely said, "No, you're going on sixteen. If I haven't raised you properly so far, there isn't much use trying to start now. I'm relying on your good sense. I think you'll find that most any man will be a gentleman as long as the girl is a lady." And then she gave her daughter a sack full of lemon drops!

After two years away at Reed College in Oregon, Mardy came home to Fairbanks in 1919. At a dinner at a friend's house she met Olaus Murie. That week they took a boat trip up the Chena River in the early evening. To her amazement, the slim, blond young Norwegian biologist answered a great horned owl and hooted it into a tree top above them. She wondered "what kind of magic did this man have?" But she didn't have time to find out then. Almost immediately Olaus left for the hills to begin his study of Alaskan caribou, and in 1921 Mardy headed for Boston and a year at Simmons College. Her first school, Reed, offered only a teaching degree, which Mardy had decided not to pursue, and she transferred to Simmons in part because her stepfather planned to be in Boston that winter.

By the following July she was home for good, and again met Murie briefly. This time she was impressed by his quietness, pleasant voice, and agreeable outward nature "with just a touch of steel within." That summer she and her family visited Olaus and his brother Adolph, also a biologist, at their camp on the Savage River near Mt. McKinley. "At the end of those five days of tramping about in a rosy haze in those enchanted mountains," writes Margaret, "we both knew there was no life for us except together." Yet their work kept them apart a great deal—Mardy was a senior at Alaska Agricultural College and School of Mines in Fairbanks (now the University of Alaska). Olaus was working in Mt. McKinley National Park. When Mardy graduated the following summer of 1924 with a degree in business administration—the first woman graduate of the university—Olaus and she decided to marry.

The timing was tricky. Olaus would be far away at the mouth of the Yukon River studying and banding waterfowl and would have a long boat trip back to Mardy. So she planned to take a steamer down the Tanana River and the Yukon and meet him in the village of Anvik. Their wedding would take place there on the afternoon of August 18, 1924 (Mardy's birthday) in a little Episcopal chapel. Olaus had trouble with his boat, and the ceremony was a little late—2:30 A.M. of August 19! By 5:00 A.M. the bridal couple was back aboard the steamer, headed upriver toward Bettles to find the husky sled dogs which had been shipped upriver earlier for Olaus's October caribou-collecting trip. A more complicated and unconventional marriage would be hard to imagine.

As for the honeymoon, Mardy writes of those two months in a one-room log cabin at Bettles, "There are no words for the happiness we felt." Olaus was engrossed in studying the distribution of small mammals (mice, voles, lemmings, etc.) and ran a trapline everyday. Then the sled dogs had to be fitted to harnesses and trained for the big trip to the Endicott Mountains after freezeup. Much of the time Mardy stayed in the cabin, made bread, and kept the fire going while Olaus went alone to check his traplines in pouring rain.

There were still long miles ahead, but from here beside Hanging Woman Creek, we would be sliding out of the wilderness, away from perfect solitude and unsullied country. [From] here on the Porcupine with the wolves, we would be leaving perfect atoneness with the untouched."

The Old Crow River was only one of many wilderness places where Margaret Murie "set up housekeeping." As she says simply, "You can set up a home anywhere. When it's outdoors, you just do it in a little different way. There's no problem."

In 1927, they left Alaska. Olaus was sent by the U.S. Biological Survey to Jackson Hole, Wyoming, to begin a study of the life history of that area's famous elk herd. At that time it was the largest remnant of these animals in a wilderness retreat. His research culminated in publication of *The Elk of North America*, a classic treatise on this species.

The Muries were to live in Jackson Hole for thirty-six years. Their second child, a daughter, was born during their first summer there, and Mardy took Martin and the seven-week-old Joanne along on Olaus's summer research expedition to Pacific Creek. Camp in a high meadow beside a small creek was her little world for the summer while the men roamed the mountains studying elk.

In the summer of 1929 they moved into the mountains near Whetstone Creek. This time Olaus's mother came along. Though she loved the outdoors, the old Norwegian lady had a deep respect for and fear of all natural forces. As soon as it grew dark she would start to worry, although Mardy assured her there was nothing in those woods to hurt them. Mardy was determined not to fret, having fought and conquered these same fears on her honeymoon.

In *Wapiti Wilderness*, the book she and Olaus co-authored about their Wyoming years, Mardy describes what it was like to live for long stretches in the backwoods with two children.

It was simpler there than in town. They were well fed, and because they were busy in the open air every moment, their appetites were wonderful; they grew and were brown and never had a sick moment that I can recall. Their clothes were simple—underwear, socks, sturdy shoes, coveralls of blue or tan denim, cloth hats to protect them a bit from the sun—there was no ironing. Their play was no problem; they were busy from morning till night with places and objects they found right there in the wilderness. I think that the only phase of camping which bothered me in any way was too much stooping, over the campfire and over the dishpan on the log where I scrubbed out the clothes, and over the little stream where I sloshed them well and wrung them out. It is well for a camping mother to have a strong and limber back!

At the same time I had no hardwood floors to wax and polish; no furniture to dust, no telephone to answer, no parties or committee meetings to attend; no problems of neighborhood children's squabbles; no dresses to starch, no trousers to press; and so on and so on.

But perhaps above all this was the plain fact that camp life suited me; it was just naturally no trouble for me to settle into it. I have always felt that if a woman does not "take" to this kind of life she should not be expected to do so, and should not be criticized if she stays behind in town. If she goes unwillingly, *making* herself be a camper, she is not likely to be a carefree cheerful companion.

Even in Jackson, the Muries' home life revolved around Olaus's work. Their house was full of wildlife. It was not unusual to be kept awake at night by captive mice frisking in their boxes; to choke on the smell of elk skulls boiling on the stove; to find vials of formaldehyde full of pickled parasites in the kitchen; to trip over antlers piled in the living room; to feed and nurse crippled birds; to find a great horned owl perched on the laundry drying rack; to discover a hog-nose snake coiled on top of a hot air vent; to uncover a fat toad in her bed. All these episodes ended in laughter, as Mardy wrote: "Since I could practically never get really angry at Olaus, and absolutely never stay angry with him, and since he was so dedicated to his work, that every project or experiment he thought important was bound to go on despite anything or anybody, it was far better just to relax and take it all as it came."

And so the years passed peacefully, passionately, productively. Olaus continued his work for the Biological Survey (now the U.S. Fish and Wildlife Service), while Mardy raised their three children (the youngest, Donald, was born in Jackson in 1931) and became involved with townspeople and local politics. They built a lovely log home near Moose, Wyoming, and hundreds of conservationists and anticonservationists came there to discuss, plan, fight, and compromise on environmental issues. As Mardy soon discovered, "People would sooner come to my house to discuss problems than attend a public meeting in a public place, and especially if they could sprawl out on the living room floor in front of the fire and have coffee and carrot cake or tea and cookies. This is where and how it happens. It all depends on tea and cookies."

In 1943 their life changed abruptly. Their older son, Martin, joined the Tenth Mountain Infantry to fight in the Second World War, and Mardy was asked by close friends to help manage their dude ranch, the Bear Paw. Olaus was away alot on a black bear study in Yellowstone National Park, so the ranch seemed like a good way to keep busy. Mardy moved there with Joanne and immediately loved the business and fun of running a dude ranch.

In 1946 the Muries purchased a seventy-seven-acre ranch, the STS, not far from Moose. At the same time, Olaus was offered the directorship of the Wilderness Society in Washington. It seemed an impossible dilemma. Mardy knew they'd never be happy in a city, so she was delighted when the Society suggested a half-time, half-pay position with their base at the ranch. Olaus accepted, and the family moved into the STS, soon to be joined by Olaus's brother Adolph and his wife, Louise. Friends thought the two Murie families slightly mad for exchanging town and all its modern conveniences for an isolated ranch with no electricity, no phone, and roads which were often impassable from December to late April. Supplies had to be laid up in fall, wood cut for the fireplaces, and skis, snowshoes, and toboggan readied for winter. But they were glad to pay the price for "the ineffable beauty and peace of this place which soon became deeply *home*." Mardy still lives on the ranch.

With Olaus as director of The Wilderness Society, there were mountains of mail to handle and conservation matters to study. Olaus was working on his own book, *A Field Guide to Animal Tracks*, and doing his delicate and meticulous illustrations for other people's books. Life on the ranch was good. In the evening, "the Tetons would be shining like mammoth rugged amethysts against the clear pink winter sunset." Margaret might come in from picking up the mail a mile away, or skiing through the willow flats by the

river for fun, and put on steaks to broil. After supper there'd be
dishes to wash, letters to answer, and books to read out loud as
Olaus did his drawings.

In 1947 Adolph Murie's work for the National Park Service took
him back to Alaska. Olaus and Mardy soon began to get uneasy
reports from him and other biologists of the changes occurring
there. It was the "age of the bulldozer," and nothing was safe.
Both Adolph and Olaus became more and more concerned about
the fate of the Brooks Range and the great herds of barren-ground
caribou. Eventually this worry resulted in a full-scale ecological
research expedition, led by Olaus and supported by the New York
Zoological Society, to the Sheenjek River region, one hundred
miles south of the Arctic Sea and surrounded by the 10,000-foot
peaks of the Brooks Range. It was just thirty years since the Muries
had approached these mountains from the south via the Old Crow
River. The journey had taken two weeks by boat in 1926; in 1956
it was accomplished by seaplane in an hour.

On this trip Olaus and Mardy were accompanied by three young
scientists: Dr. Brina Kessel from the University of Alaska, an ornithologist; Dr. George Schaller, a graduate student in zoology at
the University of Alaska who has since become one of the world's
most famous wildlife biologists; and Dr. Robert Krear of the University of Colorado. The expedition's goals were to study the vegetation, birds, and mammals of the region: describe their habitats;
group them into ecosystems; and collect specimens. Once this data
was in hand, they all hoped this area—roughly 215 miles east to
west and 100 miles north to south—would become a wildlife range
encompassing about nine million acres. It would be the one great
representative of unspoiled arctic wilderness to be preserved for
scientific research, recreation, and inspiration.

Once again, Mardy reveled in her beloved Alaska. In *Two in
the Far North* she wrote:

I lay flat on the moss and heather, hat over my face, and felt absolutely
content. This cannot be put into words. Here I was, privileged to lie on
top of a mountain in the Arctic, an observer of the richness of this short
summer pageant. Through half-closed eyes I looked across the valley to
the west and north. The mountains made an unearthly beautiful frieze

against the blue:—And then the broad valley, the winding Sheenjek, the countless lakes. It is the Arctic in its unbelievably accelerated summer life. It is also the personal well-being purchased by striving—by lifting and setting down your legs, over and over, through the muskeg, up the slopes, gaining the summit—man using himself. This wondrous mingling of weariness and triumph and sudden harmony with the exquisite airs, the burgeoning life of the bird and plant world of the tops, is part of the "glad tidings," surely, which John Muir meant when he said: "Climb the mountains and get their glad tidings."

This is the value of this piece of wilderness—its absolutely untouched character. Not spectacular, no unique or "strange" features, but just the beautiful, wild country of a beautiful, wild free-running river, with no sign of man or his structures. For this feature alone this Arctic is worth preserving just as it is. Our hope is to leave it as lovely as we found it, with every possible sign of our short occupancy obliterated.

They did as they hoped. On December 7, 1960 the U.S. Department of the Interior, under Fred A. Seaton, established the Arctic National Wildlife Range.* "It was the second time in his life that Olaus shed tears," reports Mardy, "when he read the telegram from Washington. We had certainly come a long way from Bettles in our lives.

"It goes to show what a very small group of people can do through inspiration and with good field data when they decide something needs to be done," she adds proudly. "It took us three trips, but we got the largest national wildlife refuge in the United States, if not in the western hemisphere. It meant more to us than any other piece of land in the world."

In 1963 Mardy's beloved husband died, and her world crashed. The years as companion, wife, trailmate, and secretary were over. What should she do? Deep emptiness engulfed her.

"It took several months after Olaus died to realize that the pain would always be there," Mardy acknowledges. "Then finally I realized that I would just have to build a new life on top of that void. The sense of loss would remain with me forever."

Winters she left Wyoming and stayed with her mother in Seattle; summers she lived alone on the STS. The Wilderness Society put

*Now the William O. Douglas Arctic National Wildlife Range.

her on salary and kept her busy. She wrote articles and flyers, gave countless speeches and lectures, attended and testified at hearings, and lobbied tirelessly for conservation causes. She was instrumental in getting North Cascades National Park in Washington established. Mardy has continued her association with The Wilderness Society and is now a vice president and member of its governing council as well as a part-time consultant.

Gazing at Margaret Murie's sweet clear face, her silvery hair held back with turquoise and silver clips, the wedding band formed from a gold nugget, one feels the underlying sadness. One also senses her air of quiet acceptance and gracious authority. She's a woman who can listen and understand but will never baby herself or anyone else.

"I can't imagine what other life I ever could have had," she confesses. "I was so happy and fulfilled. One of the best parts of my marriage was that I never felt any restrictions of any kind. Olaus always wanted me to do whatever I wanted, even though we were so very busy with field work and kids and mail. He was always urging me, even 'bludgeoning' me into writing my books, lecturing, and doing other things on my own. There was no pressure on me to become immersed in Olaus's studies, but it came along as a natural result of my great interest in wildlife and its habitat. I was not obliged to prove anything!"

She cocks her head questioningly, like a plump wren with alert brown eyes. "Now I just live from day to day. What keeps me going is talking to young people and helping them work out their problems. That means most of all—more than a new career, more than any honor."

And honors she's received aplenty. In 1976 the University of Alaska granted her an honorary doctorate. The U.S. Department of the Interior gave Mardy the Citizen Conservation Award; the Rocky Mountain Center on the Environment, its Edward Hobbs Hilliard conservation award. Perhaps the greatest honor came from the National Park Service, when they named Mardy an Honorary Park Ranger in 1978.

The seventy-seven-year-old grandmother of ten claims to be completely bewildered by what she has done to deserve all these honors.

Recently Mardy was invited back to Alaska to participate in a conference of women writers. Four women made up the panel. Mardy describes it as "quite a contrast. Two seemed filled with aggression and resentment toward men. The moderator turned to me and asked how I felt about men and how they had treated me through all my years in the wilderness.

"Well, I was hardly the one to ask since I'm not an avid feminist. I've never had any trouble with men. On the contrary, from the time I reached Fairbanks as a child up to now, I've been treated with respect, consideration, and warmth. As a child, I was a precious individual to all the men who had given up a home and family for the call of gold and adventure. As a teenager, I had a great advantage being one of very few girls in town. We had wonderful times with the boys; we were all one big happy mixture—no discrimination at all. And as Olaus's trailmate, I was always admired and encouraged. However, I certainly realize that other women have had other experiences, and I don't believe there should be any discrimination anywhere because of sex. I have done what I could for the passage of the Equal Rights Amendment. I only object to bitterness and extremism."

She falls into silent reminiscing, idly clasping her large, strong hands loosely, fingering the gold nugget. Then, with a wistful smile, she says, "What, after all, are the most precious things in a life? I still feel they are the same as when I wrote these words [in *Two in the Far North*]: 'We had a honeymoon in an age when the world was sweet and untrammeled and safe. Up there in the Koyukuk there were very few machines of any kind; but there was joy in companionship and in the simple things—like the crackle of a fire, having tea and bread while the rain pattered on the roof, a chance meeting with a friend on the dog-team trail.' "

Chapter 18

Maggie Nichols

Outdoor Journalism
in the Urban Jungle

MAGGIE NICHOLS AND I walked down Broadway, looking for a quiet restaurant to have lunch. A long, glossy black mink coat enveloped Maggie's tall figure and contrasted nicely with her golden-gray mass of ringlets. Feeling distinctly like a visiting hillbilly in my jeans suit and low-heeled boots, I kept asking myself, "What am I doing in New York City interviewing this woman? This is not exactly the wilderness!"

As if sensing my discomfiture and perplexity, Maggie shrugged self-consciously in her coat and said, "It's really warm. Those Russians sure knew what they were doing wearing furs."

As the author of *Wild, Wild Woman* strode purposefully along, she moved protectively toward me. "Watch your bag. There are a few pickpockets along this stretch." She sounded for all the world like a backwoods guide warning her client about rattlesnakes along the trail.

We passed an elderly woman dressed in layers of old tattered clothes. She hovered back in a doorway, guarding five or six huge shopping bags full of rags. A little further on, another old woman lay curled up on a newspaper bed, a worn blanket over her head, bags around her feet. Somehow the November wind seemed colder than ever. I shivered half from cold and half from compassion for those ragged ladies.

Maggie Nichols takes a break to appreciate the panorama of gently rolling hills during a backpack trip along the Appalachian Trail. Photo by Maggie Nichols.

"How did you come to write a book for women about the outdoors when you live and work right in the middle of this enormous city?" I asked Maggie.

"I wrote it mainly for big-city girls like me who want to get into the country as often as possible," she explained, putting out an arm to keep me safely on the curb as a careening taxi streaked through a red light. "In a way, we move from one wilderness—the urban one—to another. I'd like to see women have the best of both worlds, and with a little thought and a sense of adventure, they can."

We reached the restaurant, and Maggie swung open the door. "You see, I feel the city and the outdoors are similar in many ways. Neither is without its dangers. You have to keep your wits about you all the time—the signs are always there, and you must learn to read them at a glance. In the wilderness you watch for signals like wildlife and weather; here, for people signs. After all, it is a people place. Both cities and wilderness places demand respect."

I was fascinated with the concept of approaching city and wilderness from a common point of view. "Go on," I urged as we sat down.

"Well, just as folks like you have to learn the skills and attitudes to handle yourselves in the city—pickpockets, crowds, traffic, noise, bums, blackouts, addicts, tension—so other people have to adjust to the wilderness. They have to get over the idea that there are lots of cute, cuddly animals out there, à la Bambi and Thumper. They have to realize that accidents can occur, that weather dominates all, that hypothermia may take place even on a cool summer day, for example. They have to get over the fantasy of 'getting back to Eden.'

"You saw those 'bag ladies' out there?" she asked. "They're very independent. They have a subculture all their own. They can survive in the city just as well as the old trappers and hermits that you wrote about in your book, *Woodswoman*, manage in the backwoods. They sleep out on the streets, gather trash from garbage cans, get meals in their own mysterious ways. As I see it, both the city and the wilderness are environments which give people the chance to be individuals and to be self-reliant.

"The suburbs don't do that. They're deadly. Human beings are put in boxes, banished from nature, and insulated from almost any kind of challenge to survival. They face incredible pressures to conform and not be individualistic. Mow the lawn, wash the car, join the club, and so on."

As we studied our menus, Maggie filled me in on the background that formed her philosophy and directed her career. As assistant managing editor to *Field and Stream* magazine, Maggie Nichols is the first woman to hold one of the top editorial positions on an outdoor-sports publication. The magazine has two million subscribers and is read by eight million people every month. Now in her forties, Maggie has worked there for seventeen years as editor/ writer/photographer, seeing the magazine change from the time when she was not allowed to put her first name on the masthead— only initials so she'd appear to be a man—for fear of alienating the readership, and when she was totally deskbound. Now she travels extensively around wilder parts of this country and abroad in search of outdoor ideas and stories. Now she is writing feature-length articles under her full name and for three years has had her own column, "Especially for Women."

Born and raised in Winnetka, Illinois, Maggie attended Antioch College in Yellow Springs, Ohio, where she majored in English literature, and graduate school at the University of New Mexico. She always wanted a magazine position. After a couple of disappointing first jobs, she landed a position on *Field & Stream*. She soon decided that she really wanted to stay and grow with the publication and live in New York City. And that's exactly what she's done, mixing in liberal doses of outdoor living and adventuring.

Some of her ventures have included a float trip down the Green River in Utah, bonefishing in the Bahamas, a jeep safari through the southwestern deserts, flying lessons, driving a twenty-five-foot motor home from California to New York State "to see whether a woman would have any trouble handling it," horsepack trips in rugged western mountains, backpacking on the Appalachian Trail, deep-sea fishing in the Virgin Islands and Panama, exploring in Alaska, gliding in a balloon over the New Jersey countryside, and tarpon fishing in the Petén jungle of Guatemala.

Although she has visited and appreciates truly remote locales, Maggie is not adamant about Wilderness with a capital "W." She feels that it's possible to have a wilderness-type experience virtually in a vacant lot. Small wild places, though less spectacular than the vast wilderness tracts, may be just as important to a great many people. And if more attention is not paid them, they may disappear. The loss of these areas to housing tracts and shopping malls can be quite devastating to all concerned. In many areas, otherwise heavily built up, these pockets of wildness near towns have been rescued from development by local efforts, in many cases spearheaded by women.

The whole point, Maggie feels, is one's attitude toward being in the outdoors. It isn't necessary to climb to the top of a mountain to find nature—although such places are invaluable national treasures. It's the sense of the unexpected, the pride of self-sufficiency, and the inventiveness when things go wrong that make for a wilderness experience. And under certain circumstances, the fact that somebody once cut trees or built a cabin may not diminish the beauty of a still-wild place.

Her adventures and journalistic accomplishments have earned Maggie membership in the Outdoor Writers Association of America and the Society of Women Geographers, and a role as one of the founders of Outdoor Women, an organization dedicated to helping more women find the fun and learn the skills involved in outdoor activities.

Over steaming bowls of onion soup, I asked Maggie where and how her interest in the outdoors had begun.

"My mother," she answered simply. "Mother was a teacher and principal of an Illinois elementary school. She loved the outdoors. She grew up in an isolated part of Michigan and spent a lot of time in the woods. In fact, she and one other girl canoed on Lake Temagami in Canada in the early 1920's, which was quite an adventure back then. She also had her own .22 rifle as a young girl.

"She always made it clear that I could do whatever I wanted; that she expected me to do so. Most of my high school friends were never exposed to any such role model. All they were expected to do was get married and run a home. When I went back to a recent high school reunion, I found I was one of only a handful of the girls I'd known who'd gone out and gotten a job and done well."

As the waiter brought our sandwiches, I asked if anything else had been important in forming her interests.

"The second big influence in my life was summer camp in Wisconsin," she answered. "We had a terrific leader, Miss Palmer, a remarkable woman born with a hunchback but limitless energy and spirit. She knew about everything, from making paper flowers to nature lore, archery, horses, deportment, camping, woodcraft, and, most of all, canoeing. I figured that if she could do all that with her handicap . . . well, we kids could, too."

Maggie also learned much from early women outdoor writers and contributors to *Field and Stream,* some of whom were venturing afield in the late 1800's and early 1900's. (See Chapter 4.) In 1902 Helen Lukens Jones scaled University Peak in the Sierra Nevada (elevation 13,632 feet), clad simply in a jacket and skirt, with climbing equipment that consisted only of a tin drinking cup and an alpenstock which was used for cutting steps in ice. Florence Tasker accompanied her husband into the wilds of Labrador in 1907 for six months of canoeing, portaging, and backpacking. Mrs. Shirley Hulse walked fifteen miles and climbed over a 3,000-foot mountain the first time she ever put on snowshoes!

Following this early wave of women in the woods, activity started to taper off, for various reasons discussed in part in the introductory chapters of *Wild, Wild Woman* and of this book. Today, of course, the tide has turned, and millions of women are working outdoors and trying every conceivable type of recreational activity. It was to share her considerable knowledge of how to be safe, comfortable, attractive, and happy in the wilder parts of the world that Maggie wrote her book.

"I'll tell you one thing," Maggie said dramatically as she pushed back her plate. "The outdoor movement has toughened up women's minds and bodies. A lot of them aren't just going to give in to a rapist or mugger or murderer these days without at least thinking about self-defense!" The waiter overheard this as he halted by our table and eyed us askance as he brushed away the crumbs.

Maggie contends that she couldn't have completed her book without her husband's encouragement. Sometimes Mike Nichols accompanies her on field trips; sometimes Maggie goes alone. Not having children does make it easier, she admits. "However, if I did have them, I would not hesitate to take them anywhere I went, provided they would be of an age and state of mind to enjoy it— and let me enjoy it too. I think people should keep in mind that children are individual people, and some children may enjoy wilderness outings more or less than others. I also think it's important to remember that young children are small: they can't take great big steps, and they can't see over tall grass, and they may get tired and even bored a lot faster than grownups with more height and years of experience to trade on."

Her articles for *Field and Stream* show Maggie's commitment to conservation and sound management of fish and game. In November, 1973 she wrote a complex factual coverage of Consolidated Edison's proposed plant at Storm King Mountain along the Hudson. This scenic and historic site is an important habitat for striped bass. The article, entitled "Showdown at Storm King," pointed out that it was not a "local skirmish" between the electrical company and environmentalists, but rather "a national struggle between conservationists and industrial arrogance." In 1975 Maggie wrote a similar article on the proposed Tocks Island Dam on the Delaware River; this time the adversary was the U.S. Army Corps of Engineers. Her piece was subsequently reprinted and distributed to the U.S. Congress.

Tackling another kind of controversy in 1972, the spunky editor produced "Alice (and Friends) in Disney Land," a broadside directed at what she considered the extremism of some wildlife protection groups such as Friends of Animals and Fund for Animals. The piece called for proper wildlife education, management, and ecosystem preservation. Four years later she widened her attack to include antihunting groups in general, with damning statistics and financial figures to back up her argument. A quotation from this article shows the depth of Maggie's convictions:

You can search in vain through . . . the literature of any of these small but aggressive "animal welfare" groups for a significant word on the very real threats to wildlife's most basic habitat needs. But here is the bottom line: Land, water, wetlands, estuaries, woods, streams, fields. You name it, wildlife needs it. You name it, it is being dug up, filled in, paved over, dumped into, cut down, plowed under, built on, dammed, probed, poisoned, and used in a thousand ways by and for the supposed good of human beings. This is the danger that wildlife faces, not the much-advertised "hunter's gun." . . . Let the loss of wintering, feeding, and resting areas in the continental U.S. continue at the rate it has been going the last fifty years, and all of the wildlife species that depend on wetlands stand to be in trouble.

Such forthright statements are a far cry from the early 1960's, when Maggie Nichols was forced to use only her initials to masquerade as a male writer and to cajole an assignment out of New York City. In 1979 Maggie won the Buck Knives Award for excellence in communication, and it's a sure bet that she will be tackling other sticky issues in the future.

"Do you want to be editor-in-chief some day?" I asked as two tiny cups of aromatic espresso were served.

She grinned and said, "I'm sure our readers, 80 percent of whom are men, wouldn't go for that. And I want to do what's best for the mag, not Maggie, in this case. They'd like to see a man at the helm, and so they should. Would you like to see anyone but a woman running *Cosmo* and *Ms.*? No, I know I can make important contributions to the magazine—and the outdoors—even if I can't be top 'man.'

"Actually, I'm quite content. I'm best summed up as a woman who lives in a city, works at a desk, and enjoys the urban experience. And in my New York City off-hours, I share an active life with my husband, who's a music promoter, photographer, and moviemaker. We listen to music, eat, go out on the town. We're both Geminis, so we know how to enjoy!

"Of course, I'm luckier than most women because I have a job that takes me into the woods and deserts and mountains and gives me a chance to try a lot of different activities in different places. Whenever I can get away, I head for the open spaces. These are all important ingredients in well-balanced living.

"I think that the wilderness can be a great teacher and that it has much in common with feminist ideas. And by feminism I mean getting in touch with your own values, intelligence, resourcefulness, physical capacities, and general ability to live a rich and satisfying life of your own, not only with, but also apart from, friends and loved ones. There is nothing like severing connections to outside resources—both mechanical and human—to show a person how much she or he can really do. Since women have traditionally been taught that they cannot handle tough situations, the confidence gained on wilderness outings can be particularly valuable for them. I believe that even one weekend backpacking, even in not very difficult surroundings, can have a tremendous and lasting effect on the spirit which will carry over into all aspects of life.

"In turn, I feel that what women can offer *to* the wilderness is concern and care. The more people who love something, the more chance that something has to survive. If you learn to enjoy a walk in the woods more than an afternoon in a shopping center, you'll be willing to fight to keep precious undeveloped areas, especially near population centers, from going under concrete."

A few minutes later we paid the bill, slipped on our coats, and walked back out onto the tumultuous streets. I hesitated a moment, adjusting to the din and movement. Maggie led the way to the corner of Broadway and 37th Street. "This is a good spot to catch a cab," she counseled. Then, grimacing, she said, "Isn't this modern life a mess in many ways? Every day new information, shortages, and disasters make us feel more helpless and trapped. What possible control can we have over events? There is a limit to how much good individual sacrifice, protest, and conservation can do in the face of so many events today—energy shortages, nuclear accidents, runaway inflation, impending recession, and capricious governmental leadership. More and more, people are feeling impotent, and depression is a growing disease. One of the great things a trip to the wilderness—or a life in it, for those few who can live the way you do, Anne—does is put us back in charge of our lives, for a few days at least. It's one of the few remaining circumstances where a person really can be the master of her or his own fate. Furthermore, wits are sharpened by exercising the skills necessary to be comfortable and safe in the wilds, so people will be better able to cope with problems back home. Some people freeze to death when the power goes off because they don't know how to make a fire to keep warm. People have also been known to burn down their houses trying to heat them with fireplaces. People who have lived in the outdoors are equipped with both the experience and the gear to keep alive and well without the benefits of technology and civilization."

Just then an empty Yellow Cab cruised by, and Maggie vigorously flagged it down for me. She opened the door and gave me a goodbye embrace. Again I had the feeling of a competent guide seeing off her "sport" after a day in the bush. The last glimpse I had of her was a broad-shouldered figure in that stunning coat stalking competently past the pickpockets, bag ladies, and three-card monte hustlers on Broadway.

Chapter 19

Nicole Duplaix

The Peripatetic Zoologist

THE JUNGLE RIVER rushed and foamed among dark boulders. It was the third set of rapids which Nicole Duplaix and her two Bushnegro guides had encountered that day—one of the last in a three-week journey down the upper Coppename River in the wild interior of Suriname. Wearily, they secured the tarp over the gear piled in the center of their thirty-eight-foot dugout canoe, tipped up the outboard engine, and slid over the sides. Grasping the gunwales firmly, the three then began to push the boat forward through the rapids. Nicole groped for footholds in the tea-brown water, sliding her sneakers over moss-covered rocks. The two men struggled along barefoot. The river was up to their waists and tugging at their legs and hips. Slowly they eased the eight-hundred-pound loaded craft over the churning shallows.

Suddenly Nicole's foot slipped. She struggled frantically for balance but fell backward into the foam. The current caught her and carried her downriver a few yards, then shoved her up against a huge boulder and held her there. Without her extra support the cigar-shaped canoe slowly began turning. The two guides fought to hold its bow downstream, but the current was too powerful. With increasing speed the dugout swung broadside to the river and swept heavily downstream. Then, with a shuddering thud, the stern crashed into the boulder scant inches from Nicole's head.

She recalls the incident vividly. "My boatman, Mofo Soiso, turned from ebony black to pale gray with fright." Grabbing the craft, she managed to hold it till the two men rushed down to help. Then the three once again began tugging the stubborn boat slowly through the swirling waters.

In this laborious and hazardous fashion, Nicole Duplaix was canvassing the rivers and streams of Suriname—an Oklahoma-sized country on the Caribbean coast of South America. Her quarry was the giant river otter, *Pteronura brasiliensis,* one of the twenty most endangered mammals on earth. This seventy-pound, seven-foot species once ranged from Venezuela to Argentina north to south, and east to west from Brazil to Peru; but it has almost been eliminated from its habitat throughout South America. Only in Suriname's interior, where few people live or travel, do these creatures still survive. Nicole's two-year expedition, which she conceived and organized herself, was the first time that the behavior and natural history of giant otters was observed and recorded by a scientist.

During the first nine months the young zoologist explored eleven rivers and fifty-three creeks, but came up with only brief sightings of seventy-four otters—her observations totalling only twelve hours. Sheer frustration! Nicole tried every trick she could think of to approach closely and not frighten away the elusive, wary animals. She used blinds, sounds, scuba gear, rubber otter masks on her head while swimming—all without success. Compounding her troubles were constant breakdowns of the outboard motor and the many rapids to be traversed. In dry season the boat had to be shoved over the shallows; in rainy season there was perilous maneuvering through roaring torrents. In the quiet waters lurked electric eels capable of giving a six-hundred-volt shock, sting rays, and piranhas. Along the shores might be poisonous snakes, hidden roots to trip on, impenetrable thorny vegetation, and jaguars. "I really learned during this work that fitness is a frame of mind," Nicole declares.

Nicole was accompanied throughout her travels by her beloved Doberman, 'Pegs.' "She shared our cramped quarters in the dugout, rubber raft, aluminum canoe, and tiny tent," Nicole says proudly. "She panted in the saunalike heat and snapped at the

Nicole Duplaix with one of her favorite creatures—a common river otter (not the giant species she studied) in Suriname. Photo by Nicole Duplaix.

swarms of horseflies which always buzzed overhead on the river. But she never complained and she never disturbed the others. I think we both learned to keep stiff upper lips.

"I had to remind myself every day," recalls the petite blond woman stoically, "that the giant otter was already wiped out of Brazil and would probably disappear altogether in the next twenty years unless someone obtained reliable basic field data on the species. This would be the first step in finding a way to properly manage and protect them. The situation was critical. When my spirits really sank low, I would remember that I had an outstanding example to follow. The first naturalist to visit Suriname was a

Dutchwoman, Maria Sybylla Merian, in the early 1700's. If she could do it then, *I* could do it *now*."

After she had been in Suriname for nine months, Nicole's luck changed. A Dutch botanist told her that he had seen more otters in the vicinity of Kapoeri Creek than anywhere else. So in January, 1977 Nicole headed up the Corantijn River to the mouth of the creek, which she describes in her July, 1980 *National Geographic* article:

> Following its winding, haphazard course, strewn with submerged logs and fallen trees, we seem to enter the forest itself. The water is stained a dark brown color by the peaty soil; I think to myself, "It's like floating across a coffee cup." Tall stalks of *mokomoko*, each topped with a single heart-shaped leaf, form eight-foot high hedges on either side. Ripples among the lilypads to my right suddenly part and two black heads pop up like periscopes. We observe each other in silence. I can make out round eyes, small ears, and tufts of whiskers. One of them slowly cranes its neck and opens its mouth, the pink interior a vivid contrast. The other, keeping quite still, makes a sing-song humming sound. Suddenly, with a snort and a splash they are gone, leaving a few ripples behind. My first meeting with "the Hummers," as they later came to be known, had just taken place.

From then on Nicole was able to amass superb data. By March the pair, with one cub, was allowing her to follow them for over an hour and a half at a time. The female was shyer and would usually keep the cub close beside her while she uttered her strange humming growl for minutes on end. Gradually the otters came to pay less and less attention to the canoe and rubber raft and Nicole's observation time lengthened. Identification of individuals and sexes was easy. Both were sleek, dark brown, and beautifully furred, with large white throat patches as compared to spots in other otters. The male had a larger head and thicker neck than the female. The pair defended a territory two-and-a-half miles along the river, which they patrolled every day. The cub went everywhere with its parents, both of whom were very attentive and reassuring.

After her fifteenth month in Suriname's wilderness, Nicole had seen 249 individual otters. On the basis of hundreds of hours of observations of their behavior, such as the mutual grooming and affection in mated pairs, she concluded that the giant otters are monogamous for at least several years.

One fascinating aspect of otter behavior which Nicole discovered was their "campsites"—large, bare, open areas, up to fifty feet long and thirty feet wide, which the animals cleared themselves. They reared up on their hind legs and broke off saplings, then churned up the soil with their paws. Off to one side they set up a communal latrine where the otters in residence would urinate and defecate. This landmark signaled to passing otters that an extended family belonged here. Nicole recalls that the musky, rank odor was so strong that she could smell a campsite fifty feet downwind. Campsites along the territorial boundaries were usually the largest and best maintained.

The food habits of otters were also of concern to Nicole, so she and her guides would collect droppings for analysis. She gave a 5¢ reward to whichever man found and retrieved a pile. Mofo and his fellow guide, Jobari, thought the routine of collecting hilarious. Later Nicole would measure, weigh, and label the contents of each envelope of material; however, she despaired of ever identifying all the fish and crab remains correctly. (There are over 1,300 species of fish in Suriname—five times the number found in the Mississippi—and many have not been identified.)

At first, Nicole didn't know whether the men would take orders from a woman once the going got rough, or whether they would grow sullen and uncooperative, perhaps sit down and refuse to go on, even turn back. But her guides had utmost respect and confidence in Nicole. Mofo often said to Jobari in Takitaki, their pidgin dialect based on English and Dutch, "Dati Mama watra dagoe a sabi ala sani"—"That Mrs. Otter knows everything." And the Bushnegros' temperament—a happy, positive outlook coupled with a love for the bush and river life—took care of most problems.

"The Djuka (a tribe of Bushnegros) is in many ways matriarchal— so the respect for female authority is there once you have *earned* their respect," Nicole explains. "Within a day of setting out with a new pair of helpers, I made sure I caught a big fish, repaired an engine, and made them laugh; these three key ingredients promoted respect and team spirit. Once the loyalty is elicited, they will do anything, anywhere."

Life along the river was methodical and even pleasant and peaceful at times. In the morning Pegs would awaken first and nudge Nicole's neck until she unzipped the tent flap and let her out. Then the two would set out quietly in the small canoe to search for otters and explore. Meanwhile Mofo and Jobari made breakfast and broke camp. The day passed in observations or further explorations up creeks. Every evening the two boatmen would erect a crude shelter of branches tied with lianas under which to string their hammocks, while Nicole put up her bugproof, rainproof tent. Then, before dark, they would all go fishing, enjoying the cool of evening.

"The Djuka treated me as a team leader, a buddy, an eccentric," states Nicole, "a doctor for their ailments (treating syphilis was a rather unusual case, while sewing up a piranha bite was more difficult) and a companion to hunt and fish with.

"The skills they most envied were my ability to repair an outboard motor and to use a rod and reel with lures. There was never a problem with sexual advances—a *bakra* (white person) is normally unapproachable. Also, I never gave anything but a completely neutral feedback—anything negative would have been a challenge, anything positive an invitation. Furthermore, the team spirit put me in the same category as other male field biologists; I became, in a way, an 'honorary male'—and therefore asexual."

From time to time Nicole broke her field-work routine with trips into the capital, Paramaribo, to buy supplies, put on a skirt, and visit friends and colleagues. These included Americans Henk and Judi Reichart, who were conducting a countrywide survey of mammals and the effects of hunting and tourism, under the auspices of the World Wildlife Fund. Their hospitality and encouragement were invaluable in keeping Nicole's enthusiasm and determination high.

The logistics of a project such as Nicole's are formidable, as are the expenses. She estimated that her expedition cost $3,000 per month; fortunately, it was funded by generous grants from the National Geographic Society, the World Wildlife Fund, the New York Zoological Society, and the Rare Animal Relief Effort. Nicole gives much of the credit for the success of her expedition to three factors. One was, of course, the funding and support of these conservation organizations and Suriname itself. A country with high regard for nature preservation, it has a good system of national parks and reserves. Most of its population of 385,000 live close to the coast so that southern Suriname is still wild and pristine.

The second factor was the moral support of friends such as the Reicharts and Dr. George Schaller of the New York Zoological Society, who convinced Nicole she could do the job.

The third factor was being female. As she explains, "If a woman has surmounted social barriers to be different, if she has had the single-mindedness to reach her goal, if she has sacrificed her private life, she will be ready for any discomfort, setback, or solitude that the wilderness presents. Women are often tougher than men because they are willing to accept and overcome; they have the patience, and they know how to manage their moods and those of others.

"Female zoologists tend to be the focus of much public attention," she comments, "not only because they are groundbreakers in their special areas—for example, Jane Goodall with chimps, Dian Fossey with gorillas, Birute Brindamour with orangutans, or Eugenie Clark with sharks—but also because they tend to be very competent. Because of the sacrifices involved, female field biologists tend to be highly dedicated and single-minded."

This description applies equally well to Nicole herself, and surely had much to do with her success. Why else would a BBC television crew come to Suriname to film a fifty-minute documentary on her otter work, and *National Geographic* send a photographer to take over eight thousand pictures?

Nicole's decision to study the giant river otter in Suriname was neither isolated nor spontaneous, but rather the culmination of many years of otter work and research. She first learned the fascination of field work in the late 1960's, as an assistant to a biologist studying European species of beaver. Her work with otters began at New York's Bronx Zoo in 1964–1965, when she served as a volunteer under Joseph A. Davis, then curator of mammals and an otter expert extraordinaire. Later (1965–1966) she studied animal ecology at the University of Paris, getting the French equivalent of a master of science degree. In 1966 she accompanied her professor, Dr. François Bourlière, to the Ivory Coast to study Cercopithecine monkeys and clawless otters. It was Nicole's first experience in a primary tropical rain forest, and she was thrilled by it.

From this point on she was devoted to otter work. She was strongly influenced by meeting Gavin Maxwell and Jeremy Harris, both renowned otter specialists. Over the next ten years Nicole researched captive otters at various American and European zoos. She taught otter field courses, learned scuba diving so as to observe the animals better in their watery world, contacted otter specialists, and made field studies to determine the status of otters in Great Britain.

In 1971 Nicole married David Hall, a commodities broker, and during the next four years she led a somewhat more sedentary life in London. She nevertheless managed to visit over a hundred zoos all over the world while she was editor of the *International Zoo Yearbook* for The Zoological Society of London. In this capacity she once again had a choice opportunity to watch otters in captivity and also to act as a consultant to other zoos by designing otter enclosures and doing master plans for new zoological parks.

"David, my husband, gave me a great deal of security, loyalty, and affection," recalls Nicole, "but once I had begun sprouting my own wings with the *Zoo Yearbook*, these supports were no longer important. We have very different interests and friends. As I became more involved in my work and more aware of myself, our grounds for marriage faded away.

"He was very supportive of my professional ambition and never put me down, but he never quite realized how quickly they would snowball, leaving him suddenly out in the cold. He felt 'left out' too often and realized time and my ambitions would only make matters worse. So we decided that saving our very close friendship was more important than staying together and feeling guilty about having to put up with each others' commitments.

"David needed the security of a quiet, peaceful, loving home life and not the whirlwind of meetings, dinners, and conventions I thrive on. He needed both moral support and unquestioning adulation. I failed to provide these on a daily basis."

After her divorce Nicole moved to the United States and in 1974, when she was thirty-two, she became scientific assistant to the general director of the Bronx Zoo. It was during this period of flux and instability in her life that Nicole conceived the idea of doing a long-term field study of the giant otter in Suriname and trying to save the species from extinction.

Up to this point Lily and Georges Duplaix had regarded their daughter's preoccupation with otters more as a harmless diversion than a serious profession. Both parents were involved with the arts, widely traveled, creative, and articulate. Their main sports interests were tennis and swimming, and they had never enjoyed camping or outdoor activities with their children. Although Nicole had always been a water baby and outdoors-lover, her decision to pursue her career to such extremes was incomprehensible to them. The thought of their daughter going off to the swamps and creeks of wildest Suriname seemed foolhardy and dangerous—even insane.

Nicole says she has often wondered what it might have been like to be raised in a family of famous naturalists "like the Leopolds or the Zims of this world. I might have been a better scientist, but I certainly would not have been as cosmopolitan, artistic, self-sufficient, or well-read. As it was, my professors and colleagues gave me all the necessary scientific support. It has taken my parents six years, but they gradually have accepted my choice of lifestyle and professional interest in zoology.

"Actually my childhood was marvelous, and I was spoiled rotten. I grew up in Paris, New York City, and Palm Beach. I remember different stages of discovery and of commitment. I remember watching an ant hill with my father when I was four; earlier a pet chick followed me until I walked it to death; and I discovered the joy of fishing with grubs dug out of horse manure. The outdoor opportunities came during my parents' business travels. They did not discourage my interest in nature but added it to our world of books, art, and music. Dolls bored me, but I could sit outdoors and paint or fish all day. I just slowly became magnetized until nature was my whole life. These activities were not discouraged as being an exclusively male province.

"You can be made to view things certain ways, but the decisive factor is applying them to yourself, identifying with them. I never was forced into preconceived ideas; I was, in a way, my own person and made my own decisions very early on." Then she grins. "Some people would call me intractable."

When Nicole was a teenager, she had dreams of becoming an actress. (Born a Leo, she's not shy of the spotlight.) But her ambitions soon changed course. One influential event was going diving from a three-masted schooner in the Aegean Sea and experiencing the delight of observing sea life close-up. Another factor was reading books by Gerald Durrell about animals and also Konrad Lorenz's *King Solomon's Ring*. Her goal gradually took shape: to be a marine biologist, then a veterinarian, next an anthropologist, and finally a zoologist.

"The macho image of the male conquering the wild West," Nicole continues, "the pilgrim, the farmer, the buffalo hunter with a wife back in the log cabin—we all grew up with that concept. Yet it never occurred to me that I couldn't be that man; that I was typecast to be back in the log cabin. I still think that if a girl is good enough, believes in what she wants to do enough, she will rise above the preconceived role ideas. Then people will accept her—either as an eccentric in bigoted societies or as an innovator in others. Women will be and are becoming more themselves, daring to be what they want to be, whatever the area of interest. Those for whom it is a fad will drop out. Those women for whom it is a necessity, an uncompromising way of life, will succeed. We are already reaching a stage where the novelty, the innovation, has worn off. Now comes the consolidation period, the long-term proof that women can really succeed professionally."

Suriname is behind her now, and Nicole is once again at a desk job—this time in Washington, D.C., as Director of TRAFFIC (the acronym stands for Analysis of Trade Records, Fauna and Flora in Commerce). This is an international unit which monitors wildlife trade; it is sponsored and funded by The World Wildlife Fund. She also chairs the otter specialist group of the Survival Science Commission of IUCN (International Union of Conservation of Nature and Natural Resources), and is a member of the prestigious 1001 Club of the World Wildlife Fund (those who have donated $10,000 to the Fund). Back in 1972 Prince Bernhardt of the Netherlands, then president of the Fund, approached her for names of people who might be interested in joining, and Nicole decided that becoming a member herself would be a good way of putting her money where her mouth was. She has not regretted the decision. "I met many interesting people at 1001 meetings, giving me a better understanding of what sort of person is willing to shell out $10,000, for what reasons, and what interests them about wildlife. I feel that this rather elitist, emotional group of wildlife lovers is partly what makes World Wildlife Fund so successful. WWF is very special to me, and I would be willing to give my last penny to it."

In her spare time Nicole is completing her doctoral thesis on the comparative ecology and behavior of otters, again for the University of Paris (she expects her degree in 1980). Her list of publications on otters and other mammals is already long and imposing.

Nicole Duplaix doesn't intend to sit writing in Washington for too long, however. She is planning to travel to southeast Asia or Central America as soon as she can get away, to see what's doing with otters in those parts of the world. And, no doubt, she'll drop in to Suriname to check up on the animals and people she grew so close to.

"It won't be the same as before," she warns herself sadly. "A road and bridge already have been built along Kapoeri Creek, and the Western Suriname Development Project is nearing completion. They are putting in a railroad and a new bauxite mine in that area. The population of one small Arawak Indian village has tripled in six months and it may eventually become a city of sixty thousand people. Also, a major hydroelectric dam will be built twenty-five miles south on a major river. This will probably lower the water level upstream on the Corantijn River and Kapoeri Creek, both tributaries. But I'm encouraged that the giant otters are becoming a symbol of Suriname's concern for its wildlands and wildlife. The government of Suriname is planning to make the Kapoeri Creek area into a nature preserve in 1980 or 1981. So those otters I love can go on living undisturbed somewhere in that wilderness paradise."

Chapter 20

Joan Daniels

Homesteading on the Alaskan Frontier

A<small>T FOUR O'CLOCK</small> the long Alaskan night already was descending. A low cloud cover hung over the valley, hiding the mountains and promising more snow. Bare alders and willows made a jumble of stark black lines along the creek. The only sound was the gurgling and splashing of icy water.

Inside the large tent Joan Daniels was stoking her Yukon barrel stove and steeping a pot of tea. She expected her husband Steve back momentarily and wanted their temporary home dry and warm, a hot cup of tea and freshly baked cookies ready. He'd probably carry in a load of lumber for the cabin they were building, and arrive wet to the knees from crossing the creek and tired after the half-mile hike. Damping down the stove a bit, she relaxed in a rocker and continued her sewing. Four candles burned steadily for light. All was peaceful.

Then above the muffled rush of the river, Joan heard her husband running. She hurried to the tent door and untied and opened it quickly, guessing that Steve was dodging the belligerent old moose that wintered in their valley and often chased people. Instead of Steve, Joan saw the moose galloping full tilt for the tent! Frozen, she held the door wide open and watched the moose charge right up to the stout wooden tent platform before veering off into the willows.

Joan Daniels (right) with her husband, Steve, and the author on the front porch of the Daniels' cabin in Alaska. Photo by Anne LaBastille.

Minutes later Steve trudged up calmly, balancing two twenty-foot boards on his shoulder. Had the moose been running from this apparition and not seen the tent till the last second? Or had it been intent on attacking the tent and been frightened off by the flickering flames inside? No matter—Joan and Steve happily hugged each other and collapsed into laughter over the incident.

It was one of many such wilderness surprises that Joan had faced in the past two years. That was how long she and Steve had lived in a tent in this narrow wild valley at the edge of the Chugach Mountain range, some fifty miles from Anchorage, while building their cabin. Steve and Joan Daniels were founding members of an experimental land development group—a number of families that had jointly purchased several acres in this wild country. Each family built a home on a site of its choosing.

Joan recalls, "First we built the tent platform. Then we put up the tent, and around the tent Steve then started building the hexagonal, rough lumber-and-log, two-storied structure that was to be our home. Finally, two years later, we walked the tent out the door. Even though it was just about rotted through by then, I loved living in the tent—even at 30° below zero when my sheets froze to the walls. We were always warm with the Yukon, and we could hear everything—sounds of birds, wind, moose, falling branches. We were real close to nature living in that tent.

"The only times it was a little rough," smiles the lithe, long-haired, forty-two-year-old woman, "was when the creek flooded. I was still dancing for a living then, and I often waded to work in my hip-boots and wool lumberjack shirt, with my tiny dancing costume underneath them. We never went to bed without our boots beside us in case we had to dash out to higher ground in the night."

Building the cabin was a team effort that almost defies description. The work actually had begun long before the Daniels occupied their chosen site. As Joan relates, "I danced seven years for boards, nails, and tar paper—one year in Fairbanks, three in Seward, and the last three in Anchorage. Once we actually began construction, Steve spent 80 percent of his time transporting the building supplies on his back over the half-mile trail to our site and the other 20 percent building."

Steve would drive Joan the fifty miles into work at 5:00 P.M. and pick her up again at 5:00 A.M. in their battered, four-wheel-drive pickup. During the day they both worked on the cabin. They might spend part of the morning unbolting and transporting rusty steel beams from derelict bridges to their building site. Or carrying ninety-four-pound sacks of cement along the trail. Or nailing up ceilings, building a rabbit hutch, fashioning a door from old ship planks and a porthole washed ashore near Seward. "It was sheer survival," says Joan matter-of-factly. "There were no male-female roles, no sexual stigmas, no differences between us. Each of us did everything."

During those seven years Joan danced in ballet shows, go-go bars, even topless joints—anything to make money. Her imaginative performances and fluid movements attracted people, and favorite customers often would bring her gifts: buckets of fresh scallops, a quarter haunch of venison, big oak barrels for storing food. (Presents to the other women usually came in tiny boxes). "Sometimes other dancers were aggressively hostile toward me," grins Joan. "But the guys would be so grateful. They'd sit for hours telling me stories about their lives. I'd listen and drink with one fellow, then get up and dance. Then listen and drink with another. The men were often very serious. And *so* into alcohol. They really appreciated someone cheerful to talk to. It made me realize how fortunate I was to live with Steve in such a beautiful spot."

The contrast between Joan's days and her nights was often hard to reconcile. "I used to make up all kinds of stories to tell the fellows in the bar about what I'd been doing during the day," laughs Joan. "I knew they wouldn't believe what I'd really been doing!"

Although the Daniels have neighbors almost within shouting distance, the valley is quiet because all the families in the community want to keep it that way. They walk over to one another's homes to say hello and talk, and no one ever yells loudly or uses machines unnecessarily. Their isolation is formidable; the jointly owned property backs up to the Chugach State Park, almost half a million acres of wilderness. No one in the community has plumbing, electricity, TV cables, or telephones. However, each cabin has running water right outside the front door: the creek never freezes entirely, even at 30° below zero.

As Joan says, "Our lifestyle has required a multitude of superhuman efforts over a period of years, so we kind of lost sight of 'normalcy.' I don't prefer flush toilets—I'd rather wade through snow and crawl a bit through the alders to get to our outhouse on the hill. I like chopping ice daily along the creek bank for good clean drinking water and to keep our food cold and fresh. I hold my breath in shopping malls (the air is all *used* in there). I'd rather haul firewood than go out for dinner.

"Some of the rewards are easy to describe. We can enjoy a great variety of wildlife right through our picture windows, for instance, and we can collect berries, wild greens, and mushrooms in season. Of course, we also haul boulders, shovel rocks, peel logs, repair boardwalks over the creek, and it's hard to conceive of that kind of work as anything but drudgery. To sustain this kind of effort without a loss of sensitivity seems a worthy, if difficult, goal. Our lifestyle is a day-to-day experiment in quality living."

She gazes around the stout six-sided cabin. The Yukon stove is hissing softly while bright-colored kettles and pots steam on top. Joan's kitchen space consists of two sides of the building. Wide, long planks lie beside the large picture windows with cupboards above and below. Enamel cups, iron skillets, shiny whisks, and soup ladles hang from the ceiling. There are jars upon jars of cereals and grains, a meat and grain grinder, a pressure cooker, and a stock pot on the counter tops. Another side is devoted to a cozy day couch, a desk, Joan's beloved rocker, and shelves of books. The fourth side is taken up by the thick plank dining room table, chairs, and the stove. The two remaining walls hold the heavy front door with its porthole for ventilation, a coat rack, and the steep stairs to the second floor.

Rising up through the center of both floors is an enormous support post from which the rafters fan out like spokes on a wagon wheel. Each is held in place with handmade rivets and an iron plate which Steve wrested from the boilers of an early Alaskan sawmill. As Steve explains, "Sometimes winds of sixty or seventy miles per hour roar down this valley, so we *must* have a well-constructed cabin." This cabin is more than well-constructed, however; it's an example of superb workmanship. There is an overall feeling of strength, good taste, and individuality.

Upstairs the couple's huge bed takes up one whole wall and looks directly out back into the forest and mountains up the valley. A day couch that looks onto their front yard and the creek bed is ajumble with pillows of all shapes covered with bright foreign textiles—Guatemalan, Indian, Eskimo, Navajo. A third side is exclusively for Joan's treadle sewing machine and piles of materials. Another wall has a smaller Yukon stove and heavy plank portholed door leading to a circular porch. On the south-facing window sills boxes of tomatoes and bean sprouts are tentatively bending toward the weak Alaskan winter sun. In the corners where the six walls join, narrow shelves run from floor to ceiling and hold neat piles of clothes. The central post is hung with a pot-pourri of objects—a cross fox pelt, a stuffed pheasant, flowered parasols, and jaunty hats from Joan's dancing days.

From the cabin windows by their bed Steve and Joan can see slender willows, birches, and Sitka spruce aflutter with chickadees most of the year. While they eat breakfast, they can watch Dall sheep browsing in springtime on the steep four-thousand-foot slope which forms one flank of the valley. In the grey, bouldery creek bed dippers warble and dive. The whole scene is cupped by huge stark mountains on either side of the valley.

Often Joan and Steve walk up the creek underneath enormous cottonwoods and Sitka spruces. Moose tracks and scat are everywhere in the soft forest soil, and many clumps of willows have been gnawed and debarked by the animals. Young cottonwoods and birches have been chewed through and toppled by beaver, whose dams and lodges choke the river, forming ponds. If the Daniels climb up one of the nearby mountain sides, they can see other sharp white peaks swerving up the valley one way, and the glitter of the sea far off in the other direction.

"Your art is living," a friend once told Joan. She has made it one of her precepts. "I actively pursue grace and artfulness in wilderness living. All other living forms practice and achieve it. With their extra brain cells, why can't humans? And that's all Steve and I have time and room to do. We try to match the outdoors, rather than separate ourselves from it. Any beauty we may possess or inspire in others simply complements the beauty around us that we've been given."

Other friends, especially from the lower forty-eight, often complain about the weather and the bugs. Joan is quick to comment. "The area of Alaska that we live in is no idyllic fairyland. The weather *is* inconsistent and turbulent. My husband, my grown daughters, my friends, my garden, and the wild creatures whose territory I live in are all close to me, but the weather is my real companion! I watch for it, dress for it, and move according to it through each day. To be in disharmony with it is a killing conflict. I get tired of people who are always damning the weather and saying they can't do things because of it. That's often a cop-out. We can learn from discomforts and problems. Extremes of weather, like extremes of country, shape real character and consequently real people. You've got to be adaptable, inventive, and versatile.

"As for bugs, yes, there are jillions up here. Mosquitoes, no-see-'ums, moose flies, deer flies, blackflies, whitesocks, and more mosquitoes. So you forget about superficial femininity. You wear baggy pants, head nets, bug dope, long-sleeved shirts—and you survive."

She gets up from her rocking chair and paces catlike about the cabin, her rubber-soled boots making no sound. She normally wears jeans, a wide leather belt with a Pisces sign on the buckle, a hunting knife and a woolen sweater. Her long dark hair, touched here and there with silver strands, is usually free or in braids. To 'dress up,' Joan ties on gay ribbons or tucks spruce twigs or wild flowers in her braids.

Turning gracefully, she philosophizes for a moment. "Wilderness work and living demands physical strength, strength of character, and decisiveness. These are qualities that are often overlooked in women whose work or lifestyle is more sedate. In the woods these qualities are no longer subtle, and this often nourishes the attitude that woodswomen are tough and callous. That's a dreadful misconception. In some ways women are like doilies: complex and lacy. But in the woods they require starch."

This quality of "starch" is what has nurtured and sustained Joan through many crises in Alaska. She says she loves crisis because it knocks the complacency out of her and whets her instinct for survival. When the creek flooded and threatened the Daniels' and their neighbors' homes, Joan and her closest neighbor sewed up burlap into sandbags by night, which the men then filled with sand by day. Earthquakes are about as frequent as breezes, kids Joan. Ten per year is probably a conservative estimate.

And the wildlife is not always benign. Once, when Joan was entertaining her mother from Washington State, a grizzly appeared on her porch and began rummaging around. The two women, who had been inside sewing, began to beat on pans, clap, shout, and pound on the windows in hopes of scaring the animal away. The bear just snarled, not in the least intimidated. Joan's mother was so terrified, and the grizzly seemed so intent on entering the cabin that Joan, in desperation, picked up a rifle and fired into the air— whereupon the grizzly ran off. The Daniels have had other close calls with wildlife, such as the episode of the moose charging their tent.

Their life holds other perils, both natural and manmade. Fire is perhaps the most terrifying; Steve is a former smoke-jumper and has had extensive experience fighting forest fires in Montana, Idaho, and Alaska. His fire consciousness promotes a healthy awareness among the little community, which lives in a valley ravaged by fire thirty years ago. Then there is the freezing winter cold, the hazards of avalanches or climbing falls in the mountains, car accidents on the back roads and highways, injuries from chainsaws and axes. Luckily Joan and Steve have escaped any such mishaps; however, Steve suffers from lung congestion brought on by a combination of smoke inhalation during his fire-fighting days and a bad bout of pneumonia. Consequently, he must guard against overexertion and has found it necessary to avoid smoke, alcohol, and refined sugars, and to take massive doses of Vitamin C. Nevertheless, the tall, beautifully muscled man has extraordinary strength. He is known up and down the valley and coast as a veritable Paul Bunyan.

Did Joan Daniels grow up in Alaska, accustomed to such hardships, adventures, and perils? Not at all. Yet her fantasies as a young girl prepared her for Alaska. She grew up in Washington with her mother, a grade-school secretary who enjoyed walking, hiking, and participating in a variety of organized sports, as her sole parent. Joan describes her mother as plucky and always ready to try something new. "Mother had an eye for beauty in nature. We always had fresh flowers in the house. She would walk five miles for a branch of bittersweet. And in fall, when we still lived on our farm in Ohio, she always marched us to the woods with gunny sacks to gather hickory nuts.

"We had no TV when I was a child—thank goodness. My world revolved around frogs and cows, blackberries and blue racers, oat bugs and apple dumplings, wild violets and wiggly things in the cistern. My great ambition was to collect as many lightning bugs as possible in jars, and my great passion was fort building. My devotion to warm, dry, and secret shelters required hours of hard work and was surpassed only by my determination to stock them with enough Rice Krispies and wheat germ to keep myself and my cohorts alive forever in case of any disaster.

"My interest in wilderness was instinctive, I think. Nothing ever stirred me into more ecstatic productivity than an approaching purple or gray horizon. No moving picture could compete for entertainment with a ferocious storm."

Even as a young girl, Joan admired older people who possessed traditional skills in homemaking and country living. The vision of a woman going to bed with her shoulders and arms aching from kneading the weekly bread, she claims, would send her into a romantic swoon in those days. Her favorite adult was her grandfather, a devout Mennonite, who exposed her to a culture whose past and present are rural and even pioneering.

"At the ripe old age of thirteen Alaska became infused in my vision of my future, though I'll admit there was a period when singing, dancing, and movie stardom got serious consideration! I made a secret pact with myself to get to Alaska somehow, but it was a long time before that became a reality.

"I married at sixteen and had two dear daughters before I was twenty. This was a stormy alliance, and it detained me, but I knew the time would come, so I waited. Along the way I was discouraged by my very young husband. I naively thought that our little family was perfectly suited for going north and homesteading; he preferred the intellectual life, although he was an astute hunter (a combination I could never reconcile). And hunting was strictly his domain—no amount of pleading on my part would convince him to allow me into the woods with him. I stayed home to mind the electricity: year after year, dreaming of the cabin in the wilderness and the wonder-woodsman who was ruggedly handsome, very brave, very strong, very true, and who insisted that I accompany him on *every* hunting trip!

"Since I had been an outrageously defiant youngster, I now became fiercely independent as a mother and homemaker. I still had a clear picture of my direction, but how to get there with a balking dinosaur for a mate was a problem that called for some radical surgery. It came down to a simple emotional nightmare—divorce the balking dinosaur. That was step number one.

"Step number two was to stabilize and earn a small grubstake, manage a large house, make a lively and interesting home for my two girls, and return to school. That was another pact I had made with myself. When my youngest daughter entered primary school, I went back to finish high school. The two steps took two very full years.

"Finally I took off for the North Country on my own. When I landed in Fairbanks, I was about forty-five years old in experience, though only twenty-five years in actual physical age. And I was there in the guise of a saloon dancer. No Mennonite would have claimed me!

"I was definitely through with men. I'd spent some time on intensive research in the Prince-Rugged-Charming department, had given up, and had decided to leave all those drips in the dust. There I was, my first night in Fairbanks, dressed in my little costume, sitting in that smokey saloon when the bartender announced, "The smoke-jumpers are on their way!" All the other girls got real excited and started preening and fixing their hair. I just sat there, not knowing what to expect, and I couldn't have cared less. Then Steve walked through the door, and suddenly I cared. Those blue eyes told me we were headed straight for the woods. And so my greatest adventure began: how to get the money, the land, the necessary skills."

After the years of dancing and getting settled, Joan turned to another of her talents to help provide an income—creative cooking. She started as first cook at a new restaurant and worked a year there until the place was fully functioning. After three years of that the couple decided to stay out of the restaurant business and stay closer to home. As Steve puts it, "We went back to the creek to listen to dozens of chickadees sing all day, ice skate on our beaver ponds, take hikes up the icy creek to a waterfall, gaze nightly at the magnificent northern lights and stars, and wonder at our folly in the big and very disappointing city of Anchorage.

"We could make out O.K. by taking occasional part-time jobs, myself doing rough carpentry, and Joan working on the herring boats or catering. More and more we live off the land and sea and forests."

The Daniels have a garden area squared off and enriched with woodchips, ashes, compost, and manure that supplies them with gigantic cabbages, turnips, carrots, potatoes, and other vegetables. They have a small greenhouse for starting seeds, a rabbit hutch, and chicken pens. There's also a sawdust pile to store ice chunks, great stacks of firewood, and a tool shed. In the summer they keep their food cold in metal milk crates partially sunken in the brook. When Joan has large parties to cater to in Anchorage, she often drives out to get aqua-blue ice from one of the nearby glaciers. It melts slowly and will keep things cold a long time inside the sawdust pile.

In springtime Joan eagerly forages for wild greens. As far north as they live, the forests and fields still provide plenty. She collects stems and flower heads of coltsfoot, the shoots and blossoms of fireweed, dandelion greens, yellow cress, fiddleheads, violet leaves, mountain sorrel, and Arctic dock. Each green she prepares in a unique and delicious manner. Then she succumbs to "mushroom madness." "I'm so intrigued by mushrooms," she raves. "I experiment with them alot. My one rule of thumb is: Never eat two different varieties within twenty-four hours."

As summer progresses, there comes "berry mania." Dressed in headnets and impenetrable clothing, Joan and her daughters comb the bogs and hillsides, picking rosehips, wild cranberries, serviceberries, raspberries, currants, and crowberries. "I can't help myself," Joan grins. "I have a real primitive urge to gather. And I measure my wealth in berries and firewood."

She also augments their menus with Dolly Varden trout and salmon from the streams, occasional caribou meat in sausages and mince pie, and, of course, venison, bear, and moose meat. Joan plucks spruce tips in early spring and dries them for tea.

Joan is often called an "earth mother" by the many guests who enjoy her hospitality and admire her talent for living. She smiles and shrugs. "I just don't let people feel sorry for themselves. I give them wholesome meals and meaty conversations. Food is a universal fuel and every creature's outlook is improved by it. Sometimes I advise people to take a plane ride and look down at the earth. From that perspective, their problems will seem less significant. Then I tell 'em to *get busy* and *stay busy*."

Joan and Steve are often visited by her two grown daughters, Scarlet and Sara. Nineteen-year-old Sara is a sprightly girl with many talents and a wonderful sense of humor. Scarlet, at twenty-one, is almost the spitting image of her mother. She also dances professionally. To see them together, one thinks they are sisters. In fact, Joan confides, sometimes her girls are embarrassed by her because she's so lively and outspoken. They say she acts younger than they do.

"I've always been very permissive with my girls," she explains. "And I've taught them that they can manage anything. Once Scarlet was driving her old Volkswagen through Anchorage when it died at an intersection. She'd been having trouble with the battery and had another in the back for safe measure. So she opened up the door, hauled out the battery, and installed it by herself. People just sat in their cars and stared to see this foxy-looking girl repairing her car.

"I want them to be capable, but I don't want them to get so independent that they repulse men. There are some women like that up here in Alaska—real spitfires. I'd hate to tangle with them. They're very capable. They fly planes, drive heavy equipment, run chainsaws, log, captain fishing boats, do mechanics, enter sports marathons. They get so independent that they can't tolerate or have no need for any man who's not as competent. As a result, it seems an awful lot of men and women are just not getting together up here.

"Of course, once in a while I come upon a man who resents my independence on the basis of my sex. This man is in trouble with himself, and I immediately turn right or left. I have no interest in a confrontation on this basis. It's like challenging a retarded child, which is not a perfect analogy for the retarded child would probably learn something.

"This is not to say I have never put feminine mystique in my back pocket and marched onto the battlefield. But age does contribute to wisdom. I get stronger as I get older and less noisy."

Joan also seems to get more talented and more catholic in her tastes. She will work two weeks at sea aboard a herring boat, standing up twelve to fourteen hours a day and squeezing eggs from rotted female fish. The eggs are brined and sent to Japan.

The smell is impressive and the work exhausting. After the two weeks her arms and hands are numb from stripping thousands of fish bodies, but her pocketbook is fatter. Then she will return quietly to the cabin, relax, and work on home-made gifts. Joan loves stitchery and makes fabric pictures, a combination of applique and embroidery. One of her pieces made her the grand champion of stitchery at the Alaska State Fair in 1978.

On rare occasions she and Steve will drive into Anchorage to hear Paul Rosenthal, Alaska's extraordinary violinist. Or they may go to Homer to see an art show. One of their favorite pastimes is hunting through junk shops and trash piles. "We always find something useful and timely," explains Joan. "In fact I've often thought about having my own junk store."

Berries, moose, rhubarb, cement bags, sewing machines, chickadees, pickup trucks, tents, sourdough—this is the fabric of Joan's life in Alaska, its pattern and color imposed by the wilderness she loves so well.

"Wilderness!" she exclaims. "When I am out in it no animal, tree, or breeze identifies me as a woman. I feel a part of it, connected to its energy. It's the ultimate school for the "human bean" who has placed too much emphasis on himself or herself. Wilderness should provide us with a more balanced viewpoint of life and life systems."

Chapter 21

Women and Wilderness

W E HAVE NOW seen fifteen contemporary women living and working in the wilderness, as well as examples of several historical wilderness women. The women in the profiles are a diverse group—an outdoor-magazine editor in New York City, a university professor who dives in the Red Sea, a New Jersey housewife–mother–caver, and so on—and they may seem to have little in common. So what really *is* a "wilderness woman"?

Clearly the wilderness means different things to different women, and it molds their personalities and professional careers in various ways. However, I believe there are certain characteristics common to most women who live and work in the outdoors. My travels and interviews to produce this book and my own lifestyle, described in my earlier book, *Woodswoman,* have offered me some understanding of these qualities.

Before I describe them, it seems appropriate to further define *wilderness* as the term is used in this book. In general, most of the women profiled define it as open space that provides a habitat for wildlife and natural vegetation and lacks motorized access roads or "civilized improvements." Some women offered more details, ranging from Jeanne Gurnee's sensitive appreciation of "pockets of natural environment" in heavily populated suburban areas; to Elaine Rhode's "areas in which the only recognized 'time' is natural

287

and evolutionary, as the modern development-oriented world races past"; to Diana Cohen's "an integral energy system which has the ability to sustain itself, and within which there is no room for value judgments."

Definitions offered by men associated with the wilderness are similar. David Brower, perhaps the best-known spokesman of the environmental movement for the past twenty years, has said:

Wilderness is a place wherein the flow of life, in its myriad forms, has gone on since the beginning of life, essentially uninterrupted by man and his technology. It is a place where man respects what that life force built in the old eternity and what that same force can probably keep building well in the new eternity, and without man's help—except in his willingness to come, see and not conquer.

Dr. Stephen H. Spurr, dean of the School of Natural Resources at the University of Michigan, defines wilderness as "simply an ecosystem in which man is a relatively unimportant factor."

The values which the women profiled place on the wilderness are essentially the same as those enumerated by men. Almost all have recognized the scientific value of wilderness: as a biological yardstick or control to measure and evaluate other environmental communities more influenced by human beings; as a genetic reservoir; as a center of dispersal for species which may have been extirpated elsewhere; as a source and wellspring of clean air and water; as a natural laboratory and study area of complex and dynamic ecological relationships in fairly pristine condition; and as a sanctuary for species of fauna and flora that need vast spaces or have critically low tolerances for human intrusion.

They almost all recognize as well the cultural values of wild nature: its influence on poetry and literature, art and sculpture, music, and television. They have acknowledged the spiritual values which give human beings a sense of well-being and renewal in this age of shrinking space and clamorous civilization, as well as the sheer aesthetics, the recreational opportunities, and the psychological stabilizing power found in wilderness. Most of the women echoed the words of Sigurd Olson, the noted conservationist and nature writer:

. . . the opportunity of knowing again what simplicity really means, the importance of the natural and the sense of oneness with the earth that inevitably comes within it. These are spiritual values. They, in the last analysis, are the reasons for [wilderness] preservation.

Finally, they have pointed out that wilderness can help human beings learn survival in a world that discourages self-reliance. Maggie Nichols has written about this eloquently in her book *Wild, Wild Woman*.

One of the greatest treasuries of choice lies in the out-of-doors. Not that I dismiss the richness of cities. . . . But alienation from nature is far more widespread than alienation from concrete, and for many living in the midst of superhighways it is easy to let a lifetime slip away without discovering the deep pleasures that are to be found in the undeveloped outdoors.

Such a loss would be a tragedy. All of us need to keep in touch with wild, unruly things, even if we do it in the tamest possible way. But sadly, some are content to do their touching through the magic of television, letting nature shows do the walking, as it were. Those who know the outdoors solely through the TV or movie screen simply do not know the outdoors, any more than a man falling in love with a *Playboy* centerfold knows that woman.

Meeting nature face-to-face is worth whatever effort is involved. Besides the aesthetic values and personal joys that come from close acquaintance, or the physical and mental stimulation you get from active involvement in outdoor sports, there are other more serious reasons for learning to get along with the world out there. It doesn't take much looking to see that more than just personal lives are running toward an end. There is no longer all the time in the world for things like oil, natural gas, or maybe even food. No one really knows anymore.

People whose only survival techniques consisted of turning switches and dials to heat and light the house or driving to the supermarket for food found themselves in real trouble [during the winter of 1977], stuck without resources of knowledge or equipment to see them through. . . .

Self-reliance is the key in the end, not just to the possible demands of the future, but to a sense of well-being now. The outdoor person who knows that he or she can catch fish, get meat, build a fire, live outdoors, rig a camp, make do on lots or little, and enjoy the unexpectedness of life has a large psychological edge over the person who has never tried to live without all lines plugged in. Bad times may never happen, but if they do, the outdoor person is the one who will be best prepared.

As for the traits that characterize a "wilderness woman": if we can take the fifteen profiles as any sort of sample, I'd say these are enthusiasm, youthfulness (regardless of age), idealism, a sense of commitment, a certain disregard for convention, capability, self-sufficiency, self-confidence, love of nature, and, in varying degrees, a sense of adventure. On the physical side, without exception each woman looked far younger than her actual age and was in good physical shape.

Many women who have outdoor careers or a strong connection to the wilderness also consider themselves feminists. The two groups seem to share some goals—independence, the right to equal work opportunities, and the freedom to do what one wants. But for the most part the wilderness women lack the militancy and hostility toward men that some women's liberation groups display. I did not notice any bitterness in these wilderness women toward men. Regardless of marital status—some were single, some divorced (up to four times), and some widowed—all but one of the profiled women clearly enjoyed heterosexual relationships. Two showed strong signs of competition with men though enjoyed their company. No wilderness woman talked disparagingly about men.

Yet it is easy to see how bitterness and antagonism arise if we define feminism as Adrienne Rich does in Ruddich and Daniels's book *Working It Out*:

Feminism means finally that we renounce our obedience to the fathers and recognize that the world they have described is not the whole world. Masculine ideologies are the creation of masculine subjectivity; they are neither objective, nor value-free, nor inclusively "human." Feminism implies that we recognize fully the inadequacy for us, the distortion, of male-created ideologies, and that we proceed to think, and act, out of that recognition.

The only emotion that came close to this was expressed by the two academic women, Meg Stewart and Eugenie Clark; they, like myself, had to struggle with sex discrimination in order to achieve their doctoral status and find professional jobs.

Maggie Nichols's definition of feminism seems more pertinent to most of the women I interviewed. She says, "Feminism is getting in touch with your own values, intelligence, resourcefulness, physical capacities, and general ability to live a rich and satisfying life of your own, not only with but apart from friends and loved ones." Certainly the wilderness allows, even encourages, women to do all that. I feel that wilderness-oriented women differ from their male counterparts chiefly in the recentness of their entrance into this arena, with its accompanying challenges, risks, and benefits. Consequently, women still feel reticent about going into the wild. But the fifteen women profiled here are clearly finding and developing their own strength, endurance, and determination.

And what about the many women in America who love the outdoors and nature, but who are not heard from in this book? What does the idea of "wilderness women" mean to them? In the two years that I have been instructing a weekend workshop called "Women in the Woods" and three years of leading backpacking trips on ten-day "Wilderness Workshops" (now run by the Adirondack Institute), I feel I have gained some insights about such women. During the course of these experiences I asked approximately one hundred women to list historical or contemporary female role models that they looked to for their inspiration. The combined lists of all the participants named, in addition to "pioneer women in general," only fifteen individuals: Sacajawea, Pocahontas, Anna B. Comstock, Frances Page Jacques, Annie Oakley, Calamity Jane, Juliette Lowe (founder of the Girl Scouts), Willa Cather, Dorothy Moulter (a retired nurse who has lived alone for years on an island in the Boundary Waters Canoe Area), Joy Adamson (who worked with lions in Africa), Audrey Sutherland (author of *Paddling My Own Canoe*), Amelia Earhart, Rachel Carson, Margaret Mead, and Jane Goodall.

This hardly complete or accurate list reveals that women have not been taught very much about their adventurous forebears. If the participants had been asked to name men associated with the wilderness, their lists probably would have been far more extensive.

The other revealing exercise was to distinguish the traits that make a "woodswoman." These women listed, in order of importance and relevance: appreciation of the natural world, skill and competence out-of-doors, ability to survive in the wilderness, knowledge of natural history, self-sufficient and independent nature, and ability to be comfortable in the wilderness. Of lesser importance, and all rated on an equal basis, were: a sense of freedom, enjoyment of wilderness, appreciation of wildlife, enjoyment of being alone in the wilderness, and a need to preserve the wilderness. Traits mentioned by only one or two women were gutsiness, adventuresomeness, strong body, good spirit, lack of fear, ability to share with others, safety consciousness, need for peace, and femininity.

Although I know of no specific psychological studies that corroborate this information, I am assuming these values might be typical of most contemporary women's views of the wilderness. Having been a woodswoman for fifteen years, I would agree with them, although I would place far more value on adventuresomeness, a strong body, and safety consciousness. During the "Women in the Woods" weekends most of the participants, who were fledgling outdoorspeople, exhibited quite a bit of nervousness about not knowing what to do. They also were somewhat afraid of dirt, discomfort, injury, or ridicule at first. However, there was such a supportive and loving atmosphere among the women that by the second day almost everyone was at ease and eagerly trying new challenges such as rappelling, canoeing, nature photography, and so on.

In the wilderness workshops, which spanned ten days and included both male and female participants, the women's uneasiness wore off more slowly. I would say that this was probably because there were men present and possibly because the women novices felt inferior to their instructor. Fortunately, none of the men in my sessions were aggressively macho, and most were caring and supportive of their fellow participants.

Diana Cohen, who has worked with young women and men in the wilderness for a number of years, observes:

Very few of our students have had difficulty in a wilderness setting, but the ones who have, have been females. I can't think of a time that I had to assist a male student through rough or rocky terrain or had to coax them through a difficult backpack or cross-country ski trek. Yet over the years I have done this with women students. But I believe the difficulty they experience has nothing to do with their physical inability or stamina but comes from lack of confidence.

She also mentions that when a student occasionally makes a point of being first in line on a hike, it is always a male. My own experience also has been that women generally tend to do less showing off and putting themselves forward in wilderness situations than men.

Women who go into the wilderness for professional or recreational reasons come into frequent contact with men there. What is the nature of their interaction in the outdoors today, compared with frontier days? Chivalry, courteousness, and lack of criminal intent on the part of most men continued into the early 1900's, as we can judge from many of the accounts in Chapter 2. In recent times, however, there seems to be some slight increase of resentment, competitiveness, loss of courtesy, and even brutality in men's dealings with women outdoors. This is probably a natural reaction of some men toward what they see as invasion of previously all-male professions or lifestyles. Fortunately, it is not a widespread reaction.

The deep-seated fear of being raped or molested while alone outdoors is an ancient and perhaps a universal terror. I consider, however, that it is less well founded in the wilderness than in any other place, and that rape and assault tend to be perversions more common to the inner cities and other highly populated and stressful areas. The circumstances all point against a woman being troubled in the wilderness. For one thing, there are far fewer men outdoors than in the cities, and certainly far fewer "crazies." Somehow the wilderness isn't the right habitat for sex offenders. I have no statistics on sexual violence in wilderness settings; however, a study conducted in Philadelphia in 1967 found that of 647 known rapes, only 51.1 percent of the victims were strangers to their attackers. Furthermore, it was found that 55.7 percent of the rapes occurred in the home, 14.9 percent in cars, and 29.4 percent elsewhere, mainly in the street. This study would seem to indicate most rapes take place not in the woods, prairies, dark glens, caves or canyons, but within the domestic realm where friends and acquaintances meet. Fully 70 percent of rapes were prearranged and planned,

with only a mere 15.9 percent happening in an impulsive way.*
The only exception seems to be a totally psychotic killer or rapist
in an isolated area, a very rare occurrence.

All of the women I interviewed, plus myself, have had generally
positive experiences dealing with men in the outdoors. None were
ever raped, roughed up, or made uncomfortable by male co-work-
ers, companions, or strangers during chance wilderness meetings.
Moreover, a good many stated that if a woman acts professional,
competent, and polite, men will normally respond in kind and
treat her with respect and courtesy. Men usually show either respect and a tendency to protect a woman met on the trail, or a
shying away, as if the woman is invading their privacy. Once individuals get to know each other, these tendencies seem to de-
crease. And, not least, being in the wilderness is a demanding and
energy-consuming experience; one is usually concerned with
surviving, not about making sexual advances to a stranger.

Aside from a few minor differences, then, wilderness-oriented
men and women today interact well in this environment and relate
to the wilderness in essentially the same ways. The director of the
wilderness workshops I instructed, Dr. Jon Fairbanks, has had
over a thousand students go through his institute over an eight-
year period, and he corroborates this observation. He writes:

I have found no great distinction between the ways men and women
relate to the wilderness. Both sexes respond to the challenge—whether
it is a three-mile portage, a bushwhack through thick spruce, or a steep
snowclimb to a high summit. Men in general are physically stronger. But
it is the individual spirit that is critical. And this I have observed certainly
as much in women as in men. Conversely, men are as sensitive to the
beauty of the landscape as are the women.

At all events, I think the important point is not which sex is
better or worse, stronger or weaker, or more or less involved, in
the wilderness, but that they are both out there working, playing,
and living richer and healthier lives because of it. Women in the
wilderness is not a passing fad. It's a permanent necessity. As
Jeanne Gurnee said to me:

*Amir, Women Sexuality, and Social Control, 1978.

People are searching more and more for their roots—not ancestral, genealogical roots, but roots for themselves as human beings who are seeking out the environment that was originally created for them and which has been so greatly altered. Whereas women do not seem traditionally to have been associated with wilderness, there has been a tremendous burst of interest in wilderness-type work and recreation in the last few years. Women I know who have never set foot in the forest or never climbed a mountain have received a sense of new-found euphoria in these experiences. I believe the phenomenon is here to stay and will help people find themselves.

It has been a long evolutionary process, spanning centuries, which has brought women to their present sophisticated and sensitive level of awareness about and participation in the wilderness. In a sense, it seems to me like the closing of a circle. In prehistory, women were directly associated with the fertility and nurturing power of the earth, and in the ancient world this took the form of their incarnation as goddesses of agriculture, fertility, fruitfulness, the moon, tides, and planets. With the spread of Judeo-Christian thought in the Western world came fear about the wilderness and about the wild part of women's nature. The eighteenth century brought the first scientific study of the natural world, and the nineteenth century the romanticizing of nature, along with the exploration and exploitation of the wilderness. In this period, as we saw earlier, women's presence was a symbol of the civilizing impulse, and this usually served to alienate most women from the wilderness when they might otherwise have found it a liberating environment. More recently we have seen a growing scientific understanding of natural laws and ecological principles, and finally the realization of the environmental threats we face. In this last stage we have come to a new sense of protectiveness, nurturing, and mothering of our earth. Now women are as much concerned as men, just as active and just as effective. They have challenged the stereotypes and traditions of female roles and behavior and entered into the environmental movement. Once again they have become guardians of nature. If Louise Bogan could pen her poem "Women" today, perhaps she would begin it:

Women have wilderness in them.

Appendix A

Women and Wilderness Questionnaire

The following questionnaire was sent to fifty women who were preliminary candidates for the profiles in Part Two of this book. The final selection of women profiled was based on the responses I received as well as other factors that contributed to a broad and varied group of portraits.

1. How do you define wilderness? What would you say are the values of wilderness?
2. How did you first get interested in outdoor/wilderness activities/ work/living? Did someone "show" you? Who? Or did you discover the outdoors on your own?
3. What were your experiences along the way? Were you generally encouraged or discouraged? Please explain and give examples of your experiences.
4. What did your parents do professionally? In what kinds of outdoors activities, if any, did they participate?
5. Do you think women have traditionally *not* been associated with outdoors/wilderness work/play? If not, what reasons do you see for this? What social attitudes have you observed; and where have you observed them (for example, among friends, in media, etc.)?

6. Do you think women will enter increasingly into wilderness-type work and recreation? Is this phenomenon here to stay, or is it only a fad?

7. Do you know of any females in history who have worked, played, or lived outdoors and made reputations for themselves based on these activities? (Examples might be Annie Oakley or Sacajawea.)

8. How do you believe women differ from men in their relationship and attitudes toward the outdoors? In endurance? Strength? Appreciation? Survival ability and skills? Personal hygiene requirements? Fear? Bravery? Attitude toward wildlife? Weather? Hardship? Or do you see no differences?

9. Do you know of any books, papers, journals, articles, etc., that address the subject of women in the wilderness; i.e., outdoor-type working women or women who've associated themselves in significant ways with wilderness?

10. Anything else you have to say on the subject?

Appendix B

Wilderness Schools and Courses

A wide variety of schools, workshops, university courses, and training sessions have become available to both women and men in the last several years. They teach, according to their emphasis, outdoor skills and techniques, physical conditioning, survival, environmental protection measures and attitudes. Some offer a highly supportive environment; others may be extremely competitive, and women should judge for themselves which are best suited to their personalities. A distinction should be made between schools or courses offering actual instruction, and tour or expedition services that run unusual vacations in wild and remote settings. The latter are not included here, nor are the numerous specialized mountaineering schools that exist mainly in the West.

What follows is a limited listing. Further information can be found in the author's article "Wilderness Schools" (*Field and Stream*, June 1980). You should write in advance for details and/ or brochures.

ADIRONDACK INSTITUTE
Skidmore College
Saratoga Springs, New York 12866

Offers ten-day wilderness workshops in the Adirondacks.

CHALLENGE-DISCOVERY
Box 229
Crested Butte, Colorado 81224

A wilderness education program formally affiliated with Antioch College.

HAWAII BOUND
Box 1500
Kailua, Hawaii 96734

Exploring the coast and mountains of Hawaii while learning outdoor skills; modeled after the Outward Bound school.

HEADWATERS
Box 288P
Temagami, Ontario P0H 2HO

Wilderness canoe travel in the Canadian North.

HIGH COUNTRY EXPEDITIONS WILDERNESS SCHOOL
Nye, Montana 59061

Year-round wilderness expeditions in the mountains of Montana.

THE INFINITE ODYSSEY
57 Grant Street
Waltham, Massachusetts 02154

Teaching and practice of wilderness skills and exploration of exciting wilderness areas.

NANTAHALA OUTDOOR CENTER
Box 68
Bryson City, North Carolina 28713

Group training programs including canoeing, kayaking, backpacking, rock climbing, and skiing; also wilderness trips abroad.

OUTDOOR EDUCATIONAL CONSULTANTS
465 South Newton Ave.
Minneapolis, Minnesota 55405

General introduction to adventuring in wilderness environments.

OUTWARD BOUND
384 Field Point Road
Greenwich, Connecticut 06832

The well-known wilderness survival courses, with branches in many
parts of the country.

THE SIERRA CLUB
530 Bush Street
San Francisco, California 94108

Offers a broad range of outdoor trips and instruction; local chapters
nationwide and in Canada.

SUNDANCE EXPEDITIONS
14894 Galice Road
Merlin, Oregon 97532

River running by kayak or raft, plus fishing.

VENTURE
Cone University Center
University of North Carolina
Charlotte, North Carolina 28223

A wilderness education program adapted from Outward Bound.

THE WILDERNESS INSTITUTE
333 Fairfax Street
Denver, Colorado 80220

High country ski tours, winter camping, and mountaineering.

WOMEN IN THE WILDERNESS
San Francisco Ecology Center
13 Columbus Avenue
San Francisco, California 94111

Educational organization devoted to women's participation in the
wilderness; publishes a newsletter of its activities; sponsors and
recommends trips and outings.

Bibliography

Note: Sources referred to in more than one chapter are listed here under the chapter where first mentioned.

Introduction

Bogan, Louise. 1954. *Collected Poems, 1923–1953.* New York: Noonday Press.

Faragher, J., and C. Stansell. 1975. "Women and Their Families on the Overland Trail to California and Oregon, 1842–1867," *Feminist Studies,* vol. 2, no. 2/3.

O'Meara, Walter. 1968. *Daughters of the Country. The Women of the Fur Traders and Mountain Men.* New York: Harcourt, Brace.

Chapter 1

(For novels, journals, memoirs, and letters, please see Chapters 2 and 3.)

Alderson, Nannie Tiffany. 1942. *A Bride Goes West.* New York: Farrar and Rinehart.

Erikson, Erik H. 1950. *Childhood and Society.* New York: W. W. Norton.

Fischer, Christiane. 1978. *Let Them Speak for Themselves. Women in the American West, 1849–1900.* New York: Dutton.

Groves, Ernest R. 1937. *The American Woman. The Feminine Side of a Masculine Civilization.* New York: Greenberg Publications.

Hofstadter, R., and S. M. Lipset (eds.). 1968. *Turner and the Sociology of the Frontier*. New York: Basic Books.

Kolodny, Annette. 1978. "To Render a Home a Paradise: Women on the New World Landscapes." In *Women's Language and Style*, D. Butturff and E. L. Epstein (eds.). Akron, Ohio: Department of English, University of Akron.

Lander, Dawn. 1978. "Women and the Wilderness: Taboos in American Literature." In *The University of Michigan Papers in Women's Studies*. Ann Arbor: University of Michigan.

Keeler, John. 1978. "Interview with Paul Petzoldt: Professor of the Wilderness," *Mariah*, vol. 3, no. 3, June–July, 1978.

Lawick-Goodall, Jane van. 1971. *In the Shadow of Man*. New York: Dell.

Montagu, Ashley. 1953. *The Natural Superiority of Women*. New York: Macmillan.

Romney, A.K. 1965. "Variations in Household Structure as Determinants of Sex-typed Behavior." In *Sex and Behavior*, F. A. Beach (ed.). New York: Wiley.

Sherman, Julia A. 1971. *On the Psychology of Women. A Survey of Empirical Studies*. Springfield, Ill.: C. C. Thomas.

Williams, Juanita H. 1977. *Psychology of Women. Behavior in a Biosocial Context*. New York: W. W. Norton.

Time-Life Books. 1978. *The Women*. The Old West Series, vol. 23. Alexandria, Va.: Time-Life Books.

Chapter 2

Bird, Isabella L. 1960. *A Lady's Life in the Rocky Mountains*. Norman: University of Oklahoma Press.

Eastman, Elaine Goodale. 1978. *Sister to the Sioux. The Memoirs of Elaine Goodale Eastman, 1855–91*, Graber, K. (ed.). Lincoln: University of Nebraska Press.

Hickok, Martha Jane Cannary. 1976. *Calamity Jane's Letters to Her Daughter*. Berkeley, Calif.: Shameless Hussy Press.

Moodie, Susanna. 1962. *Roughing It in the Bush (or Forest Life in Canada)*. Toronto: McClelland and Stewart.

Royce, Sarah Bayliss. 1977. *A Frontier Lady. Recollections of the Gold Rush and Early California*. Lincoln: University of Nebraska Press.

Stewart, Elinore Pruitt. 1961. *Letters of a Woman Homesteader*. Lincoln: University of Nebraska Press.

Summerhayes, Martha. 1979. *Vanished Arizona. Recollections of the Army Life of a New England Woman*. Lincoln: University of Nebraska Press.

Chapter 3

Cather, Willa. 1913. *O, Pioneers!* Boston: Houghton Mifflin.
————. 1918. *My Ántonia*. Boston: Houghton Mifflin.
Guthrie, A.B., Jr. 1949. *The Way West*. New York: William Sloane, Associates.
Richter, Conrad. 1940. *The Trees*. New York: Knopf.
————. 1946. *The Fields*. New York: Knopf.
————. 1950. *The Town*. New York: Knopf.
Rölvaag, O. E. 1927. *Giants in the Earth. A Saga of the Prairie*. New York: Harper.

Chapter 4

Agassiz, Louis, and Elizabeth Agassiz. 1868. *A Journey in Brazil*. Boston: Ticknor and Fields. (Harvard University Press, Cambridge).
Akeley, Delia J. 1930. *Jungle Portraits*. New York: Macmillan.
Dole, Gertrude E. 1978. *Vignettes of Some Early Members of the Society of Woman Geographers in New York*. Closter, N.J.: Society of Woman Geographers.
Field and Stream magazine, early issues.
Greer, Germaine. 1979. *The Obstacle Race. The Fortunes of Women Painters and Their Work*. New York: Farrar Straus & Giroux.
Groves, Ernest R. 1944. *The American Women: Images and Realities*. New York: Emerson Books.
Huth, Hans. 1957. *Nature and the American*. Berkeley: University of California Press.
Jacques, Florence P. 1938. *Canoe Country*. Minneapolis: University of Minnesota Press.
James, E. T., J. W. James, and P. S. Boyer (eds.). 1971. *Notable American Women. 1607–1950*. 3 vols. Cambridge, Mass.: Harvard University Press.
Lamb, Dana, and Ginger Lamb. 1938. *Enchanted Vagabonds*. New York: Harper.
————. 1951. *Quest for the Lost City*. New York: Harper.
Murphy, Grace Barstow. 1943. *There's Always Adventure: The Story of a Naturalist's Wife*. New York: Harper.
Shor, Frank, and Jean Shor. 1955. *After You, Marco Polo*. New York: McGraw-Hill.
Smuts, R. W. 1959. *Women and Work in America*. New York: Columbia University Press.
Stanwell-Fletcher, T. C. 1946. *Driftwood Valley*. Boston: Little, Brown.

Chapter 5

Conable, C. W. 1977. *Women at Cornell. The Myth of Equal Education*. Ithaca, N.Y.: Cornell University Press.

Jacques Cattell Press (eds.). 1921 (3rd ed.), 1938 (6th ed.). *American Men of Science*. Garrison, N.Y.: Science Press.

Kohlstedt, Sally G. 1978. "In from the Periphery: American Women in Science, 1830–1880," *Signs: Journal of Women in Culture and Society*, vol. 4, no. 1.

LaBastille, Anne. 1976. *Woodswoman*. New York: Dutton.

National Research Council. 1977. *1977 Survey of Doctorate Recipients*. Washington, D.C.: Commission on Human Resources.

National Science Foundation. 1976. *Characteristics of Experienced Scientists and Engineers, 1976*. Surveys of Science Resources Series. Washington, D.C.: National Science Foundation.

Nichols, Maggie. 1978. *Wild, Wild Woman. A Complete Woman's Guide to Enjoying the Great Outdoors*. New York: Berkeley Windhover.

Smart, C., and B. Smart (eds.). 1978. *Women, Sexuality, and Social Control*. London: Routledge and Kegan Paul.

Sutherland, Audrey. 1978. *Paddling My Own Canoe*. Honolulu: University Press of Hawaii.

U.S. Department of the Interior. 1978. *Doors to the Future: Careers for Women*. Washington, D.C.: U.S. Department of the Interior.

U.S. Fish and Wildlife Service. "Refuge System Celebrates Anniversary," *Fish and Wildlife News*, December, 1978–January, 1979. Washington, D.C.: U.S. Department of the Interior.

Chapter 6—Elaine Rhode

Rhode, Elaine. 1979. "This Wild Goose Chase Paid Off," *National Wildlife*, vol. 17, no. 2., February–March, 1979.

Chapter 7—Jeanne Gurnee

Dole, G. 1978. *Vignettes of Some Early Members of the Society of Woman Geographers* (see Chapter 4).

Gurnee, Jeanne. 1956. "The Cave of the Guacharos," *Natural History*, vol. 65, no. 10, December, 1956.

———. 1968. "Mayan Cave Discoveries," *Explorers Journal*, vol. 46, no. 3, September, 1968.

Chapter 9—Margaret Owings

Brower, David Ross (ed.). 1965. *Not Man Apart;* lines from Robinson
Jeffers; photographs of the Big Sur coast; by Ansel Adams [and others];
Introd. by Margaret Wentworth Owings. San Francsico: Sierra Club
Books.
Owings, Nathaniel A. 1973. *The Spaces in Between. An Architect's Jour-
ney.* Boston: Houghton Mifflin.

Chapter 10—Diana Cohen

Cohen, Michael J. 1974. *Our Classroom Is Wild America.* Freeport,
Maine: Cobblesmith.
———. 1979. *Across the Running Tide.* Freeport, Maine: Cobblesmith.

Chapter 11—Eugenie Clark

Clark, Eugenie. 1951. *Lady with a Spear.* New York: Harper.
———. 1972. "The Red Sea's Garden of Eels," *National Geographic,*
November, 1972.
———. 1975. "Diving Among Sleeping Sharks," *National Geographic,*
April, 1975.
———. 1975. "The Strangest Sea," *National Geographic,* September,
1975.
———. 1978. "Flashlight Fish of the Red Sea," *National Geographic,*
November, 1978.

Chapter 12—Peggy Eckel Duke

Adirondack Park Agency. 1972, 1973. Master Plans for State and Private
Lands. Ray Brook, N.Y.: Adirondack Park Agency.

Chapter 13—Sheila Link

Link, Sheila. 1976. "Winter Wilderness Survival," *Field and Stream,*
February, 1976.

Chapter 14—Carol Ruckdeschel

McPhee, John. 1973. "Travels in Georgia," *The New Yorker,* April 28,
1973.

Chapter 15—Margaret Stewart

Stewart, Margaret. 1967. *Amphibia of Malawi*. Albany, N.Y.: State University of New York Press.

Chapter 16—Rebecca Lawton

Lawton, Rebecca. 1977. "Taphonomy of the Dinosaur Quarry, Dinosaur National Monument," *Contributions to Geology*, vol. 15, no. 2. Laramie: University of Wyoming.

Chapter 17—Margaret Murie

Murie, Margaret. 1962. *Two in the Far North*. New York: Knopf. Reprint (1978) Anchorage: Alaska Northwest Publishing Co.
———. 1966. *Wapiti Wilderness*. New York: Knopf.
———. 1977. *Island Between*. Fairbanks: University of Alaska Press.

Chapter 18—Maggie Nichols

Nichols, Maggie. 1972. "Alice (and Friends) in Disney Land," *Field and Stream*, May, 1972.
———. 1973. "Showdown at Storm King," *Field and Stream*, November, 1973.
———. *Wild, Wild Woman* (see Chapter 5).

Chapter 19—Nicole Duplaix

Duplaix, Nicole. "Giant River Otters," *National Geographic*, June, 1980.
I.U.C.N.. *International Zoo Yearbook*. Edited by Nicole Duplaix. Morges, Switzerland: International Union for Conservation of Nature and Natural Resources.

Chapter 21

Ruddick, S., and P. Daniels. 1977. *Working It Out*. New York: Pantheon.

Index

Achey, Mary Elizabeth, 71–72
Ackley, Carl, 76
Ackley, Delia, 76, 114
Adams, Harriet C., 114
Adirondack Log Building, 127–128
Adirondack Park Agency, 177
Adirondacks: and Duke, Peggy Eckel,
    173–183; and Johnson, Krissa,
    120–130
Adventurers, women as, 42–49
African Wildlife Leadership Foundation,
    144
Agassiz, Elizabeth, 76
Agassiz, Louis, 76
Aikens, Martha, 87
Alaska: and Daniels, Joan, 274–286; and
    Murie, Margaret, 237–253; and
    Rhode, Elaine, 95–101
Alderson, N. T., 20
Aleutian goose, 91–95
Aleutian Islands, 91–105
Alexandra in *O, Pioneers!*, 62–54
American Women: Images and Realities,
    66
Ama divers, 167
Amphibians, study of, 210–223
Antonia, in *My Antonia*, 62–64
Arctic National Wildlife Range, 251
Army wives, 35–39
Architects, women as, 120–130
Austin, Mary, 71
Author, background of, 79–84

B. Allan Mackie School of Log Building,
    121–122
Backpackers, women as, 146–158
Barchus, Eliza, 72
Barrier Islands, and Ruckdeschel, Carol,
    195–209
Bass, Joan, 85
Beecher, Catherine, 39
Beret in *Giants in the Earth*, 61–62
Bernhardt, Prince, 272–273
Biological roles, 16–17
Biological superiority, 17
Bird, Isabella, 42, 45–49, 73
Birth control: 16; and Sayward, 57–58
Bloomer, Amelia, 69
Boat women, 224–236
Bogan, Louise, x, 1, 295

Bourliére, François, 269–270
A Bride Goes West, 20
Brindamour, Birute, 269
Brower, David, 288
Brown, Edmund G., 135
Brown, Mrs. Pat, 140–141
Brown, Pat, 140–141
Buck, Pearl, 114
Buldir Island, 91–105
Byrd, Vern, 94

Calamity Jane, 42–45
Candler, Sam, 205
Cannary, Martha Jane, 42–45
Cape Haze Marine Biological
    Laboratory, 163
Caribbean: and Gurnee, Jeanne,
    115–117; and Stewart, Margaret,
    219–220
Carson, Rachel, 71, 137, 139
Carter, Jimmy, 206
Cashman, Nellie, 42
Cather, Willa, 62–64, 71
Caves, women exploring, 106–119
Childbearing, trap of, 15–16
Childbirth, 13
Chugach State Park, 274–286
Clark, Eugenie, 159–172, 269
Clark, James, 77
Clark, Sally, 77
Clarke, Edward, 67–68
Cleveland, Agnes Morley, 20
Clitherall, E. B., 14–15
Clothing: outdoor, 81–82, 87, 189;
    revolution in, 69–70
Cody, Bill, 42, 44–45
Cohen, Diana, 88, 146–158, 288,
    292–293
Cohen, Mike, 146
Coit, Lillie Hitchcock, 42
Colden, Jane, 72
Comstock, Anna, 72
Cortés and Malinché, 49
Council for Survival Education, 189
Covey, Earl, 125, 130
Crane, Jocelyn, 81

Daniels, Joan, 274–286
Daniels, Steve, 274–286
Defenders of Wildlife, 138

Djuka tribe, 267–268
Dole, Gertrude, 114
Doña Marina, 49
Duke, Peggy Eckel, 173–183
Duplaix, Nicole, 263–273
Durrell, Gerald, 272

Earhart, Amelia, 114
Eastman, Dr., 41–42
Economic opportunities, 67
Endurance of women, 18, 292–293, 294
Environmental Education Expeditions,
    148
Environmental Protection Agency, 153
Erikson, E., 20
Estes, Dr. James, 101
Explorers Club, 76
Explorers, women as, 75–78

Fairbanks, Jon, 294
Faragher, J., 17, 19, 21
Farr, Senator Fred, 136, 141–142
Feminism: defined, 290–291; and
    Gurnee, Jeanne, 118–119; in the
    wilderness, 290–291
Fiction, women in, 54–64
Field and Stream: 187; and Nichols,
    Maggie, 254–262
Flacke, Robert F., 86
Foote, Mary H., 71
Fossey, Dian, 269
Fowler, James, 110
Friends of the River, 226
A Frontier Lady, 23
Frontier women: categories of, 22;
    equality of, 21; and homesickness,
    29–30, 61
Fuller, Fay, 73–74

George, Anita, 166
Gerber, Barbara W., 83–84
Giants in the Earth, 60
Gold rush women, 33–35
Goodale, Elaine, 39–42
Goodall, Jane, 269
Grand Canyon environmental education
    expeditions, 148
Greer, Germaine, 71
Groves, Ernest, 18–19, 66
Guacharos, 110–112
Guerin, Elsa Jane Forest, 69–70
Gupta, Kamini, 133
Gupta, Ruth, 134

Gurnee, Jeanne, 106–119, 287, 294–295
Gurnee, Russell, 109
Guthrie, A. B., 12, 59

Hance Trail, 146
Hansa, Per, in Giants in the Earth, 61
Harrison's Cave, 116–117
Hart, Pearl, 42
Heinz Steinitz Marine Biological
    Laboratory, 163
Herpetologists, 210–223
Hickok, Wild Bill, 42, 44–45
Homesteaders: in Alaska, 274–286;
    women as, 15, 22–33
Hudson, Grace Carpenter, 71
Hulse, Shirley C., 75
Hunters, women as, 184–194
Hypothermia, 190–191

Immigrants, 13–14
Indians: and army wives, 37–38;
    marriage with whites, 49–50; attack
    by, 13; Sioux, 43; women, 3, 49–53
Industrialization, effects on women, 67
Isle of Pines, Cuba, 116

Jacques, Florence Page, 77
Jacques, Francis Lee, 77
Janzen, Victor, 123–124
Jewett, Sarah Orne, 71
Johnson, Krissa, 120–130
Johnson, Martin, 77, 218
Johnson, Osa, 77, 114, 218
Jones, Helen Lukens, 259

Kessel, Brina, 81, 250
Koford, Dr. Carl, 138
Kolodny, Annette, 14–15
Krear, Robert, 250

Labor, sexual division of, 17
Lady with a Spear, 163
A Lady's Life in the Rocky Mountains, 45
Lake Placid Winter Olympic games,
    173–183
Lamb, Dana, 77
Lamb, Ginger, 77
Lander, Dawn, 19–21, 50–51
Lawton, Rebecca, 224–236
Legal rights of women, 15, 68–69
Leopold, Dr. A. Starker, 138
Let Them Speak For Themselves, 42
Letters of a Woman Homesteader, 26–29

Lewis and Clark and Sacajawea, 51
Lindbergh, Anne Morrow, 71
Link, Sheila, 184–194

Mackie, Allan, 124
Mackie, Mary, 124
Marine life: exploration of, 159–172;
    preservation of, 141–143
Maxwell, Gavin, 270
Maxwell, Martha, 73
Mayan Indians, exploration of caves,
    107–119
McGinnis, Bill, 225
McPhee, John, 206
Mead, Margaret, 114
Mech, Dr. Dave, 99
Mennonites, 153–154
Merian, Maria Sibylla, 72
Merrill, Fannie Buss, 75
Mining camps, 33–35
Mitchell, B. W., 74–75
Moodie, Susanna, 29–33
Montagu, A., 17
Morgan, General T. J., 41
Moses sole, 170–172
Mountain climbing, 73–74
Mountain lions, protection of, 136–137
Mulhall, Lucille, 66
Murie, Adolph, 244
Murie, Margaret, 88, 100, 237–253
Murie, Olaus, 237–253
Murphy, Grace Barstow, 76
Murphy, Robert Cushman, 76

National Audubon Society, 135, 137–138
National Park Service, 87, 135
Natural Areas Council, 205–206
Natural sciences and women, 72–73
The Natural Superiority of Women, 17
New Melones Dam, 224
New York Zoological Society, 268–269
Nice, Margaret, 81
Nichols, Maggie, 88, 254–262, 289
Nichols, Mike, 259
No Life for a Lady, 20

O, Pioneers!, 62
Oilbirds, 112
O'Meara, Walter, 5–6, 49–50
On the Psychology of Women, 17
Otters: giant river, 263–273; sea,
    preservation of, 141–143
Outdoor Women, 258

Outdoor Writers Association of America,
    258
Owings, Margaret, 102, 131–145
Owings, Nat, 135

Papakonstantinou, Ilias Themistokles,
    163
Peck, Annie Smith, 74, 114
Petzoldt, P., 18
Physiological superiority, 17
Pine Bush wilderness area, 221–222
Pioneer women, 22–33, 291
Psychological superiority, 17
Psychology of Women, 17

Rafting, whitewater, 191, 224–236
Rare Animal Relief Effort, 268
Ras Muhammed, 169–170
Rebecca in The Way West, 59–60
Recreation and women, 73–75
Red Sea exploration, 160
Reed, Nathaniel, 135
Reptiles, study of, 210–223
Rhode, Elaine, 91–105, 287–288
Rich, Adrienne, 290
Richter, Conrad, 54–55
Rio Camuy, 115–116
Roe, Frances, 38–39
Rölvaag, Ole, 60
Rosenthal, Paul, 285–286
Roughing It in the Bush, 29
Royce, Sarah Bayliss: 23–26; and Gold
    Rush, 33–35
Ruckdeschel, Carol, 195–209

Sacajawea, 49, 51–52
Sadat, Anwar, 172
Safety: consciousness of, 292; in
    environmental education expedition,
    154–155
Salaries for women: in natural sciences,
    85; for teachers, 39
Save-the-Redwoods League, 139
Sawtelle, Dr. Mary, 42
Sayward in Richter trilogy, 55–59
Schaller, George, 250, 269
Scripps Institute of Oceanography, 134,
    167
The Sea Around Us, 137
Sea lions, protection of, 132–145
Shagowashcodawoqua, 49–50
Shakers, 152–153
Sharks, study of, 164–167

Sherman, J., 17–18
Shor, Frank, 77
Shor, Jean, 77
*The Significance of the Frontier in
    American History*, 21
Silent Spring, 137, 139
Sister to the Sioux, 40
Smith, Donald, 50
Smith, Karen, 86–87
Smithsonian Institution, 154
Society of Woman Geographers, 258
Speleologists, women as, 106–119
Spelunking, 106–119
Spurr, Stephen H., 288
Stanislaus River, rafting of, 224–236
Stansell, C., 17, 19, 21
Stanwell-Fletcher, Theodora C., 77
Stewart, Clyde, 26
Stewart, Elinore Pruitt, 15, 26–29
Stewart, Margaret, 210–223
Stickel, Lucille, 81–82
Summerhayes, Jack, 38
Summerhayes, Martha, 36–39
Suriname, and Duplaix, Nicole, 263–273
Survival education, 189–190

Tanamá River, 113–115
Taphonomy, 230–231
Teachers on the frontier, 38–42
Thompson, David, 49
TRAFFIC, 272
Train, Russell, 144
Trist, E. H., 14
Turner, F. J., 21
Turtles, and Carol Ruckdeschel, 195–209
Two in the Far North, 100, 237

Udall, Stewart, 135
Underwater exploration, 159–172
U.S. Government Relief Company, 25
Urban wilderness, women in, 254–262

*Vignettes of Some Early Members of the
    Society of Woman Geographers in
    New York*, 114

Walker, Mary, 16, 70
Wapiti Wilderness, 100, 247–248
The Way West, 12, 59
Wentworth, Frank, 139
Wild, Wild Woman, 254
Wilderness: attitudes toward, 70–72, 295;
    definitions of, 288–289; sexual
    violence in, 293–294; and tradtional
    roles, 66; value of small places,
    257–258
Wilderness women, traits of, 290
The Wilderness Society, 251–252
Williams, J., 17
Wolves, study of, 99, 119
The Women, 42
*Women in the American West,
    1849–1900*, 42
Woods Hole Oceanographic Institute,
    169
Woodswoman, 97, 255
World Wildlife Fund, 268

Youth hostels, 151
Yukon Territory, 98

Zoologist, 263–273